JOHN STEUART CURRY'S
PAGEANT OF AMERICA

JOHN BROWN
OF THE KANSAS BORDER
JOHN STEUART CURRY

JOHN STEUART CURRY'S PAGEANT OF AMERICA

By

Laurence E. Schmeckebier

CHAIRMAN, DEPARTMENT OF FINE ARTS
UNIVERSITY OF MINNESOTA

AMERICAN ARTISTS GROUP · NEW YORK · 1943

JOHN STEUART CURRY'S PAGEANT OF AMERICA

The color plates in this volume are reproduced
through the courtesy of LIFE Magazine.

PRINTED IN THE UNITED STATES OF AMERICA

DESIGNED BY A. A. VERSH

FOR

ALEXANDRA EMILIANOVA

ACKNOWLEDGEMENT

To John Steuart Curry my sincere thanks for his unreserved cooperation in giving me free access to the whole of his studio work, letters, speeches and reports. In the study of this material both he and Mrs. Curry spared no effort in supplying the additional information, advice and criticism without which the successful completion of this book could not have been accomplished. Mr. Harry Wickey was most kind in offering further information, particularly concerning the earlier periods of the artist's activity. For invaluable assistance in textual criticism and correction of proofs I am grateful to Alexandra Kluge and Sarah Davidson.

In the critical study of a contemporary artist whose work, writings and comments form the basic sources, bibliographical material is naturally of secondary importance. Practically all the published articles referring to Curry are listed in the Reader's Guide to Periodical Literature and the Index of Contemporary Art. In addition to this material I have referred to a number of separate, privately printed publications: an article by Maynard Walker on a selected group of Curry's works exhibited by the College Art Association, a critical introduction by Thomas Craven for the catalogue of the Curry exhibition at the Lakeside Press Galleries in Chicago (1939), and my own biographical note to the catalogue of his Madison exhibition in 1937. A series of critical comments on Curry were published in the "Demcourier" for April 1941 (Demco Library Supplies, Madison, Wisconsin and New Haven, Connecticut). I am indebted to the publisher, Mr. Norman Bassett, for permission to quote from passages written by Thomas Benton, Reginald Marsh, Grant Wood and John T. Mathiesen in that magazine.

The photographs of drawings and watercolors were made for the most part by the excellent photographic service of the Department of Visual Education at the University of Wisconsin. The damaged reproductions of the early illustrations were skillfully rephotographed by Mr. Paul Hamilton of the Minneapolis Institute of Art. Permission by the Associated American Artist's Galleries to reproduce illustrations Numbers 60, 73, 97 and 113 is gratefully acknowledged. Mr. David Pollock of Norwalk, Connecticut was kind enough to take special photographs of the murals in the Norwalk High School. Finally I wish to express my appreciation to Mr. Samuel Golden of the American Artists Group for his personal interest, patience and kindly cooperation in sponsoring this publication.

L. E. S.

This book is another volume in the series devoted to outstanding contemporary artists which was inaugurated by the American Artists Group on the premise that artists' works, in conjunction with an authentic record of their lives, constitute an irreplaceable heritage, one which could best be conserved while the subjects themselves are alive.

Posterity will itself appraise the contributions of present-day American artists. Yet it is important to that final judgment that the artist be allowed to put on record a narrative of his life, together with a statement of his beliefs and interpretations, however much at variance these may be with the verdict that succeeding generations may render.

The five volumes previously published in this series have taken their places as standard works. "Gist of Art" contains the substance of John Sloan's life-long teaching and practice in art, with an unsparing commentary on his own works. In "And He Sat Among the Ashes," William Shack tells the astonishing story of Louis M. Eilshemius, eccentric genius of American art, who achieved while still alive a victory that was well-nigh posthumous. The greatness of Jerome Myers is enshrined in "Artist in Manhattan," his autobiography, the publication of which preceded the artist's death by only three months, thus emphasizing the indispensable function of these volumes. The artist and the critic, as two aspects of a dual personality, are set forth through colorful narrative and incisive analysis in Guy Pene du Bois' autobiographical "Artists Say the Silliest Things." The basic characteristics of Harry Wickey's personality and works are established in his "Thus Far," so that the reader could understand what he believed, experienced and endeavored to accomplished in his career.

· CONTENTS ·

· COLOR PLATES

· ILLUSTRATIONS ·

ILLUSTRATIONS

ILLUSTRATIONS

ILLUSTRATIONS

ILLUSTRATIONS

ILLUSTRATIONS

ILLUSTRATIONS

ILLUSTRATIONS

INTRODUCTION

AN ARTIST's WORK has a right to speak for itself. The understanding of John Steuart Curry should not be based on personal anecdotes, news stories, and critical opinions written about him. What Curry means should be determined by the reader's understanding and appreciation of Curry's work. Curry is a painter. Whatever he has to say is best expressed in the medium he has trained himself to use with greatest skill.

At first glance the biographical aspects of Curry's career may seem to have greater human interest than the pictures. With more extended consideration, however, their importance diminishes to the rank of mere colorful enrichment of the central theme—the pictures themselves.

This book is an attempt to let those pictures speak for themselves through the medium of selected reproductions. The arrangement of the reproductions grew out of a number of logical considerations. One was the matter of particular artistic problems which the artist was trying to solve: the timeless problems of color, linear design, or the composition of forms. A second involved the varying problems of content and idea associated with those of artistic form. In the actual process of analysis it will be found that these two will usually complement each other. The works tend to group themselves into periods which follow in a logical sequence.

This is not an arbitrary process of dividing the artist's life and activity into a number of compartments and tossing each work

into an historical resting place determined by the date and signature in the corner. As every artist knows, he is not always
archaeologically wise enough to sign and date every picture or
drawing at the time it is executed so as to make the historian's
task easy and "scientific." Many of these works have rested peacefully in a dusty attic or on a work bench for years. When at last
they are exhumed the artist often has not the faintest idea when
they were done—in which case the historian will usually oblige
by telling him.

The method of presentation used in this book was inspired by
the usual experience of anyone who visits Curry's studio. The
introductory conversation is along general lines: What is art?
What do you think about this or that artist? Do you believe in
government patronage of the artist? Is art propaganda? Then it
develops along a more personal vein: Do you like our community?
Where did you go to art school? Did you enjoy Paris? Why do
you like to paint tornadoes and storm scenes? And finally: Can't
you find any beautiful things in Kansas to paint, instead of such
ugly scenes as a baptism in an open horse trough?

Artists in general find this type of question superfluous and
irrelevant. Most of them, however, are quite human about it; they
realize that people are naturally curious about those mysterious
things that are supposed to make up the artist's world. The
answers the artists give are usually as irrelevant as the questions,
equally fragmentary and utterly lacking in considered judgment.

Curry is no exception. When the questions become too insistent or too involved he gives up attempting to answer them
by continuing to puff on his unlighted pipe in silence. It is easier
to draw him out when looking at some of the dozens of paintings,
lithographs, and drawings that hang on the walls, are piled in the
corner, or in the picture rack. He will point out a compositional
idea suggested in a loose sketch, then a watercolor, then a finished
painting in which he feels that the idea has been developed to its

logical and perfected solution. With a little encouragement he will tell something of the circumstances in which he first hit upon the idea and the associations drawn from his own experience that have given it a deeper and more dramatic significance. He will describe, for instance, the funeral of his boyhood friend Private Davis and the pathetic ceremonies in the old store with the Gospel Train written across the front of it. He will show you the sketches he made in his room immediately after leaving the meeting. He has never forgotten the pathos and tragedy of those situations. They have developed through the years with ever widening implications as they have been enriched by new forms and new experiences. His observations of this sort are always clear and factual. The trends of thought and imagination that they set in motion are unlimited. That is essentially the universal quality of his art.

PART 1

PREPARATION AND GROWTH

1

BACKGROUND AND BEGINNINGS
1897-1921

SQUARELY IN THE MIDDLE of the United States, halfway between the shore lines of California and Virginia, the northern border of the Dakotas and the southern tip of Texas, lies the sunflower state of Kansas. From Coronado to Zebulon Pike, John Brown to William Allen White this region has played an important role in the political and cultural life of the American people. Its geographical position, its political history and institutions, even the racial character of its population, which has one of the lowest percentage of foreign born in the country, contributed to the distinctive background from which the artist John Steuart Curry evolved.

Curry was born November 14, 1897, on a farm near Dunavant, a small town in the northeastern part of the state, comprising now little more than a store, schoolhouse, and bus station. His parents were staunch Scotch Covenanters, both of whose families had originally migrated from the Chester district in South Carolina. In 1868, when Smith Curry, John's father, was a small boy, Grandfather Curry had gone out to Kansas from Indiana, taking the boat route down the Ohio and up the Missouri River from St. Louis. Mrs. Curry's father, John Steuart, came from Sparta, Illinois, and had served with the Union Army during the Civil War. The wounds he received at the siege of Vicksburg held on for many years and ultimately caused his death soon after moving to Kansas with his family in 1880.

Struggle and privation had been the lot of both the parents in those early years as rural pioneers, but they had prospered considerably more than the average farmer of the time. Smith Curry had attended the state university along with William Allen White and General Frederick Funston. Margaret Steuart also had a college degree. When they were married in 1895 their honeymoon to Europe was looked upon as a rash and unheard of adventure by their relatives and friends. They raised a family of five children, of whom John was the eldest. After 1908 they usually spent the winter months on the ranch near Scottsdale, Arizona, purchased because of the mother's poor health.

John Curry's youth was full of the robust activity of the average farm boy. He describes it in these words:

"I was raised on hard work and the Shorter Catechism. The stock had to be cared for and fattened for the Kansas City markets. We were up at four o'clock the year 'round, feeding the cattle, planting and plowing corn, cutting hay and wheat and in the school months doing half a day's work before we rode to town on horseback to our lessons. But we didn't mind. It was the only life we knew and I had a strong constitution.'

He went to grade school at nearby Hickey Point, then to high school at Winchester. He loved athletics and excelled in several events. He could run the 50-yard dash in 5.3 seconds regularly; the 100-yard in 10.4; and the 110-yard high hurdles in 18 seconds. Though he weighed less than 150 pounds at the time, he was rated a star halfback on the high school football team.

To excel in athletics amid the shifting influences and complexities of the average youth's high school experiences requires more than mere physical strength and aptitude. Patience, personal courage, and spiritual drive are prerequisites which the youthful athlete does not mention with regard to himself but which he is quick to recognize and to praise in others. In Curry's case such qualities were simply a part of life itself, of farm life. This accounts for a great many of his later characteristic developments.

As we have seen from Curry's description of it, life on the farm was essentially hard work. Moreover, under the social and economic standards of the time, if the work was not done the family did not survive. It is quite natural, therefore, that the uncompromising dogma of the catechism should from early youth be associated in Curry's mind with the concept of "hard work."

The twin themes of Repentance and Faith are the essential features of this doctrine of economic survival. When unaccountable and unavoidable phenomena of nature and of man's society frustrated all their efforts to cope with them, reason and the intellect could make no reply. Religion then became a primary necessity. Curry's parents were deeply religious.

Bad weather, crop or cattle disease, bank failures and financial depressions were looked upon as vengeful acts of a terrible God, hurled from on high as punishment for man's sin and faithlessness. Like the seaman, the farmer is always concerned about the weather. The terrific wind and rainstorms that are characteristic of Kansas give him ample reason to be fearful.

This unceasing conflict of fear and faith absolved in the hard struggle for existence was a family heritage that enveloped the artist from his earliest youth. It motivated the tremendous development he experienced in his subsequent career.

People have often asked Curry how he came to be an artist, assuming that at some mysterious moment of his life he decided to take up that profession. With a shrug of his shoulders he once replied, "I don't know. I can't really remember when I didn't draw. I wanted to put down what I felt about certain experiences and drawing was the clearest way to do it. As for an artist, that had always been my ambition, except for a short time when I thought to be a railroad engineer was the most exciting thing to do."

He drew everything: horses and fighting animals, railroad engines and trains, pictures of battles from the Revolutionary War, hosts of everyday things about him. He kept a scrapbook filled with newspaper and magazine clippings of cowboy and Indian scenes, illustrations by such westerners as Remington and Dunton, also hundreds of his own pencil sketches of guns and revolvers, carefully drawn from a mail-order catalogue.

There was here no "cultural" motivation. His artistic expression was not for the pure pleasure of the activity itself. He drew not for the fun of it alone but for a definite purpose; these motifs he collected because he liked them and also because they were "ideas" that he might want to use some day.

Life on the farm did not mean a frustration of the boy's interest in art. From both the home and the rural schools came direct encouragement. On their honeymoon trip to Europe his parents had seen the great pictures in the museums and had brought back many reproductions of those they liked: the works of Giovanni Bellini and Peter Paul Rubens and a whole book of illustrations by Gustav Doré prominent among them. These played a considerable role in the formation of Curry's own taste and point of view.

Mrs. Curry actively encouraged John in his drawing. The father did not oppose it, although at times he found it rather trying to see his husky twelve-year-old son drawing pictures on white paper when there were farm chores to be done.

Curry recalls with a sense of gratitude the reaction of rural school teachers to his incessant interest in drawing pictures. The traditional image of a thin-lipped and bespectacled tyrant does not fit his description of Jennie Mitchell, his first grade teacher at Hickey Point. She loved to let him draw his railroad engines for the mutual delight of himself and the class. There is a story about the eleven-year-old boy artist in a grade school in Arizona, taught by Dora Jean Coe, now Mrs. Percy Ellis, in which nine different problems in arithmetic were assigned. Curry worked studiously along with the other students and like them turned in the nine sheets, but with sketches of cows in nine different positions instead of the required solutions.

At the age of twelve the youthful artist rode six miles on horseback to receive his first formal art lessons from Mrs. Alice Worswick, wife of the county attorney in Oskaloosa, Kansas, who had the distinction of having studied art in Paris. It was she who taught him to use charcoal and watercolor and in a very kindly way encouraged him to paint life around him, farm animals, landscapes, the things that he loved. He would go home, tie up the ponies beside the barn, and coax them to stand properly so he could draw them. The exciting windstorms, rolling fields and peaceful herds of cattle were subjects that had already attracted him at this time.

"My whole life was made up of sensations," he says. "I used to go out in the garden and pull tomato vines to pieces so that I could smell them. I used to go out into the pasture to the mudholes where the doves had gathered so that I could see them fly up against the sky . . . I loved the smell of wet dust."

An intimate characterization of the boy artist was written down in later years by his mother in the following words: "Because John was a nervous child he was not sent to school until he was seven. In the meantime he was thoroughly spoiled by being read books of history and travel by his elders. The primer at school, while beyond his power to read, was far below his conception of things. The drawings in the book were another stumbling block. On one page was a badly drawn cat. John said he couldn't bear to look at it. I advised him to get the lesson and then he could go on to something else. Instead of studying the page he turned the leaf and never looked at it until time to recite.

"He was always carrying a pencil and paper with him and asking people to draw for him what he couldn't draw for himself.

"As a child John was terribly afraid of thunderstorms. I wonder why he paints so many of them. Perhaps he feels something sublime in their terrific power.

"Life was a struggle for him. While not vitally interested in the farm he did his share of the work and after a hard day in the fields, night found him at his drawing board while the household slept. Drawing, always drawing and no one to teach him except what little I could give him, and a few lessons one summer, six miles away by horseback.

"His great urge to paint and his aversion to mathematics led him away from high school and college to study art. In school, despite his love for history and literature, he was considered a poor student. However, an experienced teacher from another city came to our school and talked to me about John's work. She told me that John had a fine mind. 'But look at his grades,' I said. And she answered, 'He will never have good grades, but he has the most brilliant mind in school.'

"Perhaps what has helped him more than anything else has been his great desire to be an artist, and never turning aside because of discouragement and difficulties."

At the end of his junior year, in the summer of 1916, John left high school to enter the Kansas City Art Institute. It was a rather unhappy experience. With his farm clothes, awkward manners, and rural talk he felt out of place in what to him appeared to be a sophisticated atmosphere. Though most of them came from backgrounds little different from his own, the students laughed at him and made fun of his seventy-five cent paint box and his ambitions to become an artist. He stayed a month, then went to work on a section gang for the Missouri Pacific Railroad for two months to earn enough money to take him to Chicago. That fall he embarked, beautifully togged out in a brand new $17.50 "Style-Plus" suit of clothes, to enroll in the art school of the Chicago Art Institute.

It was with a dogged determination to make his own way that he began his student career away from home. His first job was that of selling shoes in the bargain basement of a Chicago department store. It lasted until noon when he quit in disgust because he could not bring himself to peddle the shoddy merchandise with cardboard soles to the poor people who came there to buy them as "bargains." He did not even go back for his pay, for that would be little more than taking a reward for a dishonest job.

He stayed at the Institute for two years, supporting himself by such odd jobs as sweeping floors and working in the cafeteria. He studied particularly under Edward J. Timmons and John Norton.

It was as a special student, since he had not finished the regular high school curriculum, that in the fall of 1918 he entered Geneva College, a staunch Presbyterian school in Beaver Falls, Pennsylvania, where his brother was already matriculated. Aside from service as a private in the Student Army Training Corps, his interests there seemed centered chiefly on football. At the end of the 1919 season he left for Leonia, New Jersey, to begin serious independent work under the influence of the well-known illlustrator Harvey Dunn in the near-by town of Tenafly.

One does not study an artist's early work just to show the precociousness of an infant prodigy as so often happens in music and mathematics. It is primarily to determine the specific character of the matured man as it is revealed in the simplified and unpremeditated expressions of his childhood and youth. The fragmentary remarks and stories that one picks up from the artist's parents, his relatives and early friends, as well as his own recollections can thereby be checked and evaluated against the documentary evidence which is in his work of the same period. That evidence is to be evaluated simply through the analysis of subjects he chose to represent and the means by which he was able to handle them. The problems of heredity and environment, willful self-discipline, and the accidental sequence of events can best be studied through the spontaneous expression of the youthful work of art.

These eight reproductions represent the best and most characteristic examples of Curry's early work. They suggest the normal development of an average farm boy in the Middlewest, from the exciting battle scenes of the history and adventure books to the actual experience of that excitement in real life among fighting beasts and men. The boy was reared on a doctrine of hard work yet, whether experienced in dream or reality, the pleasure of escape was more delicious than the sweat of toil. Nature, as revealed in the delicate flower, the exuberance of foliage or a landscape had always been an object of a deep-seated love and devotion. The compelling vitality of color and movement seem to have been a part of his nature long before he was consciously striving to control them as mediums of expression.

Notes on the Illustrations

1—ROUGH RIDERS. Pen-and-ink drawing. Ca. 1907. Made when Curry was not more than ten or eleven years old. Related to many similar paintings and drawings of soldiers and cowboys by Remington and Russell, reproductions of which Curry had at home. There are only a few of these early drawings remaining. Most of them are badly tattered and thrust into later sketch books.

2—STILL LIFE WITH PETUNIAS. Watercolor. Ca. 1911. Painted by the adolescent youth of thirteen or fourteen years, it shows Curry's interest in pretty colors, smooth texture, and window reflections. The delicate design of the flowers reveals the tenderness of a very sensitive nature. His mother was very proud of these watercolors and kept many of them.

1. ROUGH RIDERS

2. STILL LIFE WITH PETUNIAS

3. FARMERS FIGHTING AT THRESHING

4. THE CORN PLOWER

3—FARMERS FIGHTING AT THRESHING. *Pencil drawing. Ca. 1917.* Smooth outlines, hard drawing, lack of modeling. There are, however, many direct and expressive observations: the kicking feet and swinging arms of the fighting figures and the characteristic pose of the farmer leaning on his pitchfork on the loaded wagon. The two sketches also show interest in composition: for the same subject he tries both a vertical and horizontal scheme. In one drawing he attempts to continue the central figure design into the background by means of diagonals and in the other through a circular pattern around the figures.

4—THE CORN PLOWER. *Oil on canvas. 1917.* One of Curry's first oil paintings. It is a direct expression of what he wanted to do at that time and is still striving for today. Painted while he was a student at the Chicago Art Institute, it shows no evidence of Armory Show modernism. It represents the actualities of experience which is still his definition of "The American Scene."

The color is largely gray, its handling impressionistic. The brushstroke tends toward the circular swirls so characteristic of his later designs. The cool tones and flickering atmosphere characterize the slumbering peace of the noonday scene. The drooping heads and hip slouch of the horses—a form of equine contraposto—are details which likewise show a characteristic adherence to reality as well as its expressive possibilities.

5—STRAW STACK. *Kaw River Valley. Watercolor. 1921.* With Figures 6 to 8 this is part of a group of watercolors done during the summer of 1921 while at home for a vacation. The color is of the purest red, yellow, orange, green, and blue so often

5. STRAW STACK

associated with the western landscape in nature. Its application is not the studied spot-painting of Impressionism but a free and spontaneous brushstroke which follows a diagonal pattern from lower left to upper right.

6—CATTLE CHASING A HUNTING DOG. Watercolor. 1921. A very free sketch remarkable for its action and dramatic conception. It was done directly from life. Note the enraged charge of the steer at right, the slinking retreat of the dog. This triangular composition of forms moving horizontally in space appears in many variations throughout his later work.

7—GALLOPING COWBOY. Watercolor. 1921. Curry's love of movement in color and form is especially evident in this Remington-like figure. It shows that he has lots to learn about drawing and formal rendering but that he possessed the spontaneous combination of action and balance long before he undertook the deliberate and scientific discipline of later years.

8—HORSES IN THE BARNYARD. Watercolor. 1924. The brilliant red, orange, and yellow coloration of the tree at right is the most striking feature of this humble barnyard scene. Note the interesting attempt to combine the composition of the three horses with the receding sides of the red barn in the background. As in Figure 5 the pattern of the shadows cast by the leafless trees on the ground, the horses, and the sides of the barn is used to increase the feeling of space.

· 17 ·

6. CATTLE CHASING HUNTING DOG

7. GALLOPING COWBOY

8. HORSES IN THE BARNYARD

2

THE ILLUSTRATOR
1921-1926

WHEN CURRY FIRST STUDIED with Harvey Dunn he was very much impressed with him. To this day he considers him one who has made a great contribution to American art. This estimate is not influenced by Dunn's fame and financial success as an illustrator, nor by the fact that like Curry he is a born westerner. Rather is it the fruit of Curry's respect for those qualities in Dunn which make an artist genuine: an energy, an imagination, and a gift for invention which conceived the illustration as an independent work of art rather than an appendage to a story. To Curry, Dunn is no modern Daumier, Winslow Homer, or other historical idol, but simply an artist with an artist's feeling for those values which are native to the land, the people, and the culture that one calls American.

For the five years from 1921 to 1926 Curry's efforts and rewards lay in the profession of illustrating. Beginning under the intelligent guidance of Dunn, Curry was able to use the first-hand knowledge of his own western background in the illustration of the bloodcurdling, romantic, Wild West stories of men like Zane Grey and Max Brand which were being published serially in popular youth magazines such as *Boy's Life* and *St. Nicholas* as well as in the broader *Country Gentleman, Saturday Evening Post,* and other Curtis publications.

In 1923 Curry married Clara Derrick, a daughter of the head of the New Jersey State Home for Boys. He lived first in New York City, and then, after less than a year of Greenwich Village, moved to Westport, Connecticut (1924) where he bought a studio at Otter Ponds. For a time at this period John Steuart Curry felt that he was a successful artist.

The task of the popular magazine illustrator in the early 1920's varied between two often divergent points of view: that of elucidating a text by dramatizing single scenes or situations and that of ornamenting the printed page. Curry tried both. Some illustrations, as in Figure 11, are spread out into elaborate vignettes over two full pages. The majority, however, concentrate upon particular situations that are confined as pictures within the borders of a frame.

"The illustration should always be a picture in itself," Harvey Dunn used to tell him when he went to the Leonia studio for criticism and advice. "It should give you something to think about when you look at it."

In Curry's instance the magazine editors seldom gave specific instructions as to what scenes should be chosen, much less how they should be illustrated. He was simply given the story with the request for whatever number of illustrations they wanted to use with it. Sometimes this, too, was left entirely up to him and a choice for actual publication made by the editors after the work was turned in.

It must be remembered, however, that illustration is a form of popular art, and that the successful artist in this field must recognize certain limitations which through their very necessity can become of greatest advantage to the achievement of a more concentrated expression. One is that the illustration must attract the prospective reader to the story; the subject must be exciting and the manner of its presentation must make it more so. Another is that it must be "real," by which is meant not alone the quality of visual recognizability but the broader "reality" of experience as well. In story and illustration this must not be encumbered with too many artistic impediments. It must be quick, to the point, and without complications.

The result from the literary or journalist's point of view is the crystallization of certain universally recognized situations or emotions that are always good for a popular appeal, the extent of which is readily measurable by the cash receipts of the sales department. As in the popular cinema, it is the love scene, the romantic dream or vision, the battle of men against the forces of nature, animals, or rival human beings, that play the important roles among these commercially accepted categories.

In the choice of subject matter for his illustrations the artist likewise finds himself under considerable pressure, largely financial, to think along the same lines. Just as the language of the story writer is stylized or embellished, so too must the artist concentrate his design and mode of expression on certain realistic, i.e. recognizable, elements which he uses practically as symbols. Often these come to have a universal significance whose interpretation varies with the particular situation.

This is essentially the basis upon which Curry competed with an extensive and extremely competent field of professional artists and illustrators. From his own background he had the advantage of first-hand experience with nature and the elements, perhaps even intensified by his early religious environment and training. What he lacked in technical equipment and cleverness he made up for by his own tenacity and hard work. The difference between the artist Curry and the successful illustrator lay in the fact that once Curry became interested in a subject he wanted to stay with it, to develop fully the design that grew out of it. To turn out illustrations on a scale that is financially profitable involves a less painstaking ability to make compromises, shift, rearrange and reapply successfully motifs to any kind of subject matter. Curry's blunt honesty and emotional intensity compelled the simplified subject to become more vital, and the stylized motif to become more expressive in a steadily moving process that was essentially his development.

A number of illustrations of various types done during the years 1921 through 1925, after which he completely gave up the profession, will suggest something of the character and growth of Curry's art at this time. The spirit of the popular western story magazine is best given in the gaudy pulp jacket of Figure 9. It is a conventional cover design and cowboy pose, with all the characteristics of the Dunn school. But in any genuine western story or in the actual experience of any rural westerner, the horse is more than a mere convention or domestic animal. "Horses have a rare quality of artistic honesty," Curry has often said, in describing how he used to draw them as they stood beside the barn. In his many illustrations he found them capable of countless expressions, from the dramatic verve of Figure 9 or the wild action of Figure 11, to the dejected pathos of Figure 13.

Curry is perfectly frank about the sources of his ideas—there has never been any need to hide them. He loved the towering dignity of a stallion, and would often emphasize that quality by placing the animal in a commanding position on a hill. He has related that when seven years old he made a watercolor copy of Landseer's famous Monarch of the Glen—that is it was famous years ago, for it is now known chiefly as a trade mark for a well-advertised insurance company. Much of the youthful bravado of this Highland stag is incorporated in a story, The King of Mount Baldy, by Claude I. Barnes, which Curry illustrated for St. Nicholas magazine in December, 1922, with a magnificent horned buck towering on the snowy summit of the mountain. The same idea appeared in many illustrations and watercolors (Figs. 10 and 12) at that time as well as in later paintings (see The Stallion, Figure 146).

There were many other subjects that Curry had loved to paint and draw as a youth—exciting, romantic, almost touching in their childish sentiment. These were the motifs that clung to his memory as he attempted to perform the routine tasks of the illustrator, with the result that they were no longer routine. However awkward in form, they became dynamic, developing constantly into new forms. Follow, for example, the tense battle scenes of man and beast, or those between men (Figs. 14-16); again, observe the homely romanticism of children around the Christmas tree, or running for the school sleigh on a cold winter day, or through the fields playing ball with a dog. Comparing a typical illustration of 1921 (Fig. 20) with one of 1925 (Fig. 21) one can readily understand how it came about that he became a failure as an illustrator. These two are similar compositional motifs, but the later one is far more developed, enriched, and full of feeling that seems to flow from his own experience rather than from the story. Actually the scene has little to do with the content of the story written below it as a title; its spirit has much in common with the peaceful farm and pasture scene he loved to paint on frequent visits to Cooperstown and Lake Otsego (Fig. 21a).

From the same point of view follow the changes wrought in Curry's art from the Black Leopard (Fig. 14) to The Lightning, a watercolor, it must be noted, which was made as a "work of art," not as an illustration. Then study the first loose sketch of Hogs Killing a Rattlesnake (Fig. 23). In this painting, years before the Baptism in Kansas and The Tornado, Curry had found an expression, though no one seemed to know it but himself and a few of his friends. In it is revealed that universal quality of experience, so spontaneous and powerful that one feels that, as Harry Wickey said, "life is expressing itself directly rather than through some concoction of an artist."

Curry's illustrations show, in other words, that he could do the illustrator's job. It involved a specific technique and point of view that could be learned by any willing craftsman. There are many other illustrations like that of Figure 9 that have all the professional mannerisms of the period and one can hardly tell them apart from those of Harvey Dunn or any number of other young men influenced by him. The other reproductions demonstrate the truth of a simple statement that Curry once made to the effect that when he found a good subject or motif he liked to stick to it and work it out. The illustrator's craft was therefore a discipline which Curry used as a means to an end rather than an end in itself.

By 1925 Curry was in difficulties as a professional illustrator. The editors were complaining that his illustrations were getting to be too much like paintings. It was not that they objected to "paintings" as such. As Curry, himself, later explained, they greatly admired his work, but were forced by the strictly commercial point of view of their jobs as editors to point out that his paintings were no longer successful illustrations. They lacked the proficiency and cleverness of the contemporaries with whom he had to compete. That standard of success was marked by the dextrous handling and repetition of stereotyped patterns.

Curry's shortcomings were obviously not due to lack of ability (we have already seen that he could do it when he wanted to) but were the result of a natural and deliberate choice. He had taken seriously the idea that an illustration should in itself be a good picture. As the idea grew it enveloped new problems of content and design. These gradually became deeper and more complicated. By the end of 1925 Curry had lost most of his illustration work and had set out on the arduous road of the creative artist.

Notes on the Illustrations

9—COVER FOR WAYSIDE TALES. What may have been bright color on the original painting became gaudy on the cheap pulp of the magazine jacket: purple lettering against the orange background of the plaque at the top, blue rider against the yellow bluff, and brown horse set off by a bright green ground. The bright color with the obviously balanced action of the horse moving toward the right and the cowboy turning in his saddle in the opposite direction, the general bravado of spirit and execution are typical attributes of Harvey Dunn's followers during the early 1920's.

9. COVER DESIGN FOR
   WAYSIDE TALES

10. VIGNETTE FOR COUNTRY GENTLEMAN

10, 11—TWO ILLUSTRATIONS FOR "ALCATRAZ," by Max Brand in THE
COUNTRY GENTLEMAN, June 24, July 1, 1922. These show a typical vignette type of
design which was a common practice in such large-sized magazines of the time.
Compared with Curry's other work of the same period, these are not particularly
distinctive or individual. Nevertheless, within the conventional design, he pointed out
a number of ideas that he liked. One was the device (Fig. 10) of showing the proud
stallion in the distance as seen through the telescope of the cowboy at left. Another
was the dramatic tension that could be achieved through the balancing of moving
forms, such as the sudden reining up of the horse so that he slides in one direction
while turning sharply the opposite way. The choice of subject and design in many of
Curry's later works is often determined by these preferences.

12. THE WILD HORSE

11. VIGNETTE FOR COUNTRY GENTLEMAN

12—THE WILD HORSE. Watercolor. Ca. 1922. A tiny (3" x 4½") sketch that somehow escaped loss or destruction. Curry still likes the brilliant color of the landscape
and the proud stance of the horse. He has kept it tacked on the wall of his studio.
Notice the persistent use and variation of this pose in the distant horses of Figures 10
and 11. In later years it is developed into one of the artist's most important paintings
(see The Stallion, Figure 146).

13—ILLUSTRATION FOR "THE MAIL TO LOST MINE," by M. A. Wilson in
Boy's Life, 1923. "They caught sight of a horse with head bent, while beside him the
drifting sand covered a khaki-clad figure." The horse has much in common with
Remington's End of the Trail. Its association with the idea of storm appears in later
works such as Sanctuary (Fig. 73).

14—ILLUSTRATION FOR "A BLACK LEOPARD OF SUMATRA," by Warren
H. Miller in St. Nicholas Magazine, August, 1921. A weird impression is achieved
through the S-shape of the leopard, the angular form of the victim, and the gnarled
form of the tree. These are composed as a silhouette against the bright moonlit background. This, however, is neither the text nor the caption which states: "With a
hideous screech the leopard launched himself like a thunderbolt for their hiding place."
Curry presented the leap completed, no thunderbolt, but the catlike tension of the
beast clinging to the limb and clawing at the terrified figure to the left. The drama is
of another sort, still, tense, and even fiercer than the actual physical leap might have
been. The design and the dark tone of the silhouetted forms sustain that tension. A
similar idea is used in one of Curry's later cat compositions (Fig. 180).

13. "THE MAIL TO LOST MINE" (*Boy's Life*)

14. "BLACK LEOPARD OF SUMATRA" (*St. Nicholas*)

15. WAYSIDE TALES

15—ILLUSTRATION FOR WAYSIDE TALES. 1921. A dramatic blood-and-thunder street brawl from a World War I adventure story. The composition centers on the single plunging figure before whom the others topple in every direction. "Bewildered supermen were tumbling under a flail-like assault of beating arms," reads the caption. Curry has included even gesticulating spectators on the sidelines for dramatic emphasis. He has developed much the same action with greater refinement in later football scenes (e.g., The Line Plunge, Fig. 266).

16—ILLUSTRATION FOR THE COUNTRY GENTLEMAN. 1922. "I remember the feel of shouting, 'Where's your other eye?' But I didn't hear anything." A two-figure composition in which the interest is concentrated on the realistic awkwardness of such a brawl with a view toward achieving an aesthetic balance similar to that of the most forward cowboy in Figure 11. Note also the more effective modeling and greater action than in the fighting forms in Figure 3.

17, 18—TWO ILLUSTRATIONS FOR "TOIVO'S CHRISTMAS BEAR," by Eva E. Sorenson in St. Nicholas Magazine, December, 1922. "In their midst the young teacher glowed like a lovely Christmas angel." From remarks made later in life about his early school training we realize that Curry developed this romantic conception of the teacher from his own experience. The flickering spectacle of lighted candles and ornaments on the Christmas tree illuminating the eager faces about the teacher presents a festive mood that has none of the pulp paper cheapness ordinarily expected from such a context. It is a case wherein the relatively inconsequential subject-matter fitted the artist's technical and associated interests. It shows, too, that Curry as an illustrator was by no means limited to fighting men and galloping horses.

16.　FIGHTING MEN

"Most of the children, with the teacher, came in the school sleigh." As may readily be seen, the caption and the content of the picture have little to do with each other except for the presence in both of children and the school sleigh. Represented in the picture is the quiet stillness of a cold winter day; an old-fashioned mood (paralleled in many a Currier and Ives print) in which the homely details of wooden school house rail fence, bundled-up children, and the slouching pose of the horse lend poignancy to the scene. "This badly torn photograph is all I have of the painting," Curry said "Even now I think it is a good picture."

19—ILLUSTRATION FOR "HERO," by Albert Payson Terhune, in THE COUNTRY GENTLEMAN, March 25, 1922. It presents a joyous mood that is carried by the playing figures and also by the bright impressionistic manner of the landscape.

20—MOUNTIES SEEKING SHELTER FROM A SNOW STORM. An illustration for BOY'S LIFE, 1921. A mood picture similar to Figure 13. This involves a group of figures strung along in a continuous movement from right to left. The style is close to that of Harvey Dunn. In discussing it, Curry points out the details he has observed in real life. Such are the characteristic action of the horses with their tails down, ears laid back, and their eyes half shut to protect themselves from the snow and cold.

21—ILLUSTRATION FOR THE COUNTRY GENTLEMAN, January 31, 1925. "Bobby had not only made a house dog of his big collie, but he and his father were teaching Thor to herd sheep and cattle." As in Figure 18, this is a picture in which the literary narrative has been subordinated to a mood. Here is the mood of picturesque stillness of cows returning for milking on a winter evening. As in Figure 20, the compositional scheme involves movement from right to left. Here a sort of procession of moving forms converges into the darkness of the cowbarn. Notice the accentuation of dark figures against the light winter background, the emphasis on straight horizontal lines through the backs of the cattle, the rail fence, and the timber silhouette.

21a—GRAZING CATTLE. Watercolor. 1923. One of many watercolors that Curry painted during the summer of 1923 when he rented a cabin on the old estate of James Fenimore Cooper on the shore of Lake Otsego near Cooperstown, New York. The motif of grazing cattle and the mood it expresses is one which had attracted him in many illustrations and which he used later in landscapes (Fig. 87).

22—THE LIGHTNING. Watercolor. 1924. What Curry sought to convey here was the stunning explosion of lightning as it strikes and catches the stiffened man, beasts, and surrounding space in its weird yellow-green light. The picture was not intended as an illustration for reproduction but as an artistic expression capable of justifying itself on its own merits. Notice, however, that while the subject was his primary concern he has employed expressive means used in earlier illustrations and developed them to a greater intensity. The central motif of the composition, that of lightning striking a tree, is placed in the middleground of the picture, with the figures silhouetted against that light and the landscape receding from it into the background. The S-curve design of the stunned farmer is carried over into the outlines of the trembling horses and seems to embody something of the terror that the subject implies. These same elements were used to express a similar tension in the Black Leopard illustration of Figure 14, though the literary context was of a quite different sort. The question of "truth"— so dear to the philosopher of art—as to whether the gnarled silhouette and S-curve design actually do express that emotional state, is to be answered by the artist himself. To him, they did and he not only used these elements again but developed them into a broader and more inclusive design in this and later works (Figs. 23, 59, 161).

23—HOGS KILLING A RATTLESNAKE. Watercolor. 1925. This is one of Curry's favorite watercolors, largely because it contains a powerful, fully-realized design that developed into many variations in later years. There was the one sold to Harry Wickey in 1926 (see page 36) and the other oil paintings done in 1930 (Fig. 161).

The situation embodied in this painting is no figment of the imagination. It is a reality. Curry has seen it happen out in the pasture in Kansas. The grunting movement of such stocky, cylindrical forms racing forward is also a reality that carries the scene with startling effectiveness.

Compare this with the composition of The Lightning, Figure 22, and one can see how an expressive idea, irrespective of its content, can be developed into strikingly new forms. The tension, which in Figure 22 was centered on the streak of lightning, is here concentrated on the smaller curling form of the rattlesnake. Instead of horses, farmer, and tree forms divided between foreground and back of the picture, there is here a dramatic rush of the wild beasts from the back around the tree trunk to the point of focus in the foreground. The same type of tree is used in both compositions. In the Lightning it served to dramatize the space; here it becomes a monumental form, spreading out like an umbrella under and around which the action takes place. The same idea is later translated into yet another new form in the funnel of The Tornado (Fig. 59).

17. "TOIVO'S CHRISTMAS BEAR" (*St. Nicholas*)

18. CHILDREN AND SCHOOL SLEIGH (*St. Nicholas*)

19. "HERO" *(Country Gentleman)*

20. MOUNTIES IN SNOW STORM (*Boy's Life*)

21. TEACHING THOR TO HERD CATTLE (*Country Gentleman*)

21a. GRAZING CATTLE

22. THE LIGHTNING

23. HOGS KILLING A RATTLESNAKE

3

IN TRANSITION
1925-1927

Prior to 1925 Curry had made numerous attempts at museum pictures. There were The Homestead (1921) and The Fence Builders (1922). Both of these motifs were later used in the Department of Interior murals (Fig. 315). The Fence Builders was exhibited in 1925 at the National Academy in New York without extracting comment of any sort by critics and the press.

Curry's real love and enjoyment during this time is to be found in the watercolors he painted at home on visits to Kansas and on summer trips to the Cooperstown and the Lake Otsego country in upper New York state. These include beautifully romantic landscapes often with the most banal subjects: barns, strawstacks, towering deep blue pines along the lake shores, peacefully grazing cattle on the hillsides, fighting animals, galloping cowboys. With no particular project or patron in mind, he made several ambitious mural designs of pioneer subjects (Fig. 288 a).

All of these pictures were painted purely for his own enjoyment, though he would have liked to have sold them had it been possible, and as experiments in color, design, and the expression of ideas. Throughout this period Curry was perfectly clear in his own mind about what he wanted to express. The struggle and the uncertainty came in the problem of how it was to be expressed. Through the great part of his later work it will be found that the artist's ideas and desires remain constant as they were revealed in this early period. His prodigious development came with the mastery of expressive means, and the one accidental discovery which gave him confidence and opened unlimited possibilities in the direction he was to travel was the Hogs Killing a Rattlesnake watercolor of 1925.

As Curry lost the income he had hitherto derived from his professional illustrating, the compelling necessity to earn a living drove him to other and more ambitious commercial projects. One such was to help James Daugherty on a huge map decoration for the Cook Travel Agency's booth at the Philadelphia Sesquicentennial Exposition in 1926. This was to have an indirectly far-reaching effect upon Curry.

Daugherty had studied with Frank Brangwyn in London and commanded a great deal of respect as an artist and decorator. Curry never forgot the taunting remark that Daugherty flung in his direction: "You illustrators don't even know how to draw a flag!" It was not that the ability to draw a flag would make him a great artist, but that he felt keenly his lack of proper training and craftsmanly equipment. Daugherty insisted that Curry must learn to draw and suggested that he try the Slade School in London or Schoukhaieff's Russian Academy in Paris.

The financing of an expedition to Europe seemed to present an insurmountable obstacle. From his limited earnings as artist and illustrator Curry had not been able to save any money. His wife's family could not help him. He did not want to borrow from his own parents, since that would mean a mortgage on the farm that he knew they had worked hard to keep free of debt.

An artist in America during that prosperous period was often in an anomalous position. Under the cultural guise of "art" he was thrown in contact with people of wealth and social position. Unless he had financial resources of his own, he was dependent on them for a subsistence through the sale to them of his pictures. It was common practice for the psychology of the bargain counter to govern these purchases.

In the art colonies of Greenwich Village and Westport, Curry, coming from a farm, from the Middle West, and from the low-down profession of illustrating, was plagued by the hopeless feeling of the outsider looking in. With the courage of desperation and the disarming sincerity of the artist and farm boy that he was, he presented his case to the well-known banker and art patron Seward Prosser. It was not, however, quite as audacious as it seems, for Mr. Prosser had met Curry at the Englewood Art Club some years before and had bought some of his paintings.

Prosser loaned Curry $1500 which he was to pay back in the form of paintings done during and after his expedition to Europe. In addition, Mr. Prosser secured a job for Mrs. Curry at the Paris branch of the Bankers' Trust Company.

Another patron of a different sort for whose faith and encouragement Curry has always been grateful was the etcher and sculptor Harry Wickey. Knowing that Curry needed all the money he could get together for his trip abroad, Wickey took his new watercolor, Hogs Killing a Rattlesnake, "to sell to a friend" and gave him $150 for it. Years later Curry saw the picture on the wall in Wickey's home and realized that his good friend had probably drawn his last cent from the bank to pay for it. So it was that Curry landed in Paris in October, 1926.

The goal of the average American artist on his first pilgrimage to Europe in the 1920's was not the traditional "Grand Tour" to Italy but the inspirational atmosphere of Paris. He went there to study, to work, to become an artist amid the exhilarating freedom of the Latin Quarter and the French people. Paris, being what it was, most artists, not unnaturally, took to the irresponsibilities of their surroundings rather than to the drudgery of study and hard work—as long as their money lasted. And having enjoyed themselves they were content to go back to the hometown realities of America and continue a meagre existence in a Greenwich Village atmosphere or surrender to the exigencies of a regular job.

Like these other Americans, Curry did not travel beyond Paris.

But there similarity ends. For to Curry this expedition to Paris was a very serious enterprise. He had made many sacrifices to get there. He had, he feared, borrowed more money than he could ever pay back. His wife was working in the bank to help him pay expenses. He wanted to learn to draw the way the great masters did. That's what he had come for and he set himself with grim determination to the task.

Curry lived in the Rue Daguerre studio of the American sculptor, Hunt Dietrich, and dedicated himself to steady work in the art school of the Russian academician, Basil Schoukhaieff. There he learned hard draftsmanship and the strict delineation of form on the principle of the sphere as the great draftsmen, Dürer and Leonardo, had taught it.

Solid drawings of big heads and fat nudes show determined effort in that single direction. When an exhibition was held by Schoukhaieff's students at the Dronat Galleries on the Rue de Rennes in May, 1927, Curry's drawings were singled out by Georges Bal in the review of the *Paris Herald-Tribune* as the best of the lot and the work of the most promising artist. Most of the studies he made have been subsequently destroyed, but these two large-sized crayon drawings (Figs. 28-29) show the strong character for which he was striving.

A second art school for Curry was the Louvre museum. He had known Rubens since his early childhood at home, through studies and reproductions. To study and learn from him now through the reality of his greatest paintings was indeed a revelation. Closer and more intimate, through their very shortcomings when compared to Rubens, were the works of Delacroix, Gericault, Courbet, and Daumier. Considering Curry's own frank love of the farm and its environment, Millet might have been the most sympathetic of them all, but while Millet's work contained many promising ideas, he felt the actual rendering to be weak and ineffectual.

These studies of the great pictures in the museums which Curry added to the self-discipline of his academic draftsmanship were, however, not to bear fruit until after his return to Westport.

Curry's attitude toward what was then known as "modern" art was one of respectful detachment. He admired Matisse as an excellent colorist and designer, but a great many of the Matisse followers he considered insincere and cheap. Picasso's stylistic gyrations and the eddying currents which they set in motion were phenomena quite beyond his sphere of interest and he paid scant attention to them.

Like other young Americans of the time he enjoyed the colorful and carefree Bohemian life of the Latin Quarter. What he saw and felt about it is suggested by a number of watercolors painted in his spare time. Some of them, now hanging on the walls of his home, he still cherishes as souvenirs of his great adventure.

There are a number of typical Utrillo-like scenes of picturesque streets with the white domes of Sacré Cœur towering in the background. But most of them reveal the humor, enjoyment, and homely curiosity of an American sightseer.

On a visit to the Cathedral of Notre Dame he outdid Meryon by painting the ugliest gargoyle he could find, a bony and ferocious beast greedily devouring its young. The noontime sleepiness of a shaded square in Montmartre is seen with the nostalgia of the Cornplower or of the shaded pasture scenes he had painted in the Cooperstown country. To his surprise he found an old-fashioned merry-go-round in a street fair with galloping pigs, saddled and mounted by laughing children, and he had to make several watercolors of it. Another watercolor sketch is entitled Love is Like a Bird. It shows two tightly embraced lovers swinging through the air in the dove-shaped gondola of a rickety Ferris wheel.

One is apt to pass over these sketches as products of another American who has gone Parisian, and surrendered to the mannerisms of a Toulouse-Lautrec, Utrillo, or Meryon. But it is not true. Curry's style has nothing in common with these artists, great as they may be. The one and only thing to which Curry surrendered was the factual reality of the Paris he saw: Sacré Cœur, Montmartre, Notre Dame and the street carnival. With the same realistic detachment he drew the familiar scenes in the café—characteristic types, conversational groups, and colorful atmosphere—with no more satirical or moralizing purpose in mind than did Degas, William Glackens, or John Sloan.

To the later Curry, and to modern art in general, however, these café scenes have a particular significance that cannot be overlooked. If it were possible to look at Curry's work with the detachment of the historian, one would recognize such café genre scenes as a standard artistic motif through several generations of modern art. Beginning with the realistic picturesqueness of the Impressionists (Degas), it grew to the equally picturesque form of social decadence reflected in Toulouse-Lautrec and the early Picasso, to the bitter social satire and depravity mirrored in the German work of George Grosz. Parallel to this is the tragic pathos expressed in the work of Käthe Kollwitz and José Clemente Orozco, particularly the Mexican artist's early watercolors of the Outcasts (1917) as reverberations of the social chaos and disintegration of a war-devastated period.

What actual meaning the café scene and its associated human types had to such compelling realists as Grosz and Orozco is best revealed in the work they produced in later years. The universal tragedy and chaos expressed in the German exile's New York paintings can only be comprehended through the sympathetic understanding of his earlier work. In quite a different way, but with even greater force, Orozco developed the pathetic types of the Outcasts into the bitter, penetrating harlots of his National Palace of Fine Arts mural in Mexico City as symbols of an entire disintegrating society.

When Curry painted these café scenes he was obviously not thinking of any world-wide symbolism of a decadent civilization. Sketches like that of the Streetwalker (Fig. 27) or the Belle of the Dôme (Fig. 26) were not satirical but merely studies of types that were habitués of the Café du Dôme and surrounding locales. In later years, under entirely different circumstances, different types have a remarkably similar expressiveness to him, and Curry was fully aware of its universal significance.

Just as Curry's illustrations described in the previous chapter are important in understanding the dramatic character of his later work, so, too, are these watercolor studies of the Parisian café significant to the emotional character of such later work as The Gospel Train and Prayer for Grace (Figs. 50 and 53).

Curry returned to Westport in June, 1927. On the way home he spent a week in London made memorable by a brief but impressive acquaintance with the work of Hogarth, Turner, Uccello, and the Elgin Marbles.

Back home the struggle for a bare existence began all over again. His wife went to work and he once more tried his hand at commercial art. He painted a number of decorative wall maps, notably two for James Boring in the office of the Boring Travel Agency in New York, and another for the living room of Seward Prosser's home in Wood's Hole.

But he soon discovered that his ability to cope with the innumerable restrictions of commercialized art was more limited than ever before. These wall maps (Figs. 288-289) were interesting experiments in mural decoration and really the starting point for Curry's much later mural activity. They were limited, however, to small scenes set into a large design to permit the pasting of pretty ribbons to mark the path of the travel agency's numerous tours all over the world.

The experience of Paris had made Curry more ambitious than ever to become a great artist. Moreover, he now had a sense of what the word "great" really meant. He was willing to make additional sacrifices to achieve that end. Once again he borrowed money from his brother and sister-in-law, Marian Derrick, to tide him over for another period of hard work on his own painting.

By the summer of 1928 he had finished Baptism in Kansas. It was exhibited in the Corcoran Gallery of Washington, D. C. in the autumn and respectfully commended by Edward Alden Jewell, art critic of *The New York Times*.

The thoughtful remarks written by Mr. Jewell (Nov. 4, 1928) suggest something of the public state of mind as well as its reaction to Curry's picture. In his review, Jewell quoted a certain Britisher who, in looking over a Royal Academy exhibition, was troubled by the absence of what he called "subject pictures." Jewell went on to say that of course a recognizable story-subject is not actually necessary to the effectiveness of a picture and that there may be plenty of dramatic quality in a Vlaminck sky or a Matisse interior, but still the directly told story is never likely to go out of fashion. He then proceeded to give a careful descriptive analysis of the Baptism in Kansas, pointing out its admirable composition and dramatic content which he interpreted as a satire on the religious fanaticism of the hinterland. Though not specifically stated, one gets the impression that the critic, before this picture at least, experienced a certain weariness of the standardized Vlaminck-Matisse type of drama and felt that here was something potentially vital.

Mr. Jewell's remarks can hardly be said to have had any direct effect upon public opinion. Rather, they seem to reflect the state of mind of the museum-going public and to suggest the general trend of thought which the Baptism in Kansas set in motion.

There was no depression in 1928, no thought of a "return to the land," native art, folk customs, or those artistic and cultural values which loomed so impressively a few years later. As noted elsewhere, Curry was by no means a product of the depression.

His ideas were clear and crystallized years before the depression hit, but it took time for him to perfect the pictorial means of presenting them.

The public saw Curry's ideas for the first time fully expressed in the Baptism in Kansas. The difficult transition from the illustrator to the creative artist was complete at this time, even though it took several years before his pictures began to sell. It was this fall of 1928, too, that he became a member of the Whitney Studio Club of New York and was granted a weekly stipend of $50 by Mrs. Harry Payne Whitney to support him for the next two years. From now on his reputation grew steadily with each succeeding exhibition.

The year 1928 was a crucial year in his life and development as an artist. Underlying his outward "arrival" as an artist in this year was the hard work applied to the solution of many complex technical problems. These will be fully discussed in the next chapter.

Notes on the Illustrations

24—MONTMARTRE. Watercolor. 1927. A shady square in the older artists' quarter of Paris, with its familiar open-air pissoir, blunt-nosed Renault and dozing taxi driver. Its drousy atmosphere has much in common with the homely mood noted in the Kansas Corn Plower (Fig. 4) and some of the magazine illustrations.

25—PARIS CAFÉ. Watercolor. 1927.

26—THE BELLE OF THE DÔME. Watercolor. 1926.

27—STREETWALKER. Watercolor. 1927.
  Three of Curry's souvenirs of life at the Café du Dôme and the Latin Quarter of Paris. An American artist's reactions to types that have been common in Parisian art through several generations.

28—STUDY OF A HEAD. Black crayon. 1927. A large-sized drawing done at Schoukhaieff's Academy in Paris. The model was not an Indian, as one might suppose, but an Italian whose strong features Curry greatly admired.

29—STUDY OF A NUDE. Black crayon. 1926-27. Another typical example of the firm drawing, solid modeling, and impressive form for which Curry was striving under the tutelage of Basil Schoukhaieff.

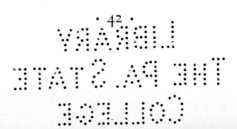

24. MONTMARTRE

25. PARIS CAFE

26. THE BELLE OF THE DOME

27. STREETWALKER

28. STUDY OF A HEAD

29. STUDY OF A NUDE

4

DISCOVERY OF A STYLE
1928

THE EXACT IDENTITY of "style" in any artist's work is seldom a closed and definable subject and the moment in his development when that style becomes crystallized is even less tangible.

There have been points in the works already under discussion where one had the impression: Here it is! Here the form speaks as the experience is felt. This is Curry! But at the same time the quality varies, not so much in accord with the subject matter, as in its clarity and directness of expression. No one was more doubtful of that clarity than Curry himself. That is why he went to Paris and to the academy.

Having set his course he proceeded to work along the same lines laid down by Schoukhaieff after his return to this country. He continued to draw big and impressive forms directly from the model. Next, he began to compose figures into groups attempting to develop a sense of movement. As Figures 31 and 32 indicate, he seemed to encounter difficulty and felt the need for a more thorough knowledge of anatomy and the structure of the human form. To that end he attended the lectures on anatomy and the human skeleton given by Dr. Stockard at the Art Students' League in New York. From the lectures and in following out the lecturer's instructions he made voluminous notes and studies which demonstrate the unbelievable industry and thoroughness with which he worked.

A number of rather significant features revealed in these drawings suggest the trend of his thinking and the artistic problems he sought to clarify. One is the simple desire to understand how a human figure is put together and through that understanding allow the structure to dictate the artistic design. To him the ana-tomical structure itself constitutes a design, a recognition which is especially evident in Figure 34.

In many drawings of this same series one can see how these two principles—the process of drawing what one sees on the sur-face of the form and drawing what one knows to be underneath that surface—seem to be juxtaposed in the drawing of the same reclining figure. Then again in later sketches one can discover instances in which his more thorough knowledge of the anato-mical structure will actually determine the particular pose that he chooses for the model. In other words, he will pose the model in what superficially appears to be an awkward position but which actually reveals a far richer design once the internal structure is worked out.

The human head and the complicated muscular structure of the face were also the subjects of numerous detailed studies (Fig. 36). It will be observed, however, that the interest in the facial muscles as a medium of expression from the caricaturist's point of view was less pronounced than the study of basic types, rather as the anthropologist would see them. He notes, for instance, the parallel forms and proportions that are characteristic of different racial types. Looking back to studies of the Italian model in Paris (Fig. 28) or the Negro head (Fig. 30), or ahead to later paint-ings such as The Mississippi (Fig. 74), one can see why type rather than the individual facial expression would be more sig-nificant to him.

In one drawing he notes certain constants: the relationship between eyes, nose, and mouth, and the whole head which re-mains invariably the same in the head of a child and that of an old man.

Curry's purpose in such painstaking studies was to clarify his own understanding of the human figure, not as scientific fact alone, but as a medium of expression. Whether the observed details are accurate or not (often they are not) is of little consequence. The fact remains that the observation of these details in their functional relationship developed in the artist a sense of certainty and self-confidence which gave him freedom to express what he wished without hesitation. That was what James Daughterty had meant when he had advised Curry to "learn to draw."

With this new confidence and technical knowledge, Curry could look at the Old Masters with an entirely new understanding. He had not forgotten Rubens, but now he realized that the best way to work out the solution of his own problems was to follow the *method* which the Flemish master himself had used: to go back to the great works of the Renaissance. The work of Leonardo da Vinci was the most inspiring and universal of them all.

Without doubt Leonardo was and still is one of the greatest teachers of all time. A profound scientific student of nature in all its aspects, he constantly made use of drawings to illustrate a theory, phenomenon, or experiment. He then kept these drawings for the use and instruction of his students. Through the development of modern means of reproduction and their application to these drawings, the number of Leonardo's students has grown from the relatively few who worked with the Master in his shop in Milan to the many thousands active in the entire artist's profession today.

As we have seen, the problem of how effectively to render a horse had fascinated Curry since childhood. Among Leonardo's drawings were hundreds of exciting examples which Curry could use, not to copy, but to help him work out problems of action and design. One can observe in Figure 40 the particular emphasis given by Curry to the pattern developed by the wrinkles of the horse's nose and nostrils, the care with which he studied the design of the eye and repeated it several times on the same page.

While Curry was now interested in movement and anatomical structure, he did not forget the solidity of the massive forms he had worked for at the academy. Neither did he surrender completely to Leonardo. It seems logical, and it did to him at the time, that the solid, aggressively active, almost brutal forms of Signorelli would have something to offer him along the lines he was following. A number of sketches from reproductions of Signorelli's frescoes in the Cathedral of Orvieto reveal just such qualities. The clarity and strength of these fighting figures are an interesting contrast to the relatively ineffectual rendering of the two Michelangelesque figures (Fig. 43) used in an earlier study of the same type. What he learned through the process can easily be followed by comparing the two versions of the same academic problem of "Fighting Warriors" (Figs. 43-44).

From all of which we may gather the impression that the year 1928 was a painfully hard one for Curry. It was also a tremendously inspiring one. He went through it perfectly aware of what he was doing and, once he had confidence and a firm grasp of the problems, he proceeded to use them for his own purpose with unbounded enthusiasm.

One example was the painting of The Bathers (Fig. 46). The subject was his own, for it was in such a leaky wooden water tank that as a boy he had first learned to swim. In Kansas during the drought season the creeks soon dry up and the farm watering tank is the only swimming hole available. From this point of view the idea is in the established tradition of other great American realists from Mark Twain (the narrative descriptions in *Tom Sawyer*) to Thomas Eakins (The Swimming Hole in the Fort Worth Museum) and George Bellows (Forty-two Kids in the Corcoran Gallery, Washington).

As an artistic problem involving the composition of active nude figures in an open space, the tradition goes back to Michelangelo's Bathing Soldiers cartoon for the Battle of Cascina mural, and has remained popular among modern artists from the time of Cezanne and Renoir to the present. The picture may be understood either from a realistic or abstract point of view, depending on what the spectator chooses to look for. To Curry the conception was essentially the same, for while the subject comes out of his own experience, its expression is based on the central two-figure group with which he had experimented in so many different ways during the year (cf. Figs. 32, 42-43). His own definition of what he considered the successful "solution" of the problem can best be seen by comparing the first sketch (Fig. 45) with the finished oil painting (Fig. 46).

At the same time Curry was working on another picture called The Return of Private Davis (Figure 276), which, though it was exhibited publicly at various times, was not actually finished until 1940. In this connection it must be explained that Curry has seldom followed a fixed and mechanical routine in the painting of a picture. He has habitually worked on a hard and steady eight to ten-hour-a-day schedule; but the time contributed to the completion of individual pictures has varied. In some cases, like one of his recent sunrise compositions, the rich and remarkably spontaneous vitality was the result of no more than two or three hours' actual work. There are many other paintings that have remained in his studio for ten to fifteen years to be patiently revised, scraped off, recomposed and developed until he felt that the idea was adequately and completely realized.

The idea of The Return of Private Davis was certainly no new invention of the year 1928, for its origin was the actual funeral of a high school friend who was killed in the Argonne in 1918 and whose body was one of the first to be brought back to Kansas after the war. For the ceremony the rural community turned out with all the military pomp and spectacle it could muster in the little Plum Grove cemetery near Winchester. Curry never forgot the scene nor its significance, for the sketch books he brought back from France contain a number of watercolor sketches of American cemeteries replete with rolling hills of gleaming white crosses and brightly waving flags. He had read the famous *Victory Ball* by the English poet Alfred Noyes and, like Ernest Schelling in his orchestral fantasy of the same name, was moved to put his own interpretation of that tragic motif into pictorial form.

While it is important to recognize the fact that Curry, like many others at that time, felt the tragedy of World War I most keenly, the real significance lay in his discovery of the pictorial means of adequately presenting that feeling. He had seen Courbet's Funeral at Ornans in the Louvre—the picture is so large one cannot miss it—and the compelling realism had made quite an impression. But Curry firmly denies any influence of Courbet on the painting of this "burial scene." "It was Private Davis that inspired that picture, not Courbet." And the sketches, as well as his recollections of how the painting was conceived show that he was right. Nevertheless history has acclaimed the famous French painter as one of its greatest realists, and in the preceding chapters Curry has been described as fundamentally a realist. One cannot help but link them together as representatives of kindred points of view.

The comparison of Courbet's Funeral at Ornans with some of Curry's original sketches (rather than the more developed painting of later years) for the Burial of Private Davis will demonstrate the basic difference in character between their respective types of realism. It will give tangible definition to the various remarks previously made that Curry's art is not synthetic and that his style grew as an integral part of his own ideas and experience.

Courbet's composition is based on the rigid alignment of strong, stolid figures before an open grave. The grave itself is lost in the shadow of the foreground while the massed figures of the mourners face the beholder and practically cut off the landscape from the scene.

In Curry's version the grave is placed back into the space at the center of the composition with the mourners spread out around it. In the watercolor study (Fig. 48) he adds the clergyman's figure as an additional aid in focusing one's attention on the center space. Instead of concentrating on individual characterizations that make up the assembled group Curry unifies them as a crowd, turns the figures about and subordinates them to the landscape in such a way as to draw the spectator into the spirit and vastness of the space.

Courbet's realism is concentrated on the plastic figures and their solid alignment. Curry appears less interested in the separate figures and more concerned with the emotional expressiveness of space. It is to this end that he chooses the strangely effective colors of gray, blue-green, and salmon pink suggested in the first watercolor sketch. Curry always liked the compositional idea of the burial scene. He used it again later in his illustration to *The Prairie* and in the Topeka murals.

It seems reasonable to believe that the spontaneous success that same year of the Baptism in Kansas was no accident. It was due to the logical if unconscious crystallization of all these compositional elements in a new and dramatic situation. The subject of the picture is the religious sacrament of the Baptism. For this particular type, however, no compositional analogy can be found in the traditional scenes of Christian art such as the well-known Baptism of Christ representations by Giotto, Verrocchio, or Rubens.

The scene was familiar to Curry from his youth at home in Jefferson County, Kansas. There revival meetings and open air baptisms were common ceremonies among those popular religious sects that make up such an important part of American rural life. Like the Saturday afternoon bathing festivities, the baptism was usually held in one of the near-by creeks, but when these were dry the performance was transferred to the wooden water tank on a neighboring farm.

Such scenes had more than a passing significance to Curry. In them were revealed to him the blind faith and religious fervor, intense often to the point of fanaticism, characteristic of such groups. They were an integral part of the rural background from which he grew. Here was no burlesque, satire, or comment of smug sophistication. The scene was conceived and executed with the sincere reverence and understanding of one who had lived it.

One might say that Curry, having been trained as an illustrator, would naturally choose such a scene as characteristically representative of American folk customs. From the study of other drawings and paintings that were in his studio at that time, however, one can readily see that Curry was working as an artist as well as an illustrator. The dramatic terror of the two central figures, the awed devotion of the surrounding crowd, the hushed impressiveness of vast spaces all speak a single and uncompromising language. The gaudy realistic details are there: the lurid color of popular mail-order clothes and the fluttering pigeons of the barnyard, those bright pink and blue counterparts to the pretty doves that floated in the yellow sunlight above the Baptism in the River Jordan represented on every Sunday school card. But their individual gaudiness is completely absorbed in the unique beauty that is Curry's Baptism in Kansas.

This is the America that was seldom thought of when students journeyed to Paris to study art. It was overlooked when the Greenwich Village Bohemians went slumming in the country and continued to delve within themselves for some new mode of expression or artistic novelty with which to compete in the art galleries of 57th Street. Here for the first time was a strong and vital presentation of rural life that could parallel the expression of city life that had already been achieved in the work of such men as John Sloan, Jerome Myers, George Bellows, and Kenneth Hayes Miller.

30. NEGRO HEAD

Notes on the Illustrations

30.—NEGRO HEAD. *Oil on canvas. 1927.* Type study of a colored youth done shortly after Curry's return from Europe to Westport. The head is an extremely dark brown, the shirt is tan, the background a luminous yellow-gold. The chief interest here, as in the Paris drawings, is in heavy solid forms which here are simplified and more direct. There is a regular recession of tone-values from the mouth and chin to the nose and cheeks, the forehead, and the receding black hair.

31—SEATED NUDE. *Red chalk. 1928.* The red chalk of this drawing produces a much more luminous effect in the original than the reproduction suggests. This and Figure 32 were done from models at the Whitney Studio Club where Curry first met Reginald Marsh. "We did a lot of quarreling," Curry recalls, "because Reggie wanted the models constantly changed so that he could draw action poses, while I wanted more time on each one to study anatomy." The sketch book from which these two drawings were taken contains many studies of big heavy nudes similar to those done in Paris. Some of them, as in this case, show an interest in greater life and movement through the use of a more transparent red chalk and a suggestion of muscular structure.

32—STUDY OF TWO STANDING NUDES. *Red chalk. 1928.* The sketch book reveals considerable interest at this time in this type of two-figure composition carefully worked out with posed models. Note particularly the luminous circular modeling of the forms and the sense of light and color. This comes out more strongly in the red tone of the original.

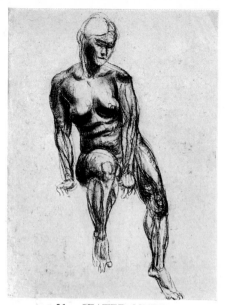

31. SEATED NUDE   32. TWO STANDING NUDES

33—STUDY OF THE SKELETON. Black crayon. 1928. An early attempt to study the human skeleton.

34—BONE AND ANATOMICAL STUDIES. Pen-and-ink drawing. 1928. Note the pains taken in the accurate drawing of bone shapes and sockets as compared to the relative uncertainty of the previous sketch. Equal emphasis is given to muscular structure and to its decorative pattern as can be seen in the plastic regularity of chest and abdomen muscles and in the sketch of the back and shoulders. This drawing and those reproduced in Figures 36 and 38 are from a book of notes and studies made while Curry was taking a course in anatomical drawing at the Art Students League in New York.

36—MUSCULAR STRUCTURE OF THE FACE AND NECK. Pencil and red chalk. 1928. Notice the observations written beside some of the sketches: "Seven vertebrae in all mammals except whales—giraffe has seven vertebrae." Concerning the muscles of the neck he notes the soft fat in front and indicates with arrows the soft skin and heavy skin and the "artery from the heart." Some high-sounding scientific terms appear here and there, such as "africuloris oculus" appended to the sketch at lower left. At the lower right beside a study of the various muscles of expression of the face is the observation that "wrinkles go at right angles to muscles."

38—PELVIC AND OTHER ANATOMICAL STUDIES. Sepia and red chalk. 1928. The particular interest here is in the mechanical structure and functioning of the pelvis. A few notes are visible at upper left referring to Rubens' use of raw Siena in the underpainting of his pictures.

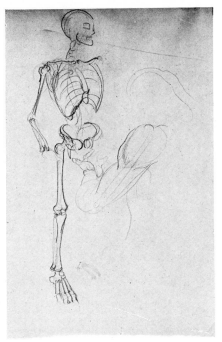

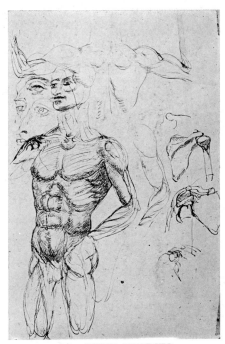

33. STUDY OF A SKELETON

34. BONE STUDIES

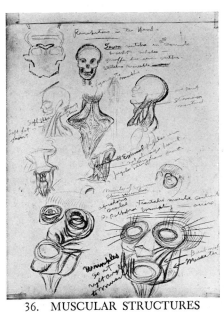

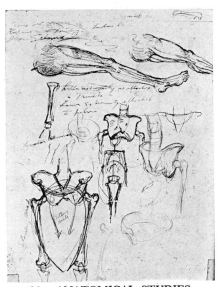

36. MUSCULAR STRUCTURES

38. ANATOMICAL STUDIES

40. ACTION STUDIES OF HORSES

41. ACTION STUDIES OF HORSES

40, 41—ACTION STUDIES OF HORSES (after Leonardo). Pen-and-ink. 1928.
Two of several sketches made from a reproduction of Leonardo da Vinci's famous
drawings in the Windsor Collection.

42—FIGHTING NUDES (after Signorelli). Red chalk. 1928. A study in figure movement made from reproductions of drawings by Signorelli for the frescoes of the Fall
of the Damned in the Cathedral of Orvieto. These drawings were done about the
same time as Curry's detailed anatomical studies at the Art Students League. Notice
the greater freedom and movement here as compared with the massive forms of the
Paris sketches.

43—FIGHTING WARRIORS. Watercolor. 1926. Done in Paris under the inspiration
of the famous lion hunts and battle scenes of Rubens and Delacroix. The composition
is based on the two equestrian figures rearing in the center. From these a number of
actively moving figures are loosely suggested receding into the distance at the left. The
poses of the two twisting nudes in the immediate foreground are taken from Michelangelo's drawings for the Battle of Cascina cartoon which Curry had studied in a book
of reproductions.

42. FIGHTING NUDES

43. FIGHTING WARRIORS

44. BATTLE OF THE AMAZONS

· 57 ·

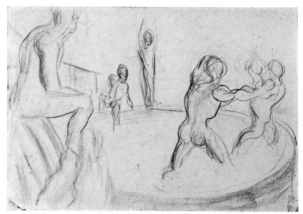

45. STUDY FOR THE BATHERS

46. THE BATHERS

44—BATTLE OF AMAZONS. Oil on canvas. 1928-29. An ambitious study in figure action based on the watercolor of Figure 43, and painted in Westport soon after Curry returned from Paris. The color is used largely as a means of unifying the design. The main tone is gray, with green in the shadows, red and white in the lights. Note the concern with anatomical structure, as seen in the male figure (a similar torso drawing was included in Fig. 34) and the remarkable contrast between this and action scenes of his illustrations (Figs. 15-16).

45—STUDY FOR THE BATHERS. Crayon. 1928. A loose sketch using the unbalanced type of composition experimented with in the two previous battle scenes. It focuses one's attention on the two-figured action of playfully fighting youths as noted in the studies of Signorelli's work.

46—THE BATHERS. Oil on canvas. 1928. Compared to the sketch and previous studies this painting shows a much more refined unity of form. The Michelangelesque posed figure of the youth at the left is pulled down into the picture and, being given greater stability it avoids the toppling oval effect that it has in the sketch. The two fighting figures are somewhat shortened and their action is emphasized by the swirling water about their legs. At the same time this design serves to place them more tangibly in the space and the circular form of the tank. Most striking is the effect of light and color in the composition. The sky is a brilliant yellow green, the figures are set off against it and the darker purple and green background by the bright yellow light of an afternoon sun.

48—THE RETURN OF PRIVATE DAVIS (sketch for) Watercolor. 1928. One of several preliminary sketches which show Curry's concern with the same basic problem of circular masses of figures in a vast open space which occupied his attention in The Bathers and Baptism in Kansas. The painting of The Return of Private Davis was begun at this time but not fully completed until 1940 (see Fig. 276).

This watercolor bears indications of the projected color composition based on gray, blue-green, and salmon pink. Other drawings suggest that the original conception was mainly concerned with the solid massing of figures around the grave. Here these acquire greater movement and organization through the loosening effect of the color, the placement of the clergyman at the head of the grave, and three single figures isolated from the mass in the open space of the foreground. The greater distance indicated in the fields behind the crowd seems to be a compliment to the recession developed in the front.

48. SKETCH FOR RETURN OF PRIVATE DAVIS

49. BAPTISM IN KANSAS

49—BAPTISM IN KANSAS. Oil on canvas. 1928. Whitney Museum of American Art, New York City. This is the picture which established Curry's reputation as one of the foremost artists in America when it was exhibited at various museums throughout the country prior to its purchase by the Whitney in 1930.

It is also the first painting in which were unified all of the various compositional problems with which Curry previously had been working. The two-figured group in the water tank is the focal point of the composition. A circular design is developed around it by the tank, the singing congregation, a half-circle of model-T Fords, which then opens up at the right to the receding highway. The angular forms and foreshortening of the barn, windmill, and farmhouse close off the scene from the background and, at the same time, emphasize, by contrast of proportions, the characteristic vastness of the Kansas landscape. The pyramidal grouping of the two central figures, as well as the opposing diagonal lines of bent heads and shoulders of the standing congregation, roughly correspond to the diagonals of the building roofs forming a pyramid which goes up to the floating pigeons and an imaginary apex in the hidden sun. Similarly the salmon pink color of the barn is carried forward into a salmon brown of the wooden water tank and the light pinkish-ochre of the woman's dress at the front. Blue sky and warm gray of the receding clouds from the top to the horizon complement both the space effect and the weird emotional tone of the color.

5

YEARS OF CRISIS
1929-1936

SEVEN YEARS OF FEVERISH ACTIVITY were to elapse before Curry was to reach his present haven of Artist in Residence. By a coincidence these years of arrival, crisis, the establishment of inner equilibrium, and expanding opportunity and achievement for the artist were the years of the great depression when the American way of life underwent changes of which we are even now not fully aware.

In the summer of 1929 Curry spent six weeks with his parents on the farm at Dunavant, Kansas. It was his first trip home in several years and the inauguration of what was to become an almost annual pilgrimage. He was prolific that summer. He did countless studies of horses, cattle, chickens, scenes from Kansas farm life in general, particularly those with dramatic possibilities, such as the floods in the near-by valley of the Kaw River. By fall he had finished the Tornado, Storm Over Lake Otsego, The Kansas Stockman, Roadworkers' Camp, and a double portrait of his parents.

In January, 1930, the Whitney Studio Club, where most of his pictures painted up to that time had been exhibited, gave Curry his first one-man show. Whereas most critics during the previous years had looked rather coldly on single pictures regarding them as provincial satire, primitive melodrama, or American small-town types, this display of dramatic power and deadly earnestness brought unqualified applause from every side.

". . . his pictures savor so splendidly of the soil that they are a positive gratification in these days when pictorial art has fallen into such traditional patterns," wrote William B. McCormick in the *New York American* (Feb. 2, 1930). He was deeply moved by the vigorous composition and engaging realism. "American art has a real meaning in the presence of such paintings as these." The critic of the *Herald-Tribune* (Feb. 2, 1930) spoke of the "keen insight into the spirit of his subjects" and the "unique effects of execution." To F. W. Eddy of the *New York World* (Feb. 2, 1930) he "weaves a story that goes beyond illustration and touches the realm of emotion." Margaret Bruening in the *New York Evening Post* (Feb. 1, 1930) said, "Curry appears like a young Lochinvar out of the west . . . convincing . . . individual in technical expression . . . blunt and refreshing."

Edward Alden Jewell's review in *The New York Times* (Dec. 7, 1930) of Curry's show the next autumn at the Ferargil Galleries brought this ringing caption: "Kansas has found her Homer" over an article praising him as one of America's foremost painters and one who was certainly headed for something even greater in the future.

It was in 1930 also that his pictures began really to sell. The Whitney Museum that year bought Baptism in Kansas, The Kansas Stockman, The Ne'er Do Well and a number of his watercolors. Two years later the Metropolitan Museum of Art bought Spring Shower, a landscape of the Heart Ranch in Barber County.

Whereas by 1932 there were these many outward evidences of Curry's professional success, actually the year was one of climax of his desperate unhappiness in his Westport environment. He needed inspiration, a new contact with life, an immediate release from the inner struggles and frustrations that threatened to break his spirit. And so literally he "ran away" as he expresses it, to join up with the Ringling Brothers' Circus on its spring tour through New England.

Huge volumes of drawings and watercolors, innumerable studies and preparatory sketches for paintings are evidences of the tremendous productivity of these three months work. It was soon after his return that the Whitney Museum bought The Flying Cadonas (Fig. 199).

In June, 1932, his wife died of heart trouble. For the next two years his entire energy was divided between his work at the studio and his teaching, at Cooper Union (1932-1934) and at the Art Students' League (1932-1936).

In 1934 he married Kathleen Gould whose personal charm and devoted encouragement is reflected in the exuberance and vitality of the work he continued to produce in the ensuing years.

It was also in 1934 that the Federal Art Project was instituted as one of many New Deal cultural and economic measures to combat the effects of the depression. Curry was commissioned to paint murals in the high schools of Westport and Norwalk, Connecticut. In 1936 he was commissioned to paint a mural in the new Department of Justice Building in Washington, D. C.

In the same year, 1936, he was appointed to an independent position as "Artist in Residence" at the Agricultural College of the University of Wisconsin. Recognition had spread from New York to the nation's capital, where in 1938 he did another mural, this time for the Department of the Interior; and from New York to Wisconsin and from there finally to his home state of Kansas, where in 1938 he was commissioned to paint a series of murals for the state capitol at Topeka.

The establishment of the artist's inner equilibrum after the crisis of 1932 was not the result of the art critics' or patrons' recognition and encouragement. It was entirely a personal matter. Many a thoughtful reader, however, will find himself recalling that darkest hour of the depression as a crisis far wider and deeper in scope than the experience of any one individual. It was a crisis that compelled the clarification of many existing social and economic problems and set the course of their development for many years to come.

Curry considers the relationship between his personal struggles and the depression as merely coincidental. From his own point of view that is probably quite true. He was painting his pictures long before the depression gripped the country and he continued to develop that style after it had allegedly passed. If, however, one looks at the period and at Curry's pictures from the vantage ground of detached, historical perspective, one realizes at once the obvious fact that an artist does not function completely divorced from his contemporary society, but on the contrary is invariably to some extent a part of it. The difficulty for the contemporary critic and even for the historian, as it is for the artist himself, is to determine the nature and the degree of the relationship.

It is neither necessary nor advisable to delve into meaningless generalities about the artist and society. It is, however, important, for an understanding of Curry's career to note a number of specific events and personalities whose influence was exerted on both the artist and his public.

One such was the persistent writing of the art critic Thomas Craven, whose *Men of Art* (1932) and *Modern Art* (1934) represent a startling attempt to bring art out of the hazy atmosphere of the esoteric down to the realities of the newspaper-magazine reading public, which the journalist as a business man was trained to respect. Craven's attacks on what he called the "curse of French trivialities" goes back as far as 1923 when he began writing for the old *Dial*, *The Nation*, *New Republic*, and other similar periodicals.

In 1926, he started a series of articles for the *American Mercury* in which the foreign artistic *ism* and the dealer-corrupted School of Paris were subjected to a vitriolic denunciation, which aptly paralleled the critical policies of Henry Mencken at the time.

Critics and artists alike rose in violent reaction against the Craven point of view, but conditions of the times and the depression were forcing art to move in new directions. From the deflating criticism of the Mencken era came a more positive appeal for a new and vital American art. It was on the point of view expressed in the work of Charles Burchfield, John Sloan, Thomas Benton, Reginald Marsh, Boardman Robinson, the modern Mexican artists, the architect Frank Lloyd Wright, and the sculptor George Gray Barnard, that Craven based the future of American Art.

Whether or not one agrees with Thomas Craven's critical methods and judgment, one must admit that he did succeed in bringing home to a larger audience than had ever before been reached the realization that the public could be exploited artistically as well as economically and that an indigenous American art could actually exist. How large that audience was can be gathered from the sales figures of the two books, *Men of Art* and *Modern Art*, which with several new editions, ran well over half a million copies. For art books in the English language this is a record and during the succeeding years it created a veritable boom in the production and sale of popular art books throughout the country.

Another controversial personality is the artist Thomas Benton. Actually he is more than an artist, for in him are combined an exciting reportorial style of painting with a literary skill and an aggressive personality whose challenge to the Parisian mannerisms also went back to the early 1920's. That challenge was based largely on the belief that the reality and function of subject matter in itself should determine the artistic form through which it is expressed, an argument that has long had its parallel in the "form follows function" slogan of modern architecture. The fact that he was commissioned to paint murals for New York's New School for Social Research (1931) and the Indiana building at the Chicago World's Fair (1933), as well as the social content he put into them, are equally significant as a reflection of the period. In the face of the abstract tendencies of the contemporary modernism, patrons again became aware that subject matter was a valuable asset to a painting which could be used to greatest cultural advantage in buildings open to the public.

The prominence given to the art exhibition at the Chicago World's Fair of 1933 is another indication of the changing times. In keeping with the general theme of the fair the exhibition was intended to represent a Century of Progress in American collecting of art works. Attendance figures broke all records but the popular interest was fixed not so much on the impressive Old Masters that American collectors had imported but on certain specific pictures. Armed guards and an iron rail had to keep the crowds back from Whistler's Mother. Grant Wood's American Gothic ran a close second in drawing popular attention. In both cases the attraction was based on an old-fashioned American love of sentiment; and while Grant Wood's picture had all the earmarks of sophisticated satire, the public took it seriously and chose to recognize in the bald simplicity of a collarless dentist and a straight-haired housewife, the fervent earnestness of typical midwestern folk. This appeal may be ridiculed as the cheap type of popular sentimentality that is generally associated with the art of the cinema, tabloid illustration, or advertising. But it drew the crowds into the museum. It brought a new element into the restricted sphere of the museum arts which needed only the artist to transform it into the higher realm of a permanent and genuine artistic form.

That fine art could have popular appeal and therefore was news copy was indeed a significant idea. The December 24th, 1934, issue of the news-magazine *Time* ran a self-portrait in color of Thomas Benton on the cover and included a dramatic account of a new school of American art which it called Regionalism. Besides Benton the article listed Curry, Wood, Burchfield, Marsh among the artists who had used their own experiences and environment for the inspiration of their painting. Obviously all these artists and many others had been in the news before. The tendency, however, had been to play up the old shop-worn inconsequentials that were supposed to be successful news copy. This involved either the usual rags-to-riches success story of an artist who has reached the top, or the drama of a virtuous public that had been ravished by exorbitant prices, or an artist's personal scandals, or the sensation of immoral, naked figures in his pictures.

In this case, however, different artists stemming from widely different sections of the country were brought together through the disrupting conditions of the depression as representatives of a new and dynamic American form of expression. It was more than just the American Scene, for it furnished a new ideal, a stylistic slogan which had tremendous influence both on the consuming art public and on many younger artists who were searching for some way out of the confused aesthetic and economic world in which they found themselves.

The public was now no longer buying French moderns. The importation of their pictures virtually ceased. A renewed and popular interest arose in such American Old Masters as Winslow Homer, Thomas Eakins, and George Bellows, as well as the living artists of the older generation, such as John Sloan and Jerome Meyers who followed in their tradition. The significance of this point of view and the consciousness that the artist's thought and production are as important to the public interest as any other activity are reflected in the prominence given to art of all types in such popular news-magazines as *Time* and *Life* during the ensuing years.

The responsibility taken on in 1934 by the Federal Government for the patronage of the arts was not a cause but a genuinely democratic result of this popular tendency. That program was originally organized to relieve the economic distress of literally thousands of professional artists hit by the depression. Under intelligent leadership the program gradually developed a consciousness of artistic quality and moral responsibility to the society for which the work is done. Regardless of political party or aesthetic creed, that is an achievement of which both the American artist and public are justifiably proud.

One more factor, and perhaps from a Pan-American point of view far more significant than any of the others, was the recognition of what the contemporary Mexican artists had accomplished, and the remarkable solutions they had achieved for many of the same problems that faced their northern colleagues. The appearance of the Mexican painters on the public horizon was very gradual and their sudden dramatization in the news from 1930 on was as much a part of the current social trends as it was their own doing.

Orozco had been living in New York since 1927; but he was not commissioned to paint his Pomona College mural until 1930. Those in the New School for Social Research in New York followed in 1931. His important work at Dartmouth College continued from 1932 until 1934, when he returned to Mexico City. Diego Rivera's career in the United States began in 1930 with his two murals in California. The New York Museum of Modern Art held its sensational—through the unparalleled attendance—exhibition of Rivera's work in 1931. He finished his decoration of the Detroit Institute of Art in 1932 and reached an exciting climax in the famous controversy over his work in Rockefeller Center in 1933. After completing the Portrait of America murals for the New Workers' School in New York he returned to Mexico the following year.

As early as 1929 and in subsequent years a number of books were published which adequately presented the social and historical background as well as the varying points of view of the government, the artists, and the public toward the problem of a national art as it had developed in Mexico.* While there was a great deal of sensational publicity about the Mexican artists at the time it did not detract from the essential value of their work. Neither did it diminish popular acceptance of the fact that art, an *understandable* art, is a necessary attribute of the cultural development of the nation.

To get a complete cultural picture of the depression years, one must observe changes in related fields other than painting. There is no need, however, to draw an elaborate cross-section. It is enough to set forth the ideas presented in two contemporary books.

One is Pearl Buck's best seller of 1931 and 1932, *The Good Earth*. Though in a sense a form of escape literature, this book actually presented problems that were not far away from home even if set in far-away China. The plaintive and sympathetic portrait of well-intentioned human beings incessantly beaten down both by the relentless forces of nature and by human avarice is indeed a far cry from the petty cynicism of a *Main Street* or a *Babbitt* of a few years earlier. These are the values which could also be recognized and pondered before such pictures as Curry's *Ne'er Do Well* (Fig. 76) and Grant Wood's *American Gothic*. They lie at the roots of an attitude of human sympathy and a feeling of social responsibility which are almost devotional in character.

The other significant book is Frank Lloyd Wright's *Auto-*

---

* Anita Brenner, *Idols Behind Altars*, (Payson and Clarke, Ltd.), New York, 1929.
Ernestine Evans, *The Frescoes of Diego Rivera*, (Harcourt, Brace & Co.), New York, 1929.
Stuart Chase and M. Tyler, *Mexico, a Study of Two Americas*, (Macmillan & Co.), New York, 1931.
Alma Reed, *José Clemente Orozco*, (Delphic Studios), New York, 1932.
Diego Rivera and Bertram D. Wolfe, *Portrait of America* (Covici-Friede), New York, 1934.
For reproductions of the Mexican murals and the story of their development, see Laurence E. Schmeckebier, *Modern Mexican Art*, (University of Minnesota Press), Minneapolis, 1939.

*biography,** which was first published in 1932. It dramatized in that artist's own distinctive way an integrated acceptance of art, architecture, and an aesthetic way of life in accordance with the laws of nature. Wright had inherited these ideas from Louis Sullivan (*Autobiography of an Idea*) ** and he had been preaching them through his architecture and his writings since the early 1900's. From this time on his social and aesthetic doctrine of a "Return to Nature and the Land" became a compelling influence on the design and social thought of American architecture. This in spite of the Chicago Century of Progress modernism which threatened to do for contemporary architecture what the Columbian exposition had done for the architecture of the last decade of the nineteenth century.

The factors to which these two books give expression do not tell the whole story, of course, but they are sufficient to indicate the breadth and character of that cultural reorientation which paralleled the socio-political revolution of the depression decade. Just as Curry's development as a youth was based on a religious background of family and the farm, so now his development as a mature artist was an integral part of that deadly earnestness that gripped the entire nation during the depression.

How was Curry consciously affected by these trends? Not at all. He had always known what he wanted to do and had concentrated his every effort on doing it. His point of view can best be found in his own words as given at a press interview shortly after his arrival in Madison to take up his duties as Artist in Residence.

"I learned that I belonged to the Regional school of art long after I had done the work as I pleased, without once giving a thought as to what 'school' it might fit. There is a great deal of

---

* Frank Lloyd Wright, *An Autobiography*, (Longmans, Green & Co.), New York, 1932.
** Louis Sullivan, *Autobiography of an Idea*, (W. W. Norton & Co.), New York, 1924.

nonsense in the critics' attempts to classify artists and their work." He was convinced, he went on to tell the reporters, that art is a powerful instrument of propaganda, but that he did not go in for the communist conception of the class struggle. He preferred to portray the farmers' struggle against uncertain nature. He loved to paint the exciting scenes of the circus, but he believed that his really vital work consisted of the paintings he made of the farm lands of his native surroundings. In Wisconsin he hoped that he could bring farm people in the state as well as students on the campus to an understanding of their environment through an art that people could really understand.

A study of Curry's work will show that there is nothing synthetic about his own personal character or about the art he produces. It is motivated by basic religious concepts that are rooted in the Bible, the family, and the home and he has never been ashamed to admit it. Obviously he does not represent the traditional religious themes as did the Old Masters of Europe. He is a modern artist in the true sense. His ideas spring from the factual world about him. It is the realities of life, directly seen and experienced by himself that fire his imagination and determine the character of his expression.

From early youth Curry's development has followed a remarkably straight line. He seemed to know just those Old Masters and the academy teacher who could help him express what he had to say. Changes of outward circumstances have not materially affected his art or his mode of thinking. From Kansas to New York, Paris, Westport, and Madison his painting shows a consistency of purpose and design that easily penetrates the varying outer forms that identify each setting.

This independence of character makes it difficult to isolate and clarify those qualities in Curry's art that are associated with his immediate environment, his desire to produce an art that is understandable, or his interest in ideas that have some significance to society. One could go to such murals as the John Brown in Topeka and the Justice Defeating Mob Violence in Washington and point out values useful to society. It is conceivable that by means of statistical apparatus employed by poll takers one could get a good sampling of public opinion and even determine the effect of these pictures on law and public morality. More important, however, are those values that manifest themselves through the deeper creative experience that his work inspires. The situation that evolved about Curry at Wisconsin after he had been established as Artist in Residence may furnish a new interpretation of the term "socialized art."

6

ARTIST IN RESIDENCE

1936

THE IDEA OF AN ARTIST IN RESIDENCE had been floating about in various educational institutions for several years. In most cases an artist was simply hired as a regular instructor to teach courses in painting and drawing or the appreciation of art. At Dartmouth the Mexican José Orozco was employed not to teach but to paint a mural, and it was understood that he would mingle and converse with the students while the work was going on. At Wisconsin no restriction whatever is imposed on Curry. He is free to come and go, meet students or not, paint, talk, travel through the state as he pleases. Curry is thus the first true Artist in Residence.

It is to be remembered, however, that Curry's salary does not come out of the state educational budget but from the private donation of a trust fund established by the late Thomas E. Brittingham of Madison. Moreover, the startling degree of freedom and independence enjoyed by Curry is not without local precedent.

Both the position and the title were used by the famous Experimental College at Wisconsin years before. At that time it was merely a matter of a visiting artist associating with the students, allowing them to watch him work, discuss the various problems, and in general providing an artistic stimulus through personal contact. The idea was but one phase of the entire educational experiment, the principle being one of informal and personal instruction rather than the formal course curriculum of traditional institutions.

The year 1936, however, presented a vastly different academic atmosphere from the relatively irresponsible days of 1927 and 1928 when the Experimental College was in vogue. The position of artist in residence was now associated with the Agricultural school whose dean soon became one of Curry's most devoted friends and whom the artist admired as a personality and an educator.

One of Dean Chris L. Christensen's convictions is that the purpose of a state university is essentially to serve the state through the twin functions of training its youth and carrying on research to increase its productivity. While heretofore it was the scientist in the laboratory, the teacher in the classroom, the extension worker in the field who were all seeking to improve the economic lot of the people, now the presence of Curry opened up the vast and relatively unexplored field of the cultural growth of rural men and women.

The point of view is best expressed in Mr. Christensen's own foreword to an exhibition of Curry's paintings held at the Wisconsin Union in Madison during the fall of 1937:

"Education, if it is to serve us to the fullest, must include many things besides learning methods of increasing our financial income. We are all realizing that income is but a means to an end, and that end is the good life.

"So it is that our educational process needs to deal with subjects that contribute to the growth of the cultural side of life, such as literature, art, music, and history, as well as with practical training for the vocations.

"In our agricultural education, both on and off the campus, we aim to help rural people create an economy which will give farmers a standard of living capable of promoting cultural growth.

"With the presence of John Steuart Curry on the campus in the capacity of Artist in Residence, we are giving expression to the desire on the part of the University to help stimulate a more generous appreciation of art, and to relate it more directly and intimately to rural living. Mr. Curry's own life and work is rooted in the soil and expresses in itself a profound understanding of the lives of the people of the land."

Curry's position, then, is not only one of association with the faculty and students of the university but also with the citizens of the entire state. The university and the state have benefited enormously by his presence even though his activity is not defined by the routine requirements of a "job." Viewed in their broadest sense these benefits are of national significance.

The position having no preconceived form to begin with soon crystallized after Curry arrived and went to work. Actually, the artist's contact with the university students as a professional art teacher was negligible. He gave some lectures to students, particularly the farm boys in the Short Course. University classes in art appreciation occasionally made an official tour through his studio, guided by an instructor, and were given a chance to see various drawings, cartoons, and paintings in process of execution. Many students interested in becoming artists went to him for advice and help, but few of them were far enough advanced to work with him, so they were directed to the proper studio classes of the university.

Practical experience has shown that if an artist is to become a cultural influence among students by personal contact, that is by discussion, demonstration, and general mingling with the undergraduates, he ceases to be an artist, for he has obviously little time left to himself in which to paint. Curry's main interest was and is in his own work and he insisted on contributing an average of ten hours a day regularly to that alone, with the result that at the beginning those other activities were restricted to an absolute minimum.

On the other hand, his presence among students in certain activities and sports became a well-known habit which was to exert considerable if indirect influence. When Curry first arrived, he headed straight for the Stock Pavilion on the Agricultural campus and spent several weeks sketching the giant stallions that were being groomed for the coming stock show. For two months during spring football practice in 1937 he was a regular attendant for the full three-hour session every afternoon. He studied and drew each player's stance, the various shifts, and the total action of the team in running off plays. He became a part of the routine. The boys became as used to having him around as to the coaches themselves. This sort of contact between the artist, the players, and the game is the experience which, in itself, is the work of art in the making.

Curry's contacts with the people of the state have been of a similar nature. He has given lectures to those conventions and farm meetings that are often held under the auspices of the university on the Agricultural campus. He has traveled all over the state, particularly during the spring and the fall seasons. Here too it has been the irresistible power of experience, the rich vitality and the movement of vast rollings hills so characteristic of the Wisconsin landscape, that has enveloped the artist. Compared to this the cultural propaganda speeches that he sometimes felt obligated to make were arduous labor.

Through his public lectures, radio interviews, and frequent contacts with the press Curry has constantly emphasized three main features. One is that art belongs in the realm of everyday life; that it should be comprehensible, and that comprehensibility should be motivated by genuine love and affection. Secondly, artistic form is not something to be applied to an object; it is the object itself. Its perfected expression grows out of understanding and the artist's control of his medium to render it successfully. Thirdly, it is the artist himself who creates his own standards of artistic excellence. He is to be judged by these alone, not by outside canons or stylistic measurements.

This appeal for an understandable reality, an organic form, and an independence of judgment in art is reflected in Curry's own personality. He is sincere in his belief that these qualities are to be found in his own work, but he is never too sure. His genuine sincerity, quiet humor, and gentle open-mindedness toward other people's ideas and strivings are apparent to anyone who converses with him. This is one reason why the frequent accounts of him in the press have been so consistently free from the petty bickerings and sensationalism that too often characterize art news.

Curry's fame does not rest on publicity, his artistic pronouncements, his teachings, or on the support of the university that employs him. It rests solely on his work. News items about him of both local and national scope are almost always accompanied by illustrations, and these are frequently in color. The anecdotes, told both in fun and in deadly earnest, which Curry has so often repeated about himself for popular consumption, have only served to deepen the understanding and widen the appeal of experiences so plastically presented in his paintings.

That popular appeal is not passive. It is a slow-moving, but active, potentially dynamic thing. When he first arrived in Wisconsin few university students knew who Curry was or what his pictures looked like. Through the years, however, a popular interest developed to the extent that the 1941 student year book, *The Badger*, was dedicated to him and a considerable number of his pictures were reproduced in it.

Not only the university students, but the gas station attendant, the truck driver, and the farmer now know the artist and his work. Moreover, their understanding is not that of the urban dilettante who has taken a college course or read a book on art appreciation. On the contrary, their understanding has about it a quality of stubborn independence. It recognizes in the terror of the storm, the exhilaration of a spring landscape, or the peaceful satisfaction of grazing cattle experiences that are their common property. Not only are such experiences clarified and even dramatized in the pictures, but they also serve as inspiration to at least a degree of self-clarification on the part of the spectator.

It can be said, therefore, that just as the scientist, the economist, and the educator can increase the material productivity of a society through research, so can the artist increase that capacity for spiritual self-clarification, or better, self-realization which is as good a definition of culture as any. From Curry's point of view rural society has an advantage over the urban and suburban because in it the ancient ties of religion, family, and home are more thoroughly integrated with the stability of the land.

There is evidence to indicate that Curry's work has already served such sociological function. Many younger artists had developed years before under his influence at Cooper Union and the Art Students' League in New York. They have won prizes and some have become famous, but they cannot be justly labeled a band of little Currys or even his "pupils." In Wisconsin Curry has encountered numerous artists, admired their work, and seen to it that they have had the chance to exhibit in New York. In many instances their success was immediate and richly deserved.

These are individual cases. Far more important is the development of an amateur spirit that encourages masses of people— society—to take up art both for the simple love of craftsmanship and for the visual satisfaction of an accomplished work of art. There is a remarkable increase among students at the University of Wisconsin taking the various practical as well as critical art courses that are offered.

A state-wide exhibition of rural art was organized by Curry and Professor John Barton of the College of Agriculture in 1940 and held at the Wisconsin Union Gallery. It attracted paintings from dozens of rural amateurs scattered all over the state. Few of them had had the advantage of professional training and all of them painted because they wanted to express themselves.

A year later another similar exhibition was held. It resulted in a far greater number of participating artists with a considerably higher standard of achievement. Newsmen even began to discover well-rounded personalities whose work the art experts could begin to dramatize as "American Primitives." An article describing the artists illustrated with color reproductions of their work was published in *Life* for March 31, 1941.

The following is Curry's report to a Madison audience on the first exhibition of rural art in Wisconsin:

"During the last twenty years the American artist has turned his eye for subject matter to his native land. He has begun to understand the American scene and to apply this understanding to design.

"The first rural Wisconsin art exhibit brought forth works from heretofore unknown artists in the state—those from the farms.

"Dean Chris L. Christensen of the Wisconsin College of Agriculture felt that the talent of farmers and rural people should be given a hearing in a sympathetic setting. He appointed Professor John Barton of the Department of Rural Sociology to head the committee to select and arrange this showing. Professor Barton working through the county agents got in touch with the artists and in certain counties the agents arranged county exhibits.

"Professor Barton has made the following resumé of certain aspects of this project:

" 'Thirty rural farm people from thirteen counties contributed works of art for the first rural Wisconsin art exhibt in the Memorial Union, January 29-February 2, during the annual Farm and Home Week. Personal information has been secured from twenty-two of the thirty of whom nine are men and thirteen are women. All of the men are farmers, although one has just left the farm to study art, another has part-time employment as a welder, and one part-time painter was formerly a country blacksmith. Five of the nine men are single and their average age is forty-four.

" 'Seven of the thirteen women are single and their average age is forty-three. The occupational status is more complex for the unmarried women as one might expect. All the married women are keeping house for farm families, and average fifty-four years in age. Of those unmarried, two are teaching school, one is employed as a county nurse, one is a professional artist living on a farm, one girl of twenty-one teaches music, another is studying at the Layton School of Art, and a thirty-three-year-old farm woman is running a 40-acre farm. The median age of this group is thirty-one.

" 'Nationality backgrounds show little correlation with state proportions. Fifteen of the forty-four parents were listed as of German origin, 4 Polish, 2 English, 2 Bohemian, 6 Irish, 1 French, and 1 Norwegian.

" 'Seventeen of the twenty-two have lived in Wisconsin all their lives and of the other five, the shortest period of residence in the state is ten years.

" 'Ten people had had no previous art training and half of the twelve who listed such training described it to be of a very fragmentary nature. One woman who painted one of the best pieces, did the painting after she had taken a correspondence art course from Minneapolis. Five have had private teachers, one of whom was a farm girl's mother. Only one of the nine men has had any formal training.

" 'Some of these rural farm artists were discovered for the first time. Only six had exhibited their work before in some general exhibition. Nine had placed work in some local or county exhibit, and seven had never exhibited anywhere.

" 'The motivation for such art work is predominantly creative self-expression or what is often called creative leisure-time activity. Seventeen gave such motivation to their activity, while three gave a distinctly religious interpretation of their art. Four of the twenty-two sell enough of their work to help with their livelihood, and one young girl hopes to become an art teacher in country schools. Only one plans to become a professional artist in the city.'

"It was interesting to me from a craftsman's point of view to see the effects some of these artists attained with the most primitive tools and poor painting materials. A great part of the painting was on wall- or cardboard with a coat of flat white for a ground.

"In talking with some of the artists their technical problems were uppermost in their minds. Their chief aesthetic concern was to achieve a true effect of nature as they knew it. This attitude contrasts strongly with the modern sophisticated idea of bending the form of nature to fit a preconceived mannerism or theory.

"Most of the designs were made from a knowledge of the subject and were not as might be supposed, literal copies of nature."

This is evidence of cultural growth, the responsibility for which falls directly on the artist and the art schools of the state. His position in this respect is best described in an address he delivered before the American Country Life Association in Manhattan, Kansas, on October 15, 1937:

"There has been in the last few years a definite change in the attitude of the American farmer and the educators in agricultural states towards cultural interests.

"There was a short time ago a general feeling among farmers themselves and educators that outside of a rudimentary education the only good use farmers could put their time to was to work and sleep.

"In these last few years, fostered by enlightened state administrators, music, the drama, and now painting have been encouraged in addition to the knowledge of how to raise bigger and better crops and animals.

"The aim of the University of Wisconsin and Dean Christensen in this new educational venture—the establishment of an "Artist in Residence" in the Wisconsin Agricultural College—is well set forth in a statement made by Dean Christensen a year ago when I moved to Wisconsin. Dean Christensen said, 'I feel very definitely that education in our agricultural colleges must be broad and include many things beyond those methods and practices used in making money. Our educational process needs to deal with good literature, art, music, history—the cultural side of life—as well as the practical training for better farming. An understanding and appreciation of art, I believe, is an important phase of an enriched cultural development among rural people.

" 'It is in line with this general philosophy that we here at the University of Wisconsin are making a place on our staff and on our campus for John Steuart Curry with the assignment as Artist in Residence in the College of Agriculture.'

"The College has provided me with a studio on the agricultural campus and I am free to devote my time to creative painting in the studio on exactly the same basis as other members of the University staff devote their time to research work in the laboratories or teaching in the classroom.

"In Japan on certain days the whole people from the Emperor to the common laborer will compose poetry to the cherry tree, or the cricket, or Spring. You can imagine here if you appeared in the restaurant on Saturday night and told the boys you had been composing an ode to the spring wheat that they might raise an eyebrow. But it can be said this superior attitude towards cultural pursuits is disappearing in both rural and urban America.

"It will be of practical value for the people of an agricultural state to erect public buildings that have style and beauty. It will be of practical value that, in these they project on the walls paintings that mean something to the people themselves.

"Last winter I attended the dinner given to the farmers and the housewives honored by the College of Agriculture of the University of Wisconsin and it occurred to me it would be a fine and fitting thing if their communities had portraits of these honored people. It would be a lively and fitting thing if a community which had raised a well-bred and excellent herd of cattle or a prize-winning horse or developed an unusual food product if it could have these celebrated in good painting on the walls of the community buildings.

"The people of the state should expect the art departments of the University and the art schools of the state to provide them with artists capable of executing these designs.

"I received a letter not long ago from a school principal in a Wisconsin town asking my advice on the selection of a subject for a panel in their school. They had so far acquired such things as the Pyramids, the Acropolis and Gothic cathedrals and were debating between the Lincoln Memorial and the Cathedral of Cologne, and all of these were hand-painted by some firm in Oklahoma City. Now my advice was that it would be more interesting and appropriate if they acquired something to do with their own life and community and perhaps used some Wisconsin artist, who could paint Paul Bunyan and Babe the Blue Ox to their great pleasure and advantage.

"I do not despise the classic and accepted form of our civilization, but it is time that people realized they have in this day a more magnificent life to use and to view in our creative efforts than that of any other age."

It would seem obvious that the institution of an Artist in Residence has been more than justified and is a success whether we view it from the angle of the artist, the students, or the citizens of the state and the nation.

PART II

THE WORK

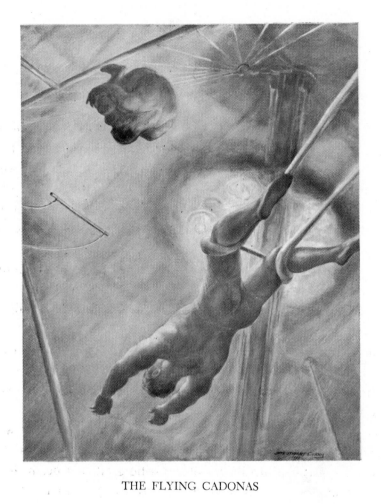

THE FLYING CADONAS

1

INTRODUCTORY

An artist's development is not always a simple matter of his progressive growth from a lower to a higher station on the road to perfection. The romantic desire of some critics to emphasize a dynamic evolution from the plastic form of the early Titian to the coloristic emotionalism of his late period, or El Greco's development from the Venetian realism of his early work to the Greek-Spanish mysticism of his matured style, or again the evolution of Rembrandt from the technical pedantry of the young man to the expressionistic impasto of the aged genius, tends to obscure the intrinsic quality of the individual picture in exploiting its psychological "significance."

Curry's stylistic changes are often influenced by extraneous factors: the patron for whom the picture is painted, the locality in which the artist resides, or the particular fashion of the time. Sometimes they are determined by the subject matter itself.

We have seen the natural ability revealed in his earliest work develop first into the narrative, popular art of the illustrator. We noted that in giving up that profession he gradually began to fix his attention on new objectives and ideals. We followed him through the years from Westport to Paris and back again as he worked his way through a series of problems that pointed to a solution which, once discovered, established the artist on an entirely new level of achievement. We observed how the change of location from Westport to Wisconsin created new possibilities and increased the significance of his own ideal of an indigenous

· 87 ·

rural art. We shall see later that when mural commissions began to come his way his development reflected the new objectives inherent in that medium.

Nevertheless and without detracting from the validity of these considerations, it must be admitted that there is one picture in which, as has been intimated, Curry found himself: The Baptism in Kansas. In it we recognize the matured artist as opposed to the student experimenter. For the thirty-one-year-old man this was a parallel to acceptance as a master in the painters' Guild of St. Luke in the days of the Renaissance. From that time on Curry felt aesthetically free to express himself on any subject in any way he wished. For Curry, however, that freedom created a self-imposed responsibility: to paint the magnificent panorama that is America.

There is nothing cheap or jingoistic about this patriotic urge. The pictures deny it. They show that Curry's patriotism is clear, critical, honest and genuine. It is associated with the geographical location of his home state. It is fortified by the intense religious atmosphere of his farm-home environment. The terse war patriotism of 1917-18 as well as his own service, however short, in the United States uniform, impressed the attitude still deeper on his mind and heart. Certainly his experience amid the social and artistic instabilities of Paris could not help but strengthen his pride in America and the background from which he came. This type of patriotism has had a long tradition in America. It has inspired the efforts of many another creative artist from Walt Whitman to Thomas Eakins to Louis Sullivan.

Freedom, then, meant the elimination of technical doubts and difficulties, the attainment of confidence in his own artistic ability. It meant that he had learned a language and could now speak it fluently. The object of his speech, however, was not personal. It was to express America as he saw it and experienced it for the benefit of the public and society.

There are some who may consider this feeling of social responsibility artificial. One has only to talk about it with the artist himself or, better still, to follow his work to be convinced of his sincerity.

In this connection it is interesting to note that while Curry painted many watercolors and small oils that might be suitable for the decoration of the rooms in a private home, most of these were preparatory sketches for something larger. His important works are all large. They are intended for museums or public buildings. He wants his work to reach the people rather than the individual owner. That is why when the Federal Government inaugurated its program of decorating public buildings Curry eagerly seized the opportunity and through it subsequently developed his art into a genuinely mural style.

In examining the many different types of pictures that Curry painted in 1929 and the years thereafter one will find that they follow a very limited and logical pattern. Each year he went home for an extended visit to his parents. He traveled about the state making sketches of whatever happened to interest him, but he found most of his material right on the family farm. In the paintings done from these studies the progressive development from one year to another becomes less important than the variation and enrichment given to the particular problem or type.

Influences can be traced at given times. Such, for instance, as the glazed technique which John Sloan and his students were using at the Art Students League. This was fully explained in Max Doerner's book* translated into English for the first time and published in 1934. Here was clearly described what many well-known American artists had never fully understood: the basic principle of the mixed technique of oil and tempera painting used by Bellini, Titian, Rubens, and all the great colorists. Since then Curry's best work has been done with this method.

---

* Max Doerner *The Materials of the Artist*. Translated by Eugen Neuhaus. Harcourt, Brace and Company, New York, 1934.

For the purposes of this book it appears most practical to follow the work which Curry has done since the Baptism along the various iconographical or compositional lines that he himself has had in mind. Though not always apparent at first, there is logic in the sequence, for as he worked one idea led to another, the solution of one problem suggested a new one.

The vast parade of experience that Curry has marshaled in works of art during these years constitutes an impressive Pageant of America. The specific facts, dates, and descriptions of individual works are confined to the analytical captions associated with the reproductions at the end of each chapter. The general ideas, artistic problems, and their associations are grouped in the following chapters and their subdivisions.

2

FOLK RELIGION

FROM THE SUBJECT MATTER of the pictures Curry painted in 1928 and 1929 it would appear that religion was more important to him than anything else. One wonders why. An obvious reply would be that it was a natural reflection of his background. That was not unique. Religious training in varying degrees of intensity was the experience of most of the artists and laymen of Curry's generation, despite the lamentations of religious reformers to the contrary. The significant point is not whether the modern artist had any religious scruples within him, but that neither he nor his public saw any excuse for their expression.

Curry did have an excuse. The much talked of prosperity of the years before October, 1929, meant nothing to him. He was poor. He was working hard against adversity, trying desperately to reconcile the conflict between his ambitions and his seemingly insurmountable shortcomings. When a lucky stroke of fortune liberated him to the inspirational atmosphere of Paris he found no aesthetic joy-ride there, but an intensification of the same struggle. Faced with his sometimes unbearable feeling of inadequacy and frustration he, like Van Gogh, sought a spiritual release through the intensified study of reality and form which in turn found expression in representations of man's struggle with his own emotions, i.e. in the religious scene.

In America such a genuine religious impulse could never find expression through the established Biblical subjects of the Christian church. Organized religion follows a time-honored practice of either condemning the religious representation as idolatrous and therefore evil (unless as an historical museum-piece it becomes a "work of art"), or of simply buying pictures that are produced commercially as practical objects of devotion. From an historical point of view the religious achievements of individual painters like John La Farge remain pathetic exceptions.

On the other hand, certain metropolitan institutions like the museum, the art gallery, and the art journals have maintained the public's respect for the artist and his ability to express what he sees, feels, and experiences in life. That is why the combined drama and pathos of such human situations as the Baptism, Gospel Train, and Prayer for Grace could establish Curry as a competing artist and, under pressure of the times, they could even achieve a considerable degree of popularity.

This popular tendency toward folk religion was not Curry's creation. During the late 1920's a wide interest had developed in the Negro spiritual with its unquestioned sincerity, deep resonance, and unsophisticated form. Its character had inspired Mark Connelly's famous and highly successful play, Green Pastures (1931), and while the play can hardly be called a product of the depression it did embody a spirit which was basically sympathetic to the new values developing in that period of economic and social dislocation. With the reorientation that accompanied the new government of 1933 these values grew into determining factors of national scope.

There are many historical parallels that might be cited in this connection as a means of more sharply focusing the situation in proper perspective. One is the now historic development of a new and modern art in Mexico during the early years of stable government after the Mexican revolution of 1910-1920. The idea of comparing Mexican aspirations, experiments, and achievements of a social or cultural nature with our own is not an unwarranted procedure. It has been common practice since the publication in 1931 of Stuart Chase's well-known book on Mexico.*

Many cultural idealists of an older order in the United States have resented the very existence of Mexican art, calling it communistic, atheistic, or just bad art. Their opinions to the contrary notwithstanding, what Mexico has achieved is not only great art but something that has proved to be of considerable cultural profit to the United States.

There were, of course, many factors in the birth and development of modern art in Mexico. The main one is that it was an integral part of a national reconstruction program following ten years of revolution, foreign intrigue, and frightful self-destruction. The "renaissance" movement was sponsored by the government as a conscious effort to build up public morale and national self-confidence. To this end native artists were employed to decorate the walls of public buildings with Mexican subjects. Though these artists were fully aware of what "modern" art was, they prided themselves on speaking in general a native language to a native public.

In the process of the work there were many manifestoes issued, personal rivalries exploited, and arguments as to the procedure, but out of the confusion appeared a number of basic solutions that will bear critical examination, if not always as works of art, certainly as ideas.

Walking through the National Preparatory School of Mexico City one will find that on a majority of the walls that were first painted by the group there are religious subjects. These deal with local variations of established themes that cannot be otherwise interpreted than as Mexican folk religion. (For example: Orozco's Madonna and Child or St. Francis; Rivera's Creation; Revueltas' Allegory of the Virgin of Guadalupe; Siqueiros' Christ; Leal's religious festival of the Feast of Chalma) .

* Stuart Chase and M. Tyler, *Mexico*, (Macmillan and Company), New York, 1931.

A second type of subject is the battle scene in which narrative historical detail is completely absorbed in the contemporary symbolism and the dynamic form (Charlot's Fall of Tenochtitlán). A third is concerned with the representation of characteristic scenes from the everyday life of the farmer and laborer (The decorations of the Ministry of Education by Rivera). A fourth type is the Mexican landscape which has remained the particular subject of the most inspired painter-patriot of the whole group, Dr. Atl. It has had little vogue among the mural painters.

Curry speaks with considerable respect of the Mexican artists. He feels that they have been a powerful liberating force on himself and on the general patronage of art in the United States. He does not care for what he calls the "bended back style" of Rivera or for the social idealism that Orozco has dramatized on the walls of the New School for Social Research in New York, but he does have great admiration for the artistic quality of Orozco's work, particularly such mural compositions as the Trench and the Franciscan, which he has seen in reproduction. Unquestionably the fame and activity of the Mexican artists were directly responsible for the liberal attitude of both private patrons and the Federal Government in permitting American artists to paint new and unorthodox ideas on the walls of public buildings.

One will search in vain, however, for direct influences of the Mexican artists on Curry. He admits only one possibility: The Fugitive, which might be related to the idea of Orozco's Franciscan. In 1928 Curry hardly knew that the Mexicans existed. It was precisely in that year that his style became fully crystallized.

The significant observation to be made here is the fact that Curry, out of his own individual experience and idealistic conception of what should constitute an American art, independently chose just the same four basic types that the Mexicans had developed. Many of his earlier pictures were of a popular religious character; while the interest in battle scenes was not the historical

THE LINE STORM

representation, it was translated into the conflict of men, beasts, and the elements of nature. His folk scenes were those of home and the farm; and he considered the landscape the most fruitful and genuine medium of a national expression.

One can see, therefore, that Curry's sense of values, his choice of subject, and artistic motif run deeper than the mere expediency of painting a picture. They have certain universal qualities that one can discover in the work of many artists in as many different countries. The examination and comparison of these values as they appear in different situations is very useful in clarifying the particular problems in Curry's work.

Such comparisons are not to be understood as an eclectic process of identifying values. Curry once remarked that it was very flattering to be compared with an Old Master, but what of it? "I'm no Rembrandt, Mexican, Homer, or anyone else; I'm myself, or at least I try to be." Just as one is in the habit of juxtaposing various literary or musical works as a means of comparison, so it is profitable to compare pictures and ideas as a means of clarifying those values which are Curry's. There are many influences of Old Masters on any artist—no artist has ever existed in a void—but those influences are not literary or historical. They grow out of the inspired contact between the artist-pupil and the Old Master through the unembellished picture that hangs in the museum.

Curry's attitude toward the museum and the work of other artists is best reflected in remarks he made to a group of young art students in 1937: "Do not make the mistake of closing your mind to the accomplishments of other artists, but when the artist begins to stuff his ideas into the form of another, then the idea is very likely putty and will never be a strong thing . . . If you have an ideal, stick to it and pay no attention to what is said for or against it . . . there is no political or aesthetic bandwagon that goes the whole way, and for the true and determined artist no Jesus on whose breast to lay his curly head."

There are many broader values in Curry's religious pictures that go beyond the particular realistic scene represented. The central motif of the Baptism in Kansas is the two-figure group, in The Gospel Train it is the single dancing figure with outstretched arms that stands out and is dramatized by smaller figures around it. The gesture was undoubtedly seen as the sketch shows, but it is an expression of prayer, supplication, pity, or helplessness that was commonly used in Medieval art (the orant gesture). It appears in almost every popular religious demonstration and is standard with any inspired rural pastor today. In The Gospel Train it carries a spirit of hypnotic ecstasy; in Prayer for Grace it is a more subdued gesture of prayer used to complement the group to the right of the picture.

A small watercolor sketch like that of Figure 56 for the Prayer for Grace can be more effective in explaining the devotional content of this painting than pages of descriptive text. As the sketches show, there were two complementary points of concentration in the picture: the praying figure and the woman sobbing in repentance. The kneeling pose and the soft texture of the light and shade recall many similar figures in the work of Rembrandt, such as the sorrowing mother of Tobias, the Repentant Magdalene, or the Woman Taken in Adultery.

Ignoring for the moment the fact that Rembrandt is one of the greatest artists of the seventeenth century in Europe, and Curry is a modern from the American Middlewest, one will appreciate that Rembrandt, too, was a stubborn nationalist, who lacked the superficial refinement of the Grand Tour to Italy. There is no doubt that Rembrandt knew the works of the great Italian masters and copied them whenever he could, but from the point of view of the well-traveled gentleman he could not compete with a Rubens or Van Dyck. Rembrandt, too, was a

54. PRAYER FOR GRACE (*First Sketch*)

55. PRAYER FOR GRACE (*Another Sketch*)

53—PRAYER FOR GRACE. Oil on canvas. 1929. A painting related to the Gospel Train but based on a group of sketches done in Kansas on another occasion. Instead of the hysterical excitement worked up by the singing, prancing mob, the situation here depicted is that which immediately follows, resulting from the physical exhaustion and emotional breakdown of pathetically sobbing figures. Compositionally the interest is centered much more on the grouped figures themselves than the larger space and gesticulating figures of the Gospel Train. The color composition is based on a weird green and purple, with the kneeling woman a muddy blue, the men at her left and right a red-brown and purple respectively. In striking contrast to the dark tone of the other figures the little girl toward the left is painted a bright pink with gleaming yellow hair.

56.　WEEPING WOMAN　(Study for Prayer for Grace)

54—PRAYER FOR GRACE. First Sketch. Blue ink. 1929. Note again, as in the Gospel Train sketches, the attention given to certain expressive details: the kneeling figure with outstretched arms and the type studies of faces. Observe that the two group suggestions are made, one a general view down the sawdust trail to the pulpit, the other the climax group when one of the crowd breaks down and is ministered to by the leaders.

55—PRAYER FOR GRACE. Sketch. Red chalk. 1929. A development of the small group around the sobbing woman suggested in one part of Figure 54.

56—WEEPING WOMAN. Pencil with watercolor additions. 1929. A study for the central figure in Prayer for Grace. The color indicated is a rich, soft beige at the face which changes to a warm gray at the waist and to a deep purple at the feet.

Among the many detail sketches which Curry had made for the Prayer for Grace composition, this rough and quickly executed watercolor is especially revealing in its simple pathos. It is not the subject alone. It is not the fact that he accidentally discovered an effective expression in the pose of a woman kneeling with her back to the spectator. It is the remarkable character of the color by means of which he has expressed these things.

57—THE PRODIGAL SON. Watercolor. 1929. A theme and composition which Curry liked but never developed into a major painting.

58—BAPTISM IN BIG STRANGER CREEK. Lithograph. 1932. As a composition this scene is more related to the Roadworkers' Camp and State Fair (Figs. 78, 181) than to the Baptism in Kansas. Sketches show that the scene was actually observed and not composed from memory as was the Baptism in Kansas. Note the emphasis given to the space through the forest interior, the winding river into the background, and the progressive descent of figures from the right foreground into the stage-like space at the center. The forward parade of the figures from the crowd on the opposite shore is another compositional innovation that is developed in later murals (Fig. 332).

57. THE PRODIGAL SON

58. BAPTISM IN BIG STRANGER CREEK

3

RURAL STORMS

To ANY FARMER, as to the seaman, the storm is more than just another weather item. Sometimes it is a matter of life or death. Often it may mean the destruction of his property; success or failure of his crops.

Few regions of the world have been more lavishly endowed with violent extremes of weather than Kansas. It was a terror to the hardy immigrants during pioneer days and is so described by Francis Parkman in *The Oregon Trail*. It is quite natural that among the early settlers, by nature a religious folk, the storm took on those religious aspects which have persisted to this day.

Something of the point of view of the storm as retribution for man's evil deeds hurled from on high by God, the great Avenger, frightful and terrifying to His wayward children has already been described in a previous chapter. During the depressed mood that possessed Curry in the years immediately following his return from Paris, this point of view was a powerful motivating force behind his storm pictures.

Though today he is no longer fearful or superstitious about it, he invariably experiences a thrill before the grandeur and drama of lightning and the thunderstorm. It alone seems to embody that supreme Power which the prophets praised and which the artists of other times painted in their Moses figures, Last Judgments, and and their Conversion of Paul scenes.

Such was the symbolism and the temperament that focused the artist's attention on the youthful memories of The Tornado. But it was no revolutionary invention of Curry's. New York's

Metropolitan Museum exhibits a number of storm pictures of various types. One is John Sloan's Fifth Avenue Dust Storm (1906), with its running figures, threatening dark cloud overhead, and the towering form of a skyscraper in the center background. Another is Winslow Homer's Gulf Stream (1899), with its funnel-shaped waterspout receding over the horizon. A third is El Greco's storm-swept view of Toledo with its dramatic color and light pattern.

Curry knew these pictures but did not "copy" them. What makes an artist is neither the subject nor the compositional motif of his painting, but his skill in handling both. The richness and consistency of his imagination can be followed through the many storm pictures which he has painted. The compositional idea of a cylindrical form silhouetted in the center, with a dark area overhead and figures on either side can be traced from the somewhat faltering but dramatic style of Curry's illustrations to The Lightning (Fig. 22) and The Tornado (Fig. 59). Years later it was dramatized into mural proportions in the decorations of the Kansas State Capitol.

Once the Tornado was perfected innumerable new variations sprang from it. The objective form of the storm developed from the clear distant space of the Storm over Lake Otsego to the thick choking atmosphere of the Dust Storm, the circular cloud wall of the Line Storm, the waving sheets of flame in the Prairie Fire, and the relentless, slow rise of flood waters. Against those forms the terrified groups of animals and human beings are juxtaposed with equal dexterity and inventive genius.

The Tornado was painted from memories of such storms in his youth, the later works based on the vivid experience of actual observation show possibilities of new developments. The horrible scenes of desolation which he saw near his home in 1930, together with the exciting stories of those who had lived through the storm made a deep impression. Many of the paintings executed depict objective facts, with dramatic contrasts of details and a weird emotionalism in the design that many critics have identified as Surrealist (e.g. Fig. 67). The projected new painting of The Tornado in action, for which he made several drawings, (Figs. 62-64) never materialized, but the sketches show something of the tremendous power the composition embodied.

The horror, desolation, dramatic action, and social implications of The Tornado may be read in a remarkable description written by his mother, Margaret Curry, shortly after this particular storm had passed.

"We in Winchester had come to believe tornadoes and storm caves a phase of life of an earlier day. But in the late afternoon of May first there was a heavy rain, accompanied by a sudden warm, humid period; then a dead calm during which hail fell. We could look up into the heavens and see the big stones, some nine inches in circumference, falling slowly. Because of the calm they did little damage.

"After this the sun almost shone and the air was fresh, a welcome change from the mugginess preceding the shower.

"Going outside, we noticed a large flat cloud, rather dark and spreading out, in the southwestern sky. The edges of the cloud waved with a restless undulation. Then a roaring began in the heavens; the center of the cloud started to swirl, then dropped in a cone toward the earth. The roaring increased. Another cone seemed to shoot upwards from the earth and the two met. In a moment the funnel formed. As it proceeded the lower end of the funnel swung like a pendulum. It came to earth and the earth came up to meet it in a wet and steamy cloud. Once the funnel parted, but came together again and began to move over the earth.

"The funnel was firm of outline and a yellow-white in color. It towered high to the cloud above. At its base was a great, boiling fountain of mud from the recently wet ploughed land. As it moved the earth vibrated as if a heavy train were passing and the whole heavens shook with the grinding roar.

"At the destroyer's approach the trees bowed down toward it, then disappeared into the black fountain. We could see a neighbor's farmstead blotted from view, then the barn appeared above the boiling mass and seemed to explode into a thousand pieces.

"After traveling about a quarter of its forty-mile course, a part of the cloud broke off and from this another funnel fell, moving in a parallel course to the parent for some miles and doing great damage. A path from two hundred to four hundred yards in width was marked as if a great muddy mop had been passed over it, blotting out every blade of grass and covering every object with a plaster of black mud. The fields were strewn with boards and rolled and matted fence wire. Some great trees were uprooted and stripped bare of leaves; from others the limbs were wrenched off, leaving torn and ragged stumps. Farm homes and buildings were swept away leaving bare foundations and a tangled wreckage of lumber, furniture, clothing, farm machinery, automobiles, and the dead and mangled bodies of chickens, hogs, cattle, and horses.

"Mr. John Miller, with his wife and daughter were severely injured when their farm home was destroyed by the tornado. Mr. Miller had stepped out on the porch to repair a window broken by the hail, when he saw the tail of the twister not a hundred yards away. He was knocked unconscious and an eighteen-inch splinter driven through his hand. Regaining consciousness, he found himself against the farther foundation of the house. Upon hearing the cries of his family he pushed the splinter through his hand by pounding it against the foundation, and went to their rescue. His daughter suffered a fractured skull; his wife terrible bruises, a burned shoulder, and a severed Achilles tendon. They were so covered with mud as to be unrecognizable.

"At the Everett Pence's place the barn was completely swept away, but left the cows unharmed in the stanchions, although almost every other animal on the place was destroyed. When the cows were released, the stanchions fell over.

"The body of another house was completely wrecked and swept away. The floor of the kitchen was moved twenty feet from the foundation, stripped bare with the exception of part of the wall and the cupboard shelves, on which were kitchen utensils and two oil lamps with glass globes intact.

"Most of the people sought refuge in storm caves. One family ran to a ditch and threw themselves face down in it. Another group ran out of the direct path of the tornado and by clinging to trees saved themselves from being drawn into the terrific suction. In other homes, the occupants, unaware of danger until too late, were all severely injured in the wreckage. A man and his wife, caught in their house, were killed. His body was found a mile away.

"Those escaping from its direct fury have vivid remembrance of the dreadful noise and the sulphurous stench of the tornado. One man who observed it at close range estimated the opening of the funnel to be twenty feet across and in and out of this opening shot clouds of black vaporous stuff.

"This community, which had sent thousands of dollars to starving Chinese, stricken Armenians, and the needy of the world, was confronted by a disaster in its own dooryard. The Red Cross immediately organized the relief work, collected money, food, and clothing, and started giving help to the most needy in rebuilding and replacing destroyed property.

"The neighbors and men from surrounding towns began the task of cleaning the debris from the fields and piling the wrecked lumber. The warden of the state prison at Lansing sent two gangs of men to help with the work. So, slowly the damage of a May Day storm is being repaired."

The experiences and their associations which Mrs. Curry has thus written down in such dramatic form can be followed in a totally different medium through the work of her artist-son in the reproductions, Figures 62-75.

59. THE TORNADO

Notes on the Illustrations

59—THE TORNADO. *Oil on canvas. 1929. Hackley Art Gallery, Muskegon, Michigan. The Tornado is Curry's best known and in many ways his greatest painting. It is one which, Harry Wickey wrote, "fulfills Walt Whitman's hope and prophecy of a truly great native art growing out of American life. . . The Tornado is a masterpiece in any age and easily stands in America today as a strong link in the great chain of the art of all time."*

The scene is a dramatic event from the rural life of Kansas, illustrating, as Curry described it, "how we used to beat it for the cellar before the storm hit." The idea

60. STORM OVER LAKE OTSEGO

is closely related to the earlier The Lightning (Fig. 22). Here, however, the emphasis is placed on the tense moment before the storm breaks rather than on the crash itself. The composition is changed from the yellow-lighted tree trunk between the figures in the foreground to the swaying cone in the distance. The result is a heightened tension.

The focal point of the composition is, therefore, the funnel-shaped form of the tornado advancing over the distant horizon. This is framed to the left and right by the barn, tool shed, cyclone cellar, and the back porch of the house, all of which are sharply foreshortened to heighten the dramatic effect of the space and the forward movement of the tornado. The figures are hurrying to the cyclone cellar, yet seem to be suspended for a moment as the farmer looks back in terror at the oncoming storm. This look, the dominating proportions of the farmer's figure, the foreshortening of the family groups to his left and right, the farmer's wife and baby and the children with their pets, even a group of frightened horses in the distant pasture, are all used for the same dramatic purpose as the exaggerated perspective.

The color composition is based on the lurid light characteristic of such storms. The storm cloud itself, receding above and behind the funnel, is a deep purple, which is carried forward to the brighter purple dress of the chalk-faced farmer's wife. The lighter patch of the sky is a blue-green which is continued in the darker green of the pasture, the tree at the right, and the grass in the foreground. With the exception of the purple dress at the left, the figures are painted a luminous blue which sets them off from the light brown of barnyard, wooden path, and steps. A cold whitish pallor is woven through various patches, from the steps and chicken to the cellar opening, the fence,

61. HORSES RUNNING BEFORE A STORM

farm buildings, and finally the storm-funnel itself, to heighten the unearthly terror of the scene.

Notice the choice of realistic details for their human interest value which at the same time function in the artistic design of the picture: the child's wagon and a beady-eyed chicken in the foreground are used as part of the circular pattern as well as a dramatic contrast to the action in the center. The white-faced mother clutches her child, the children grab their pets, and the dog runs after her puppies. As they lunge excitedly to the left they form part of a diagonal pattern that extends from the foreground figures to the tornado funnel in the distance.

It is interesting to note that when the picture was originally exhibited in the Corcoran Gallery in Washington, the tornado funnel was painted in the shape of a wildly dispersed waving mass. Later it was changed to the more plastic revolving cone-shaped form it has in its present state.

60—STORM OVER LAKE OTSEGO. Oil on canvas. 1929. Collection of Mrs. Polly Thayer Starr, Boston, Massachusetts. This picture was painted at Westport shortly after The Tornado. It was based on sketches made years earlier in the Lake Otsego region near Cooperstown, New York. Notice that the object of terror takes the form of the lightning and storm clouds over the space at right while the action is concentrated in the excited figures and the tree designs in the foreground and left in positions comparable to those of The Tornado. A greater emphasis on space in general is given through the subordinated position of the figures and the winding design of the road from the distant right around the foreground and deep into the woods at left.

61—HORSES RUNNING BEFORE A STORM. Watercolor. 1929. Whitney Museum of American Art, New York City.

61a. HORSES RUNNING BEFORE A STORM (Lithograph)

61a—HORSES RUNNING BEFORE A STORM. Lithograph. 1930. A motif based on the excited group of horses terrorized by the approaching storm used in the pasture in the background of The Tornado. Note the similarity of some of the poses here to those of the early illustrations (Fig. 11). The development of their combined balance and tension into an abstract pattern is far more effective here than in Storm Over Lake Otsego. This principle is developed further in the lithograph of 1930 than in the watercolor of 1929; otherwise the two pictures are very similar.

62-3-4—CRAYON SKETCHES OF A TORNADO. 1930. Three of an extensive series of sketches made on a visit home in the summer of 1930. Shortly before he arrived a tornado had passed through the Winchester neighborhood only a few miles from his father's farm, causing considerable damage and loss of life. Like a regular news reporter or photographer Curry not only sketched the particularly striking scenes in the devastated areas, but also tried to reconstruct the actual appearance and effect of the storm from descriptions of farmers who were in it. Reportorial accuracy, however, is coupled with artistic effects as the described event is set on paper. Notice the tree-like shape of cloud and funnel in Figure 62 which in Figure 63 is expanded into a low ceiling. From this hover the suspended tentacles of other spouts far off in the distance in a manner similar to the receding forms in the earlier storm picture (Fig. 22). As in The Tornado, these studies, even though they are little more than a reporter's sketches, show the forward-moving funnel as the motivation for the action. Notice, however, the new effects he tried: the diagonal placement of the architecture in Figure 62 at right angles to the forward movement of the funnel. In other sketches, running men and galloping horses appear to be rushing out of the depth of the picture rather than across the front, as the figures do in The Tornado. Curry has always intended to paint a new Tornado based upon these sketches and the compositional ideas experimented with here.

67—AFTER THE TORNADO. Oil on canvas. 1930. A characteristic dramatization of certain realistic details: the parlor chair with the doll in the foreground and the twisted debris piled into several decorative forms that recede into distance from the foreground at the left. The typical gaudy colors of such parlor furnishings, a poisonous pink and green chair and bright green rug are contrasted to the purple-brown floor and to the blue-gray of the background. The sky moves from a dark slate blue to an eerie greenish-yellow at the horizon.

68—DUST STORM. Watercolor. 1930. A very sketchy watercolor which he painted while on a trip to Oklahoma City the same year as the tornado sketches. The main compositional feature and motivation is a dull yellow haze that envelops the farm buildings and the pallid sun. Its artistic possibilities are more limited than the dramatic forms of The Tornado and The Line Storm. He had used the idea in an early illustration (Fig. 13) and attempted it again later in the Topeka murals (Fig. 317).

69—THE LINE STORM. Oil and tempera on panel. 1934. Collection Sidney Howard, New York. This is the second of Curry's three greatest landscapes, the other two being Spring Shower (Fig. 86) and Wisconsin Landscape (Fig. 90). Grant Wood, a great admirer of Curry's work, called the Line Storm "one of the most moving creations in American Art." The storm motif here, in contrast to the tree-like design involved in the funnel and cloud composition of The Tornado, takes the form of a heavy rim of clouds moving horizontally over a wide area of the plains and enveloping them ominously within its dark blue-green shadow. The emphasis is upon the space and the figures are subordinated to it, galloping in terror in a reaction similar to those

62. STUDY FOR THE TORNADO

63. STUDY FOR THE TORNADO

64. STUDY FOR THE TORNADO

67. AFTER THE TORNADO

68. DUST STORM

in other storm scenes. The real drama, however, is effected through compositional means: note the striking contrasts of bright yellow light on the hayrack, farm buildings, and wheat fields against the dark storm cloud; the jagged streaks of lightning; the huge form of the cloud as opposed to the small scud clouds at its edge receding from the top of the picture around to the distance at the right.

The Line Storm is one of the first examples in which the mixed technique of oil and tempera, stimulated directly by Max Doerner's book, The Materials of the Artist, was used to achieve a more solid modeling of the forms and a greater luminosity of the color.

69. THE LINE STORM

70—THE PRAIRIE FIRE. *Color illustration to James Fenimore Cooper's The Prairie, Limited Editions Club, 1940.*

"Huge columns of smoke were rolling up from the plain, and thickening in gloomy masses around the horizon. The red glow, which gleamed upon their enormous folds, now lighting their volumes with the glare of the conflagration, and now flashing to another point, as the flame beneath glided ahead, leaving all behind enveloped in awful darkness, and proclaiming louder than words the character of the imminent and approaching danger"—The Prairie, page 255.

The composition which Curry used is slightly related to that of Figure 69 with particular emphasis given to the dramatic figures in the foreground. The storm cloud is translated into a wall of flames, the color a glowing red and yellow with heavy black clouds of smoke above instead of the blue-green and white rim of The Line Storm. The spaciousness of The Line Storm's green fields is quite a contrast to the flat dry brown of the prairies, whose horizon line is set considerably lower. The dark brown figures of terrified horses and men are sharply silhouetted against the brilliant red flames. The result is that the whole spectacle appears not only to move majestically to the right but also to bear down much more dramatically upon the beholder of the picture.

71.   KANSAS FLOOD

72. SANCTUARY

73. SANCTUARY

74. THE MISSISSIPPI

71—KANSAS FLOOD. Watercolor. 1929. Curry made several sketches similar to this one of a flood in the Kaw River valley near Lawrence, Kansas, while home in 1929. The idea and symbol of the "flood" runs parallel to that of The Tornado but the artistic possibilities of such a scene are extended to an expression of mood as well as to the drama of action. To achieve the mood he uses the horizontal lines of the flood waters, gray color tones, and a composition of isolated, soaked, and dejected figures.

72—SANCTUARY. Watercolor. 1933. A study for oil painting of the same name (Fig. 73). It was based on drawings of the floods in the Kaw River valley of which Figure 71 is typical.

73—SANCTUARY. Oil on canvas. 1935. As in the Horses Running Before the Storm (Fig. 61), Curry depends on the design and gestures of the victims to carry the drama of the flood. In this case it is the pathetic plight of farm animals marooned on the only remaining patch of land. The general color tone of the picture is a warm gray which is focused on the dappled gray mare in the center. The purplish red of the hog in the foreground is repeated in the darker tones of the two cows and mule behind the horse, while the black and white of the cow and hog on either side is continued in the black of a third animal seen through the legs of the standing figures. Curry's gentle sense of humor is revealed in the parade of thoroughly soaked skunks—mother and a trail of young ones—crawling up the log at the right, to the dismay of the hog turning to look at them. When asked about them he remarked that he had always liked skunks: "They will never bother you if you leave them alone." A whole pack of them used to live peacefully under his studio in Westport. The skunk idea was not thrown in just for a laugh but, like the chicken in The Tornado, performs an essential task for the composition. The parade of skunks creates a diagonal movement that leads into the group of larger animals from the right and continues out into space through the head of the lowing cow at the left. The watercolor sketch, Figure 72, shows that these gestures were an intrinsic part of the compositional idea from the beginning. The sketch also reveals many of the basic features of the design more obviously than the finished painting.

74—THE MISSISSIPPI. Oil and tempera on panel. 1935. City Art Museum, St. Louis, Missouri. The subject is related to the songs and spirituals dealing with the tragedies of Noah and "Ole Man River," but the composition is based on the same series of Kaw River sketches mentioned in the discussion of Figures 71-2-3. Note how the weird and pathetic tone of the scene is intensified by the color: Carmine red, light blue, white, luminous brown, and yellow in the figure group on the roof set off against an eerie background of purple, yellow, and green. The pathetic head and hapless gesture of the father praying for mercy is set against the circular pattern of the light patch in the sky. The lowing gesture of the cow to the left in Sanctuary performs essentially the same expressive function.

75—FLOOD VICTIMS. Tempera on paper. 1937. One of several sketches painted the year of the disastrous flood of the Ohio River for an illustration requested by the SATURDAY EVENING POST, but rejected. The composition is based on The Mississippi but it is changed from a horizontal to a vertical frame. The figures are consequently packed in a taller group with the father standing and the pitched roof used further to accent the vertical composition. To heighten the dramatic effect, the illumination from a bolt of lightning is substituted for the soft light and praying gesture of The Mississippi. The skunk family of Sanctuary is here replaced by the well-soaked family cat that adds a touch of homely realism and pathos.

75.   FLOOD VICTIMS (Sketch for Saturday Evening Post)

4

FARM LIFE

In General

THE POPULAR RELIGIOUS SCENES and the storms were exciting events that Curry liked to dramatize in pictures. Though quite genuine, these events had something of the incredible and the-atrical about them. They were not the normal aspects of his annual visits to the farm life of Kansas. That was a moving pano-rama of people at home and in the fields, of the changing seasons and the weather in its more benign moods, of the growing grain, of trees and flowers, of domestic animals in yards or pasture, and of the pets about the house. These were the everyday things of rural life which Curry recognized as beautiful in themselves. The pictures he painted of them through the years constitute an almost Olympian reply to the naive criticism once made of the Baptism and The Tornado that "Curry paints only the seamy side of Kansas life. Why can't he find something beautiful?"

There is a contrast, to be sure, between the artistic seclusion of Westport and the farm in Kansas. To Curry Westport was a place to work whereas Kansas was home. His periodic return was not only to fatten up on his mother's cooking, but an opportunity to gather material and ideas about that life and environment which had been his own from childhood. Moreover, as a professional artist he grew to believe that such an attitude would be financially profitable given enough time and patience for his work and the public somehow to get together.

The point of view of his return to reality is best expressed in a talk which Curry gave in 1937 to a group of students at the University of Wisconsin:

"For a long time American painting has been strongly influenced by outside styles and trends: first it was the school of Munich; then French Impressionism, the various succeeding mannerisms of the so-called School of Paris; and in the last few years the famous Mexican artists. Now, however, there has been growing up a tremendous impulse among American artists to express a more direct reaction to the physical and social environment in which they find themselves. This has led to a striving after other and different forms both of idea and painting technique. To a large extent it has taken the direction of a realistic portrayal of the visible world and through this to translate the disturbed and fluctuating spirit of our times into permanent form.

"This striving for a more vital expression has been strongly directed by the work and example of many American artists of whom I think seven are the most influential to artists of the present time, namely Howard Pyle, George Bellows, John Sloan, Edward Hopper, Charles Burchfield, Grant Wood, and Thomas Benton."

He then went on to cite the examples of many younger artists who had succeeded in recent years (that was before 1937) in winning prizes and public recognition by painting the actualities of experience.

"This return of the young artist to reality, the reality of his experience, clears the way for a new and distinctly American painting. It is my contention that in this way only can we achieve a painting that is worthy of foreign respect."

With regard to public opinion he went on to say:

"There are a great many people who are interested in art as long as it means nothing. It is the new attitude of the young artist that has put a revitalized meaning into it which was heretofore lacking. I do not envisage in this new painting a depressing and continued ugliness but an awakened liveliness that embodies the shock of vital subject matter. Recently the donor of a well-known art prize is said to have complained to the judges that the prize was awarded to a so-called modern painting of unconventional subject matter instead of to a competing work of abstract nature by a very successful artist. Such people fail to realize that to the younger artists of this age an awareness of their social significance and economic situation provides a more exciting and real subject matter than what in former times was provided by the contemplation of abstract nature; and furthermore that this change of attitude has interested, even excited the general public."

Many critics have disputed and ridiculed this point of view as mere academic realism that produces nothing but bad art. There is no need to argue the question here. The significant facts are that in giving advice to young artists Curry gave a sincere expression of his own convictions regarding the artist's subject matter and methods and named those American artists that he felt had already done important work along these lines.

Curry's own attitude was not merely one of periodically taking trips into the country for subject matter—painting the American Scene, as it was popularly phrased—but one of returning home: he wanted to express himself, and to do so he felt he should use those things which were his own by birth, training, environment, and faith. The oft-repeated element of experience is what differentiates the standardized, old-fashioned folk scenes of Currier and Ives from the personal interpretation of rural life that is to be found in Curry's work.

The pictures will demonstrate this procedure much better than a verbal description; they prove too that Curry's approach to a subject was with the eye of an artist, for its possibilities of expression as well as association. Actually it will be observed that after 1929 the subject came to be chosen more and more for its design possibilities than for its illustrative subject matter. The Ne'er do

Well (Fig. 76) represents a social phenomenon that had aroused considerable thought among farmers already in those days—long before it was so dramatically presented in John Steinbeck's *Grapes of Wrath*—namely the instability and social uneasiness of migrating farm workers driven at that time by drought and mortgage foreclosure from Oklahoma and Arkansas to the relatively profitable fields of Kansas and Nebraska. Their pathetic plight naturally aroused the sympathy and compassion of the artist. But the first sketch he made (Fig. 77) indicates that it was the possibilities of the curious profile design that interested him, as much as it was the subject; and through a series of successive studies to the final painting that element was never lost. From a religious point of view he might have labeled this a Flight into Egypt or related it to the Prodigal Son, but the rural characterization as a Ne'er do Well was much more honest and direct.

A somewhat similar rural scene, but without social implications, is the Roadworkers' Camp (Fig. 78). In contrast to The Ne'er do Well, the interest here is concentrated on the moving figures loosely composed into a free, almost exuberant space. In his landscapes, in particular, Curry uses space to express moods that vary from the utter physical abandon of this picture to a quiet spiritual, almost romantic dreaming or even yearning.

Notes on the Illustrations

76—THE NE'ER DO WELL. *Oil on canvas. 1929. Whitney Museum of American Art, New York City. A "Grapes of Wrath" subject drawn from the same social material used by John Steinbeck in his famous novel published ten years later. The composition is essentially the same as recorded in the first sketch (Fig. 77) made in the summer of 1929 as Curry watched these migratory families trek past the front door of his father's house. The placid mood of dejection is consistently carried through the many details: the flop ears, drooping head and lower lip of the burro; the shuffling bent-kneed stride that continues a part of the design from the legs of the burro to those of the man walking beside it and even to the dog that trots habitually in the shade under the rear axle of the wagon. With the emphasis on the profile design, the figures are set off against the barren background of the prairie. Only the tufted clouds recede into the distance.*

76. THE NE'ER DO WELL

77. THE NE'ER DO WELL (*First Sketch*)

78. THE ROADWORKERS' CAMP (Sketch)

77—THE NE'ER DO WELL. *First sketch. Ink. 1929. Notice the profile design that is achieved through simple line and the suggestion of modeling given in the opposing diagonal loops of the harness collar and the flap of the tarpaulin.*

78—THE ROADWORKERS' CAMP. *Sketch. Ink. 1929. One of many ink and water-color sketches showing his interest in figure groups, waving foliage, and the crossed diagonal composition of forms in space.*

79—THE ROADWORKERS' CAMP. *Oil on canvas. 1929. F. M. Hall Collection, University of Nebraska, Lincoln. This is one of the three (the other two are Baptism in Kansas and The Tornado) most important pictures exhibited by Curry in his first one-man show at the Whitney Studio Club in 1929.*

The subject is the temporary camp of a road-building crew and accompanying families which Curry had seen on his trip to Oklahoma in the summer of 1929. Many preliminary sketches, of which Figure 78 is characteristic, indicate that the subject offered considerable possibilities from a compositional point of view. The chief problem was the organization of active figure groups through the luminous atmosphere of a landscape, and as such falls directly in line with works of Brueghel and Rubens (the Kermess in the Louvre), which Curry had studied and liked. The earlier concern with two-figure groups is here expanded into many combinations which move freely about in a circular space of the foreground. The hub of the action is the big gnarled tree in the center and through the shadows of the waving foliage a vast space recedes swiftly from the right foreground past the diagonal tent down the road to the distant horizon at the left. A variation of the same type of problem with an entirely different solution is to be found in a contemporary work, State Fair (Fig. 181).

79. THE ROADWORKERS' CAMP

Landscape

The romantic mood of the dreamer is expressed in First Snow (Fig. 80). One can follow the various experiments with the design, the framing of the scene, and the direct concentration of the beholder through many preparatory sketches, such as Figure 83. To reconstruct the "meaning" of the picture or perhaps better to reassure himself of the accuracy of his interpretation, the spectator might compare two other compositions done before the same window. In a sense they mutually explain each other. One is the homely Still Life with Apples and Bread (Fig. 103) and the other is the portrait of Stanley Young (Fig. 112) in the half dreaming, half struggling gesture of the creative artist. While there is a certain element of humor in the latter pose, the implications are nonetheless genuine. Curry has often spoken of the quiet view from his studio window across the river in winter. He associates it with the frugality and creative effort that characterized his life there.

A particular feature of the preliminary sketches for First Snow is the prominence given to the tall facade of a house as a focal point for the framed composition. While the idea is considerably subdued in the finished composition, it is a motif that appears again in the Kansas Wheat Ranch (Fig. 84) for entirely different purposes. The absence of framing trees, the diagonal road from the left, and the oblique turning of the house-form gives to the whole composition a sense of open, sweeping space as well as a feeling of quiet vastness through the contrast of proportions. The same function of the house-form as a focal point and unit of measurement appears again in the Spring Shower (Fig. 86). Now, however, a red barn is thrust far into the distance and reduced to correspondingly smaller proportions.

Like Rubens and many of the seventeenth-century Dutch landscape painters Curry spent considerable effort on the design of the sky as well as that of the landscape itself, and what distinguishes his work is the way in which these two designs are worked together. It has been observed in the comparison of The Lightning with The Tornado that regardless of whether it is a tree, a streak of lightning, or a tornado funnel, the function of this vertical form in connecting the design of the sky with the ground is the same. Similarly, the wavy mass of foliage in the Roadworkers' Camp, with its clean atmospheric space underneath, has its parallel in the cloud masses of the Spring Shower and carries much the same spirit of freedom and abandon though on a far vaster scale.

The fact that Curry felt he had discovered the "typical" Kansas landscape, that is to say he had invented a design which for him most adequately expressed the beauty distinctive to that terrain, is indicated by his constant use and variation of the Heart Ranch drawings in his many landscapes and sunrise compositions. When he arrived at Wisconsin to take up his new position at the university he found that Wisconsin was not Kansas and his interpretation of a Wisconsin landscape must of necessity be quite a different one. Proof of Curry's consistency in trying to paint the "actualities of experience," as well as a definition of what the phrase means, can be found in a group of landscapes he has painted since his arrival there in 1936.

Anyone who has lived in Madison or its environs, even if not romantically inclined, cannot escape the magic spell of its natural beauty. The city is built on an isthmus between lakes with the capitol hill and its shining white dome commanding the rolling countryside in every direction. These picturesque surroundings have aroused the patriotic pride of the native inhabitants, the students and intellectuals of the university, and, at times, of even the legislators. That pride has been expressed in many ways. Always, however, the determining factor has been the country's basic character rather than its mere external appearance.

This is the region that inspired some of the most beautifully descriptive passages of William Ellery Leonard's famous poem *Two Lives*. The hills of near-by Spring Green cherish one of the most picturesque shrines of modern architecture, Frank Lloyd Wright's home Taliesin. In the architect's autobiography is described with touching affection the vitality of that landscape from which this architecture grew. Wright would obviously ridicule the capitol dome in Madison as a false symbol of a false officialdom, but its design and associations are easily softened by the spacious atmosphere. If one drives along the river road toward the hills of Taliesin and watches the towering windmill (Romeo and Juliet), which he built years ago on the topmost crest, one can sense something of the inspiration that this infectiously beautiful countryside affords.

Such was the character of the region into which Curry moved in 1936. The question of how an artist is to express the spirit of his surroundings cannot be answered in one picture. It took time and much experimentation before these new problems could be solved. When he first arrived in Wisconsin his main efforts were concentrated on the big canvases for the Department of Justice murals. These he set up on huge stretchers in his studio and continued work on them until the following May. At the same time, that is through the winter months, he spent considerable time in the Stock Pavillion sketching the prize Percherons and finished The Stallion (Fig. 146). Only when spring and warmer weather came was he able to get outside to sketch landscapes. These, together with the Spring Flowers still life (Fig. 104) and Flora (Fig. 129) are parallel reflections of that fresh invigorating period of his first spring in Wisconsin.

In comparing the View of Madison with the Kansas Spring Shower, one can readily recognize the differences not alone in the composition, but the intrinsic character of the land, its life, and the society it fosters, as factors determining that composition.

Where in the one case the point of focus was the red barn nestled in the diagonal rolling movement of the fields, here the white capitol dome is placed in the center and silhouetted on the horizon. There are movements left and right but they are horizontal and planar in character, the clouds and rainbow tend to stabilize and dignify the capitol and scene.

Curry was sometimes in doubt about this first View of Madison. Was it not too stiff and formal? The choice of setting and composition in the Brittingham picture (Fig. 89) indicates a much freer movement. The capitol dome is subordinated to one side, the forms of clouds and hills are much more plastic in a wider and clearer space. The later Wisconsin Landscape (Fig. 90) might be considered a perfected solution, not so much to the "capitol landscape," but to a Wisconsin regional landscape as contrasted with the Kansas Heart Ranch. For here the farm buildings are embedded in wide fields of pasture and grain, not sweeping off into space, but balanced between two other groups further in the distance. A sense of the diagonal space is there, but the movement is enclosed and stabilized within the frame of the composition.

There are several personal elements which have some bearing on these last two pictures. Both were definite commissions by people who wanted a "portrait" of a landscape which had some special significance to them.

Thomas Brittingham, who commissioned the first of these two pictures and was one of those responsible for Curry's position at the university, was born and raised in Madison. When he moved away it is understandable that he would want such a landscape as the central decoration for the living room of his new home. Recalling what has already been said, it is characteristic, perhaps, that the landscape was not a view of the family estate itself, which is one of the most beautiful in the entire region, but the magnificent panorama of Lake Mendota and the city which Brittingham had seen daily from his home. With this point of view Curry was in complete sympathy.

The Wisconsin Landscape was commissioned by the Alexander Legge Farm Foundation as a "portrait" of what that well-known idealist had called "the most beautiful farm landscape in the world." In keeping with that spirit the painting was intended to hang as a memorial in Mr. Legge's office. Though actually the picture went to the Metropolitan Museum as a purchase prize, it is significant in that the reason for its existence is again not the desire of the artist to express himself but the will of a patron to have a work of wider, even idealistic implications created. Such an idea was not new to Curry, but its realization in a pictorial form was something that gradually developed under the favorable conditions—largely created by Dean Christensen—of his surroundings.

The various trips throughout the state that Curry took with Mr. Christensen were not sightseeing tours but had to do with the inspection of state-sponsored land reclamation projects, soil erosion and conservation, crop rotation, as well as the hundreds of experiments in fertilizer, cross breeding and cultivation that are carried on under the agricultural research programs of the State University. Out of many impressions and detailed sketches this, the finest of all Curry's landscapes, embodies something of the spirit and social idealism of that activity.

Notes on the Illustrations

80—FIRST SNOW. Oil on canvas. 1930. Collection of Wellwood Nesbit, Madison, Wisconsin. A view across the Saugatuck River from the artist's studio in Westport. As in The Ne'er Do Well the design is strictly planar. The bare tree branches and stems are used as are the wing designs of the State Fair (Fig. 181) to help characterize the romantic mood of the view across the water. The color is predominantly a soft, warm gray which, with its delicate variations of blue, brown, lavender, and ochre, give the scene its emotional tone.

83—FIRST SNOW. Compositional study. India ink. 1930. One of several studies in design and texture. They vary from the straight lines and cross-hatching of some to the solid black of this sketch which already hints at the soft mirror-like water tone that is the essential feature of the finished painting.

80. FIRST SNOW

83. FIRST SNOW (*Sketch*)

· 134 ·

84. KANSAS WHEAT RANCH

84—KANSAS WHEAT RANCH. *Oil on canvas. 1930. Collection of Charles F. Stein Jr., Baltimore, Maryland. This picture is unique in its embodiment of the typical in both prairie landscape and rural folk architecture of the Middlewest. The use of such expressive vertical proportions of the forms has been noted in The Ne'er Do Well. Here the house is not the flat surface of the house in the First Snow sketch (Fig. 83) but is turned obliquely to lead into the space. The same tall proportions are repeated in the forms of the outhouse, model-T Ford, and the truck, then continued horizontally into the vast prairie with its windblown waves of heavy wheat receding into the far distance. The romantic mood is remarkably close to that of the First Snow studies, yet is much more absorbing in its expansive conception of space.*

85—HEART RANCH, *Barber County, Kansas. Crayon. 1930. One of a series of drawings made on a visit to this ranch and important in clarifying a basic type of landscape design which Curry has used in some of his finest paintings. Characteristic of the design is the raised foreground, with a road leading diagonally into a lower middleground, in which the white house, silo, and red barn of the homestead are nestled. The hills, creeks, and lines of trees roll in loose arabesques back to the sweeping horizon and its strong imposing buttes.*

86—SPRING SHOWER. *Oil on canvas. 1931. Metropolitan Museum of Art, New York City. The first of Curry's three most important landscapes (cf. The Line Storm, Fig. 69, and Wisconsin Landscape, Fig. 90) and the one which he considers the most complete realization of the fresh vitality he loves in rural Kansas. It was painted from sketches of the Heart Ranch (Fig. 85). The color is remarkably light and fresh. From a rich salmon red of the clay road and luminous green in the foreground it leads back to the shining gray-blue sky and clouds and yellow sunlight of the distance. Particular emphasis is given to the moving design and form of the clouds, with their resulting distribution of light and shadow patches over the rolling hills. The shining red barn acts as a sort of focal point for the rich undulating movement that runs diagonally through the space.*

85. HEART RANCH

86. SPRING SHOWER

87. THE CLOUD

87—THE CLOUD. *Oil on canvas. 1930. Collection of Mateel Howe Farnham, West-port, Connecticut. In Curry's sketch book are to be found many sketches of these so-called "headers" that on occasion loom so impressively in the blue skies above the Kansas plains. The composition is less rich and varied than in the later Spring Shower. The painting is more sketchily done. On the other hand, it is more dramatic and magnificent in its sweeping horizontal form.*

88—VIEW OF MADISON. *Oil and tempera on panel. 1937. This is the first of a number of Wisconsin landscapes begun shortly after Curry's establishment there as Artist in Residence. The shining white dome is that of the state capitol building as seen from Picnic Point across the brilliant blue of Lake Mendota.*

During the process of painting, the rainbow caused a good deal of trouble. When left as a full arch in its brilliant colors it stood out as too theatrical. When it was divided or obscured by the clouds it appeared as two broken fragments. The shortening of the arch, its composition into a heavy cloud mass, and the extension of the rainbow colors into the atmosphere through the oil and tempera medium afforded a solution which Curry considers satisfactory.

89—VIEW OF MADISON AND LAKE MENDOTA. *Oil on canvas. 1937. Collection of Thomas Brittingham, Wilmington, Delaware. A panorama of Madison looking east from the hilltop of the Brittingham family estate, "Dunmoven," commissioned by Thomas Brittingham for an overmantel in his new home in Wilmington. The capitol dome is here seen through the shade of an elm tree at the right and the recession is accomplished through the rounded bluffs, the tufted clouds, and foliage across to the vast distance at the left.*

88. VIEW OF MADISON

89. VIEW OF MADISON AND LAKE MENDOTA

90. WISCONSIN LANDSCAPE

90—WISCONSIN LANDSCAPE. *Oil and tempera on panel. 1940. Metropolitan Museum of Art, New York City. Probably the finest landscape Curry has ever painted. From works of the nation's best artists it was awarded first prize in the gigantic* ARTISTS FOR VICTORY *competition held at the Metropolitan Museum in 1942. A short while after it was finished Thomas Benton wrote of it: "Looking back over the landscapes I have seen I can think of nothing comparable to this Wisconsin landscape of John Curry. It is likely to stand as a sort of unique performance in the history of American Art just as the Mont St. Victoire series of Cezanne stands in French Art." (From the* DEMCOURIER, *Madison, April 1941).*

It is a huge panorama of the rich farm land situated a few miles from the old Alexander Legge farm near Belleville, Dane County, Wisconsin. The composition is based, not only on sketches made at the spot, but also on Curry's various trips throughout the state with Dean Christensen. The resulting crystallization of that which is "typical" of Wisconsin parallels the process noted in the Kansas Spring Shower, with a number of significant differences: the farm land is not cut up by meandering creeks and red clay fields lying fallow, but is neatly ordered into mutually productive areas of grain, pasture, and wood-lots. The ensuing design is, therefore, much more regular and controlled, rather than the loose arabesques of the Kansas farm. The main farm buildings are set squarely below in the center framed by sharply foreshortened trees, pasture, and a cattle herd. While there is a slight movement into the distance at the right, there is little of the breathtaking sweep of the Kansas spaces. The main feature here is the balanced recession directly back into the lush grain fields of the valley. Instead of the shining red buttes of Kansas the accent here is on the rich blue-green patches of trees, which are contrasted to the glowing yellow-orange of the ripened grain fields. The cloud design serves to dramatize the opulence of the harvest spectacle through the unending movement of light and luminous shadow areas both in the sky and over the checkered fields.

Sunrise

Though Curry constantly uses recognizable details in his land-scapes they can never be classed as mere realistic portrayals of nature. Whether by contrasting forms, rolling hills, bright colors, terrifying storms, or fresh windblown clouds, the scene is somehow dramatized through the movement of the total design. "Art," he once said in a radio interview at Madison, "is, to my mind, struc-ture and movement; one applies form and color to give animation, and movement to obtain an effect." There is reason enough, there-fore, for his particular interest in sunlight as an artistic mode of expression comparable to these other means.

Sunlight from Curry's point of view was not the physical prob-lem of light filling in or creating space and atmosphere, nor was it the irridescence of a many-colored reflection as the Impression-ists saw it. For to him light was a medium, not an end in itself, and he chose to use the sun as an objective focal point from which this medium, that is his design, could be worked out.

Besides the problem of design there is that of content, which naturally leads to the question of why one should use an object which in nature is so powerful that the naked eye can hardly look at it. That characteristic of power, of the sun as of the storm, was precisely what attracted Curry in this instance as it had in many of his other works. Ask him why and he will usually answer that he likes it, just as did many other artists whose paintings hang in the museums. One will find the sun used many times in widely different periods. The works of men like Claude Lorrain and George Inness reveal a classic balance of forms in a vast space that is filled by the soft, all-pervading light of the setting sun. At the museum, too, one will find such contrasting personalities as Wil-liam Turner and Vincent Van Gogh whose conception and use of light is much more dynamic and expressive. To the Claude-

Inness classical conception of light as a mood, and the Turner-Van Gogh type of romantic expressionism through light patterns, contemporary artists have added a new note of symbolism such as that found in one of Orozco's frescoes in the New School for Social Research, New York. There the rising sun is represented between idealistic portraits of Lenin and Carillo Puerto as symbolic of a new social order for which these great leaders of Russia and Mexico struggled.

These three types of interpretation are cited, not to show any "influences" on Curry, but to clarify the artistic possibilities of the problem just as any artist must do as he works out his own solution. Curry's various solutions may be followed in the selection of characteristic paintings and drawings included here. One of the first was the Sunset of Figure 91. It is obvious that with his interest in a more aggressive and dynamic design, the "sunrise" motif would be iconographically more compatible than the sunset. In any case, this was the only example of a sunset he actually painted. The form varies from a greater emphasis on a flat and more bluntly forceful yellow-white light, as in Figures 91 and 97, to an exhilarating design in the sweeping western clouds of pink, yellow, and blue (Fig. 92). He tried variations in the dramatization of space as seen in the sketches (Figs. 93-96); then a greater feeling of exultation through the singing thrasher on the tops of the Osage orange trees, or the soft quietude of the mourning dove in its nest bathed in the brilliant light of the rising sun.

It is curious to see many remarkably personal and poetic situations develop out of such a basic design. One idea was the introduction of the top branches of the Osage orange to increase the effect of space and the early morning exuberance (Figure 98). With it came the glossy yellow and blue-green of its coloration, the choppy invigorating design of its foliage. The introduction of a purely romantic subject matter like the singing brown thrasher (Fig. 97) and the nestled mourning dove (Fig. 100) is an attempt to make the abstract design and even the scene more directly comprehensible to the spectator.

There are certain events in Curry's own life that would justify the spirit reflected in these sunrise pictures, and it is not forcing any romantic interpretations to be at least reminded of them. Curry has admitted many times that much of his interest in the fearful storms in nature and among men was closely associated with the struggle and turmoil that was going on in his own mind during those difficult years from 1928 to 1932. It is, therefore, not too much to assume that the happiness he experienced during 1933 and 1934 as a result of his friendship and subsequent marriage with Kathleen Gould may have had much to do with the boyish enthusiasm of the sunrise pictures.

In many ways the sunrise theme is another form of artistic self-portrait. Since that time it has become his common practice good-naturedly to add a rough sketch of a sunrise over his signature whenever anyone asks for his autograph.

It will be remembered that the general spirit of these years 1933-1934 was very different from the depressed gloom of the previous Hoover era. From the prancing jig of the popular "Happy Days Are Here Again" to the resolute reply of the Roosevelt Administration to the people's demand for action, the New Deal of 1933 provided an enthusiasm and a freshened national outlook that was as boundless as the traditional American Frontier.

The association had certainly appeared in Curry's mind just as it had in the political and social writings of the time. Sunrise, the Frontier and its eternal promise of future happiness had been one of the leading motifs in James Fennimore Cooper's *The Prairie*.* It is not accidental that Curry used the Sunrise as a frontispiece when the opportunity came in later years to illustrate that famous story of the American frontier.

* "It is glorious! . . . Glorious and heavenly is that streak of vivid red, and here is a still brighter crimson; rarely have I seen a richer rising of the sun. . . . Surely it contains a promise of happier times!"—THE PRAIRIE, page 251.

91. SUNSET

Notes on the Illustrations

91—SUNSET. *Oil and tempera on panel. 1934.* An extremely simple composition in which the focal point is no longer the house or barn as in the previous landscapes but the sun itself from which point a vigorous design of light streaks outward. The ground recession is effected by opposing arcs of reddish brown and green. Several years later the composition was changed somewhat by the addition of clouds in an irregular arc at the top and in a straight line just over the horizon to increase the effect of space. This is the only real "sunset" that Curry ever did—just why he does not know, except that the active and vigorous design he likes is more appropriate to a sunrise than a sunset.

92—SUNRISE. *Oil and tempera on canvas. 1934.* Based on the Heart Ranch sketches, the composition is no longer a "landscape" but a sunrise, as is shown in the prominence given to the sun and the dramatic design emanating from it. From this point of view notice the contrast to the "sunset" of Figure 91, and the active space absorbing capacity of the light streaks not only as they define the cloud forms but also envelope different levels of the vast terrain. The color scheme evolves from the brilliant yellow white (tempera) of the sun to the pink and blue cloud streaks and the red and green landscape.

92. SUNRISE

93. SUNRISE (*Sketch*)

94. SUNRISE (Sketch)

95. SUNRISE (Sketch)

93-4-5—SUNRISE SKETCHES. Sepia. 1934. A group of very loose and freely exe-cuted sketches that reveal some of the various design possibilities that Curry was experimenting with at the time. Notice the long wavy sun rays of Figure 93 with an indication of the Heart Ranch in the middle ground similar to the painting of Figure 92. In Figure 94 the horizon line is raised, bluffs are indicated in the foreground to drop the space more effectively backward, the light waves are straight, and separate masses of cloud are suggested to parallel the bluffs. This idea is again used in Figure 95, with a heavier accent to the bluff in front, and fluffy little clouds sketched on either side of the sun along the horizon.

96—SKETCH OF A SUNRISE. Sepia. 1934. A study that suggests an entirely differ-ent solution to the sunrise design. Instead of focusing the spectator's attention on the sun and strengthening the impression through space-contrasts or cloud designs, the composition here is unbalanced by a tall bluff and road at the left. The effect is

96.   SUNRISE (Sketch)

dramatic in a different way, allowing a left to right movement into an extended space and, at the same time, possibilities of a richer integration of the sunlit atmosphere and the landscape as can be seen in the developed form of Figure 98.

97—MORNING. *Oil and tempera on panel. 1936.* Though this panel was not completed to its present state until 1936 (and the artist still considers it incomplete), the compositional scheme belongs to this 1934 series. The landscape itself is a variation of the Heart Ranch sketch. The significant feature is the undefined mass of yellow-gold light that envelopes both sky and landscape. Against this a form is silhouetted at the left, with much the same purpose as the bluff of Figure 96 but using the more linear and decorative idea of waving top branches, the Osage orange tree whose short shiny green leaves and yellow fruit catch the gleaming sunlight. The singing brown thrasher perched high on the top branch offers a much more tangible expression to the exuberant mood of the scene than does the tree on the bluff in the drawing.

98—MORNING II. *Oil and tempera on panel. 1936-41.* Another large-sized sunrise composition parallel to Figure 97. It is the most perfect solution to the many problems developed in this series of paintings. The movement is accentuated by means of the foliage at the left. One's attention is held to the focusing point of the sun and is not swept off into undefined space. The clarity of the space is retained. The brilliant light is allowed to penetrate in all directions without obscuring either the space or design (note the patch of still water in the foreground to reflect the light and prevent its absorption by the ground). The Osage orange foliage is worked into a much richer and more expressive design than in the previous example (Fig. 97). The color extends from the yellow-gold light that strikes the clouds and contrasts with their pink shadows against the bright blue sky to the warm red, brown, and green of the landscape and the rich blue-green of the shaded Osage orange. The exuberance of color and composition seemed adequate to speak for itself so that the singing thrasher used in Figure 97 here appeared unnecessary and was left out.

100—OSAGE ORANGE. *Oil and tempera on panel. 1934.* This, so far as is known, is the first time that the Osage orange tree has ever been used as the subject of a

97. MORNING

98. MORNING (II)

painting. Of all the items of the flora and fauna of the Southwest that Curry studied, it proved the most romantic and stimulating. The color in this painting is dominantly the blue-green of the leaves. There is a rich red-brown in the wood stems and a lemon-yellow in the fruit and in the reflections of the leaves. The home-like mood of peace is concentrated on the soft gray mourning dove. Note the difference between this painting and the first sketch of the idea (Fig. 101) in which the sun is composed as a disk to be repeated in the round forms of the fruit. Its omission in the finished painting gives greater sublety to the expressive mood through the softer light that encircles the nest and the glistening reflections from the leaves.

101—OSAGE ORANGE. First Sketch. Ink. 1933. Though very loose and sketchy in execution this study shows the clarity with which the basic design was seen. The realistic details are developed in the finished painting on that framework without loss of the deign's essential character.

101. OSAGE ORANGE (First Sketch)

· 148 ·

SUNRISE

Still Life

Curry remained somewhat aloof from the idea of painting studio still lifes even though he knew they were among the most marketable subjects that an artist could paint. His aloofness was due in part to his one-time antagonism to studio subjects in general as decadent and incompatible with the blood and thunder vitality of fighting hogs and roaring tornadoes.

Once freed from these artistic inhibitions the idea grew to magnificent proportions. The frugal boldness of earlier forms (Figs. 102-103) developed strength and movement in the later flower groups. It will be noticed, however, that such flower or fruit still lifes were not used as simple exercises in color vision and composition, for the bold Apple and Bread forms (Fig. 103) are seen to be a part of the same dreamy landscape that had stimulated his First Snow. In all the massive exuberance of the seasonal still lifes there persists a characteristic tenderness and delicacy that was seen in the earliest flower watercolors of the youthful artist (Fig. 2).

The Wisconsin Still Life has a great deal of personal appeal. Curry loves to hunt and does so during the season on the small farm he bought in 1939 just outside Madison. There are several hunting and shooting stories which his friends tell with delight. Some of them are worth repeating here. On one of his first visits to the dairy farm of acquaintances shortly after he arrived in Madison, he stood out in the fields watching the gentlemen of the family shoot clay pigeons. It was a gray Sunday morning. It was obvious that they were not doing very well. Partly out of politeness and partly to divert attention from their own shortcomings they asked Curry if he would like to try a shot. He nodded sleepily, took the proffered gun and to the mounting consternation and amazement of the group scored a dozen perfect hits in a row. This may not be a dramatic feat for a trained marksman, but it was quite a jolt to these outdoor men who had expected something vastly different from one of those people who paint pictures.

With this same group of men he went pheasant hunting in the fall of 1940. Having shot their allotted quota, they had difficulty in getting Curry to return to the car at the edge of the field; he continued to hunt, muttering to himself: "Gotta have a rabbit, gotta have a rabbit." Apparently there were no rabbits to be found and he was about to give up when, as they approached the automobile, a huge jack rabbit suddenly spurted from a near-by bush. Curry got his gun into action and blasted away at the zigzagging prey, only to find when he reached the spot that he had been peppering holes into the tires of the car, quite forgotten in the background. It came out in the subsequent ribbing that all afternoon he had been planning a Wisconsin Still Life composed of two pheasants and a rabbit, and in the end had to be satisfied with his two pheasants and the gun.

There is a purpose in repeating these stories. They point up the extremely personal quality of the still life. There are other indications that the subject, at least in its conception, is an entirely personal, sometimes poetic thing. Curry's excuse for painting the Spring Flowers (Fig. 104), for instance, was the serious illness of his wife. After a solid week of hard work he carried the big picture into the hospital and presented it with the unaffected pride of a youngster as his substitute for the traditional sick-room bouquet.

On the other hand Curry was perfectly conscious that such a still life could and should have significance to someone other than himself. Actually it will be found that the studies and paintings he did of "still life" motifs outside on the farm loom far more important in his work than the studio flower pieces, which are relatively recent. There are many studies of such ordinary plants as the lowly rhubarb (Fig. 136), cabbages and sunflowers (Fig 107). Without obligation to decide which is the "better" artist, the comparison of Russian Giant (Fig. 107) with Van Gogh's many sunflower pieces will show something of an affinity. It will reveal also the vast difference between the strong indoor still life of Van Gogh and the outdoor vitality and essentially monumental strength of Curry's picture.

The sunflower, like the hollyhock, is apt to be looked upon and enjoyed with the nostalgia of old-fashioned rural decoration. Corn too has a distinctive beauty of its own, but it also has significance. The point of view may vary with the farmer, the agricultural scientist, the economist, or even the politician, for in certain states its importance does reach such proportions. It is with these implications in mind that one must appreciate the research and experimentation that Curry had made, in 1933 especially, to find that particular form which would adequately carry the beauty which the proud farmer experiences in surveying the waving field of a successful crop of corn. Curry felt he had it in the Wichita picture (Fig. 110) and the design was used for one of the proposed panels for the rotunda of the Topeka capitol murals. Though it involves another subject, others forms and associations, the towering Oak in the pasture is to be regarded from the same point of view.

Notes on the Illustrations

102—BACHELOR BUTTONS. *Oil on canvas. 1929. Collection of Helen Hokinson. A vigorous design of purple-red flowers thrust into the heavy form of an aluminum kettle; these set off against the blunt red, blue, and yellow diagonal stripes of the table cloth and the yellow ochre of the background.*

103—STILL LIFE WITH APPLES AND BREAD. *Oil on canvas. 1934. Collection of Stanley Fike, Kansas City, Missouri. A diagonal composition based on the contrast of warm colors—the light brown bread, salmon can, bowl of apples and red flowerpot —against a cold winter blue and gray outside the window. The view across the snow-covered garden and river is from the artist's Westport studio and is the same one used in the First Snow (Fig. 80). This painting was done in 1934 but is derived from a crayon sketch dated 1932 which has exactly the same composition.*

102. BACHELOR BUTTONS

103. APPLES AND BREAD

104. SPRING FLOWERS

104—SPRING FLOWERS. Oil and tempera on panel. 1937. Collection of Mrs. Paul S. Russell, Chicago, Illinois. A rich and exuberant composition that is a remarkable contrast to the frugal barrenness of the earlier still life (Fig. 103). The color is deep and strikingly luminous: a silver-gray pail as the center with a heavy red glass forward to the left, the rich forms of lavender lilacs, red and yellow tulips, and irises are set off from a deep purple background and move with the green leaves in a waving circular pattern. A superficial resemblance to Renoir serves only to emphasize the sharpness and delicacy of the drawing (as seen, for example, in the spray of forget-me-nots in the foreground), as well as the plastic modeling of Curry's forms.

105—SUMMER STILL LIFE. Oil and tempera on panel. 1940. The comparison of these three still life compositions, Spring Flowers, Summer Still Life, and Wisconsin (Autumn) Still Life, gives one the impression that Curry had deliberately set out to paint a series of the "seasons" as did Brueghel in his seasonal landscapes. This was not the case, however, for the real motivation here is the distinctive beauty and character

105. SUMMER STILL LIFE

of an armful of flowers as they are brought in from an old-fashioned rural garden. There are two preparatory crayon sketches for this painting, one roughly indicating the general light and dark tone, the other a more careful drawing of the flowers into the proposed design, with the actual identification of each flower by name written at the side: zinnias, black-eyed susans, household phlox, flame, and peonies. Notice particularly the clear linear definition of the flower forms and the loosening of the composition around two main groups to facilitate a freer space.

Color reproductions of this painting and the Wisconsin Still Life were used commercially for the backs of playing cards by the Western Playing Card Company.

106—WISCONSIN STILL LIFE. Oil and tempera on canvas. 1940. An autumn still life with the feathered game composed into crossed diagonals before the vertical forms of tree and shotgun. The color is a rich, medium-toned brown, with bright red and blue-green spots in the head and back feathers that glow with a soft irridescence and flow with contrasting whites into the warm brown and gray tones of the tail feathers. From the waving yellow-ochre grass of the foreground, the color recedes to the bright red, yellow, and orange of the autumn foliage set off against the gray tone of the sky.

107—RUSSIAN GIANT. Oil on canvas. 1929. Collection of Carlyle Burrows, New York. A homely, everyday flower whose individual character has been given the monumental dignity Curry felt it deserved. The plant is crowned by the bright yellow sun-

106.   WISCONSIN STILL LIFE

flower, but the wide leaves are worked out in varying planes about the central stem
to create a massive form. Rows of cabbages in perspective, several smaller plants, an
arbor over the gate, and the receding clouds combine to emphasize the impressiveness
of the sunflower in the old-fashioned farm garden.

108-9—CORN STALKS. Pencil and watercolor sketches. 1933. These are two characteristic examples chosen from a sketch book full of corn studies. Some of them are
separate stalks done in pencil or pen-and-ink with an emphasis on the crisp, delicately
outlined character of the leaves. Others concentrate on the waving, rustling mass of
tall corn as one sees it from the roadside or walks between the rows themselves. The
color pattern goes from the warm brown of the earth below to the fresh green and
yellow-gold of the tassels at the top.

107. RUSSIAN GIANT

108. CORN STALKS

109. CORN STALKS

110. CORN

110—CORN. *Oil and tempera on canvas. 1935. Wichita Art Museum, Wichita, Kansas. Of the various solutions this emphasis on the wavy motion of the masses of corn seems to be the most successful. Though it concentrates on one or two individual stalks, it relies chiefly on the continuous design and color of the whole for its expression rather than the linear clarity of separate forms or the space. An equally effective lithograph was done of this same subject.*

Portraits

Curry's portraits must be considered in the light of his rural background and idealistic belief in what a genuine American art should be. He has painted very few commissioned portraits. This has not been due to any inability on his part to produce acceptable likenesses. The success of a modern portrait painter is as much, if not more, the result of social and commercial promotion than of inherent qualities in his portraits themselves. From what we know of Curry's temperament and training it can easily be understood that for him such prerequisites to success were well-nigh impossible of attainment.

The portrait sketches of his father and mother (Figs. 127-128) show his ability to present the character and dignity of people who he felt had those qualities. The development of the artistic form as a personal or idealized expression seems to have greater significance than the attributes of a sitter's personality or position.

The numerous self-portraits are very revealing in their clear statement of a character consistent with his interpretation of other subjects. One motive for painting one's own image from a mirror is that the self-portrait is a gallery feature which has good sales value. The public naturally wants to see what the artist looks like. In presenting his features however, the artist has to make a choice of those characteristics which he believes are his and which he wants the public to see. The introspective process of sifting and weighing these values, together with the artist's means of presenting them, make up essentially what one can call the "problem" of the self-portrait.

The self-portraits of 1927 and 1937 reproduced here are probably the best that Curry has painted. They represent a development, not merely from a full head of hair to a bald pate, but from a proud dignity, even arrogance, that is somewhat theatrically

presented by a disdainful stare down at the mirror and the spec
tator, to the balanced self-confidence of a mature artist. Even in
this later picture the matter of confidence, expressed through the
rigidly vertical composition, clenched hands, and stern look, seems
to be associated with the self-imposed determination and will-
power that have made his career both difficult and remarkable.
His portrait of the writer Stanley Young (Fig. 112) before a type-
writer at the window of his studio is undoubtedly an adequate
representation of the struggling artist, but at the same time it
reveals a half humorous, half sympathetic attitude of the painter
which takes serious form in his own self-portrait.

Friends criticized his self-portraits for being too grim and
formal, so Curry felt obliged to do a more relaxed pose in the
lithograph of himself as a hunter (Fig. 115). Much more revealing however are the little sketches he is in the habit of doing for
the amusement of his family and friends. The group of sepia
drawings included here (Figs. 116-121) is taken from letters
written to his wife in Madison while he was at work the summer
of 1940 on the murals in Topeka. They were not intended for
publication but their husky humor is indeed an interesting counterpart to both the romantic love and earnestness of his major
paintings.

Curry's approach to the group portrait problem of the old folks
at home was with the modernist's eye for the expressive use of
light and color. The subject is of course one that the true modern
artist has long shied away from, largely because of the absurd sentimentality that has popularly been lavished on such mediocre
paintings as Whistler's Mother (Paris, Louvre). To Curry love and
admiration for his parents at home on the farm was a genuine
thing which he was neither afraid nor ashamed to express. While
the subject can have a popular and sentimental appeal its artistic
rendition has a long tradition in American art, from the romantic
genre of Eastman Johnson to the Currier and Ives prints and

George Bellows' (not Whistler's) strong portrait of his mother in the Chicago Art Institute. The peace and equilibrium which he so respected in his parents he sought to express later on with a self-portrait of his own family painted after he had achieved the stability of a settled life in Madison.

Mention was made in an earlier connection (page 88) of a certain relationship in point of view between Curry's work and that of Rembrandt and it seems profitable to venture here a few additional remarks that grew out of a conversation with Curry on the subject of the great Dutch painter. To avoid misunderstanding it must be remembered that in artistic creation as in criticism there are two methods of approach to the Old Masters in the public museum. One is the sharp-eyed recognition of an effective pose, design, or idea that is capable of rearrangement into new situations or contexts. The other approach is concerned with the aesthetic function of these elements within the total complex which is essentially the work of art. It involves a deeper and more extended understanding of personal or social background as well as intended or accomplished effect. The bare existence of that understanding makes such a rearrangement of the isolated motif described in the first instance difficult if not impossible.

In the history of art both approaches to tradition have always existed, but the progress of art, as of civilization in general, has depended on the creative thinker, not on the eclectic. The great accomplishment of the modern artist has been the destruction of that mystic reverence for the "Old Masters" which has made a cult out of their appreciation and has transformed the museum into a temple. To a critical artist like Curry the Old Master has become a teacher and fellow craftsman whose practice and experience can lend valuable aid in the solution of new problems that constantly appear with the passage of time.

Fundamentally there are two great teachers whose methods have determined the thought and expression of modern art. One is the Italian, Leonardo da Vinci, whose combined scientific and critical approach to nature as revealed in his writings and drawings, aim toward the intellectual clarification of the basic problems of pictorial expression. It is with this methodical clarity that the modernist's eye has roved through the history of art in search of adequate modes of expression: the formal discipline of Giotto, Uccello, Piero della Francesca, and Cezanne; the spiritual expressiveness of primitive and Negro art; the coloristic effectiveness of Medieval stained glass, Persian miniatures and the great colorists from Giorgione to Renoir.

The other great teacher, not as much intellectual as spiritual, undisciplined and human, is the seventeenth-century Dutch master Rembrandt. The influence of Rembrandt on modern art is seldom recorded, yet there is hardly an artist today who does not know him intimately. His story has often been told in popular biographies, and it can be read even more convincingly through the portraits, the religious pictures, the engravings and drawings reproduced in books that are among the most popular in the art libraries. Through them Rembrandt, the humanist, has become an educator in the broadest cultural sense. His portraits show ordinary men and women as Christians of dignity and character. His religious pictures—for the most part engravings that were intended for wider distribution than the religious altar piece affords—seek to explain the human side of the traditional theme and situation: the humble son and grateful father of The Prodigal Son; the cruel responsibility of Abraham in the story of his Sacrifice of Isaac; the homely happiness of a Mother and Her Child in the Nativity scene. Through Rembrandt's long career, his pictures and hundreds of drawings reveal a personal struggle for freedom of expression as well as for a bare existence in the face of unappreciative society—a situation which the modern artist, from his own experience, can well understand.

Curry's attitude toward Leonardo has already been described

(page 47) as one phase of a self-disciplinary process in learning how to draw. The influence of Rembrandt is not one of discipline but a compelling respect for reality. There is little evidence of direct influence in the sense of Curry's copying of a Rembrandt motif, but there is a profound sympathy for the attitude of the Dutch master which is especially clear in the study of Curry's portraits.

Compare the work of the two artists, again, not to prove that one is as good as the other, but to clarify those qualities that are specifically Curry's: both are provincial individualists whose personal experience as expressed pictorially is justified by tradition, and tradition is not based on perfunctory travel and academic training but on the higher cultural plane of spiritual understanding which transcends these material advantages. Both are realists whose respect for nature has something of a combined religious and romantic fervor, as can be seen in their portraits of mother and father, the landscapes, and the various reinterpretations of traditional religious themes. To both family life is something sacred, human and worth the dignity of representation. Thus one expresses the exuberant happiness with his beloved Saskia in a portrait of himself with her; the other not only does such a family portrait but carries that exuberance consistently into his other work as well. The landscape is developed into a dramatic medium of significance beyond that of personal expression. In both cases the self-portrait reflects the conflicting doubts and compensations of an aspiring artist: the earlier ones proud and arrogant; the later ones calm, matured, and touchingly human.

Three examples serve to illustrate Curry's development of the portrait into a subject of wider significance through the dramatization of both design and subject. From the peace and dignity of Mother and Father (Figs. 122-124) he develops a dramatic tension in the watercolor of the Folks at Home (Fig. 125) which belongs to a series of flood studies that was painted in 1938, in-

spired by the disastrous Ohio floods of the previous year. Contrary
to the form of the Mississippi (Fig. 74) where the terror of the
flood is focused on the family huddled on the roof top, the family
here is safely secluded in the front parlor, while the lightning flash
and weird illumination from the windows parallel other storm
scenes, such as The Tornado and the Prairie Fire, in dramatizing
an approaching danger.

A second type is the portrait of his daughter, to which, like
some of Rembrandt's portraits of Saskia, he gives the classical title
of Flora. Whereas the Saskia portraits are richly bedecked with
jewels and drapery, Curry's Flora has a material freshness that
makes it his own romantic allegory of youth and spring.

A third example is to be seen in the portrait of his father as
The Stockman (Fig. 130). This massive figure, together with the
forms and space surrounding it, has a compositional strength that
matches the strong character portrayal given in some of his preparatory sketches (Fig. 128).

There is some significance to be attached to the fact that this
picture was purchased by the Whitney Museum in 1930. This
was not a recognition of the artist alone, but a reflection of the
rising tide of social conflict and consciousness that characterized
the period. This new spirit, together with the growing interest in
Mexican art, placed new requirements and problems before the
American artist. Thomas Benton's mural decoration in the New
School for Social Research (1930) was one reply; Curry's Stockman was another.

Among the liberal and left-wing writings of the early 1930's
there developed the practice of labeling the various social groups
as peasants, workers, the white collar, and the capitalist class for
political and doctrinary purposes. In the corresponding art of the
so-called social-conscious painters a similar practice developed.
To the detached political observer, however, these classifications
were false applications of foreign doctrines and their artistic inter-

pretation was inspired largely by outside artists, particularly the Mexicans.

In his relationships with other artists Curry was exceedingly shy of the politically-minded social-conscious groups. Such paintings as The Ne'er do Well (Fig. 76) indicate, however, that he was well aware of the great issues confronting the nation at the time. Rather than apply imported styles and classifications he sought to build new forms out of local tradition and individual experience.

Curry's method of approach can best be studied in My Father's Hands: (Fig. 123) the oil sketch is a detail and preparatory study for a larger painting, but the fascination and expressive character of these bronzed, weather-beaten hands of a working farmer are in themselves a fitting tribute to the dignity of rural labor.

Having been brought up on the farm, himself, he is firm in the belief that the American farmer is no "peasant." As a proud individual the American farmer claims the right to own his farm unmortgaged, pay his taxes, raise and market the vital crops, educate his children, and above all to live and act as a free and independent citizen. That is what Curry saw in his father and idealized in The Stockman. Again it is an ideal of conduct that goes back to the pioneer and the American Frontier, and it is not surprising that Curry later on should choose to illustrate Cooper's quaint description of Ishmael Bush as the pioneer leader in The Prairie as one of the important (second only to the sunrise) illustrations of the book (Fig. 131). It is also the basis for the rural landscape used as a mural design in the Kansas state capitol (Fig. 318).

It is only a step of twelve years from the portrait of Curry's father as the Kansas Stockman to his portrait of Chris L. Christensen, Wisconsin's Dean of Agriculture. Curry has often expressed his admiration for the dean as a great idealist and educator. The portrait has no colorful, flowing robes to grace the academic halls of fame. It was neither solicited nor commissioned by anyone but was the artist's own choice, for in subject as in composition it

WISCONSIN LANDSCAPE

FIRST SNOW

embodies both the personal character of the earlier idea and the significance, social, political, or otherwise, of leadership as interpreted in the portrait of the Pioneer in Cooper's novel.

112. PORTRAIT OF STANLEY YOUNG

Notes on the Illustrations

112—PORTRAIT OF STANLEY YOUNG. *Oil on canvas. 1932.* A portrait, conceived half humorously yet with deep sincerity, of a young writer who loved to dramatize himself as a great artist. The heavy arm and clenched fist, the hand supporting the head are well-known gestures that imply such a "struggle." The placement of the figure before the studio window with the hazy landscape outside, however, carries many of the same associations noted in the studio *Still Life* (Fig. 103) and the *First Snow* (Fig. 80).

113—SELF-PORTRAIT. *Oil on canvas. 1925-1929.* An imperious composition whose strength relies on the unbalanced framing with the edge of the mirror shown at the right, the high placement of the figure with respect to the spectator, the strong coloration based on the green lumberjack shirt, the pink contrasts in the flesh tones, and in the light from above.

113a—SELF-PORTRAIT. *Oil and tempera on panel. 1935. Collection of Irving Blumenthal, New York.* The most naturally conceived and freely composed self-portrait that Curry has painted. The decorative figures in the background are details (in reverse) from the *Washington Bicentennial* mural (Fig. 291) which remained in the artist's studio for some time before he destroyed it.

113a. SELF-PORTRAIT

114—SELF-PORTRAIT. Oil and tempera on panel. 1937. Painted with the View of Madison, Spring Flowers, and The Stallion, during Curry's first year at Madison. The comparison with his own earlier representation (Fig. 113) shows not only the more prominent bald head, but also a self-imposed dignity and confidence that does not rely on the spectacular pose. The color is based on the warm brown of his corduroy coat with luminous and well-modeled forms in the glazed flesh tones, gold light striking

114. SELF-PORTRAIT

115. SELF-PORTRAIT

the chicken hawk at the left and an irridescent pink in the painting at the right. The hawk was no accident but was used both to relieve the vertical rigidity of the main figure and to compliment the design of the hair.

115—SELF-PORTRAIT. Lithograph. 1939. A more informal and humorous pose of the artist as a hunter. The corn fields are those to the west of his small farm outside of Madison which he bought that same year.

116

119

117

120

118

121

SELF-CARICATURES

116 to 121 inclusive—SELF-CARICATURES. Sepia. 1940. A group of comic sketches on letters written to his wife during the summer of 1940 from Topeka where he was at work on the State Capitol murals. The sketches tell the story of what the artist is doing and thinking much more vividly than the written text: Figure 116 shows the half-bald, fuzzy-haired artist as cupid with a big pipe in his mouth chained to his work while John Brown toasts him with a mug of 3.2 beer—the strongest allowed in Kansas. For recreation he takes up golf, Figure 117; another sketch (not included) shows him almost breaking his arm in a violent swing that missed the ball. It is very hot in Topeka (Fig. 118) and he is counting the days to September 26, when he plans to come home (Fig. 119). Finally, he is on his way, a flying cupid with a pipe, golf bag, and suitcase (Fig. 120). The inside of that last letter is embellished with a Rubens theme of satyr in the academic robes of the Artist in Residence chasing nymphs through the woods (Fig. 121).

122. FATHER AND MOTHER (1929)

122—PORTRAIT OF FATHER AND MOTHER. *Oil on canvas.* 1929. The subject of the "folks at home" has a long tradition in popular American song and literature as well as in painting. Its conception here involves a compositional problem that has been a favorite of Matisse: an interior with figures flanking a window which opens out upon a brilliant exterior view. The contrast of a Matisse view of the sunlit Riviera and a home-grown Curry view of a Kansas barnyard is striking enough, but Curry's carefully drawn plastically modeled forms in the clear space are quite apart from the brilliant color design of the French modernist.

123—MY FATHER'S HANDS. *Oil on canvas.* 1929. A rough oil sketch for his father's hands in the double portrait of Figure 122. The heavy bronzed forms bespeak more eloquently the character of one who lives by the work of his hands than does perhaps the total figure itself.

124—FATHER AND MOTHER. *Oil on canvas.* 1933. Painted from a number of sketches that were made at the same time as the corn and sunrise studies. Though both parents seem to have taken on a few more years, the chief interest lies in a more active and freer composition. A table is substituted for the window in the center, and two light openings are used to set off the heads of each figure. These too, are more active in pose and slightly unbalanced into a diagonal, as opposed to the balanced arrangement of Figure 122.

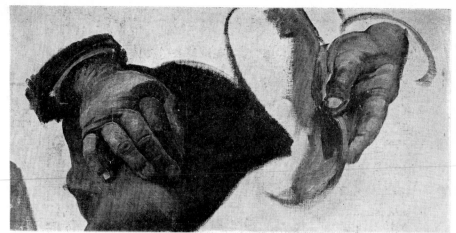

123. FATHER'S HANDS

124. FATHER AND MOTHER (1935)

125—THE FOLKS AT HOME. Watercolor. 1938. A variation of the family group composition, done about the same time as the flood scene of Figure 75. Instead of a quiet domestic scene the artist presents the terror of the family waiting for the storm to pass. This mood is dramatized by the blinding yellow flash of the lightning as it penetrates the soft blue-green interior.

125.   THE FOLKS AT HOME

127.   MOTHER

128.   FATHER

127-8—MOTHER. *Red chalk.* FATHER. *Black crayon. 1929. Curry's painted portraits tend more toward his own personal expression as pictorial compositions rather than representations of physical features. It is not a matter of the artist's ability but his deliberate choice. As character portrayals his first sketches show both his ability to produce a physical likeness and his remarkable sensitivity to the less obvious traits of character. These two studies of his parents speak for themselves as the most impressive character portrayals he has done.*

129. "FLORA"

131. ISHMAEL BUSH (On the Prairie)

130. KANSAS STOCKMAN

129—"FLORA." *Oil and tempera on panel. 1937. A small portrait of the artist's daughter in which the likeness is far less important than the deliciously fresh and lively spirit of an adolescent girl. The brilliant flesh colors are glazed with alternating warm and cool tones characteristic of Rubens' early work. The luminous red dress, warm brown hair, and purple lilacs set off the figure from the moving green and yellow design of the background. The shining eyes and the slight forward tilt of the pose give the figure tension and buoyancy. These attributes make the painting something more than merely a "portrait." They justify the title "Flora."*

130—KANSAS STOCKMAN. *Oil on canvas. 1929. Whitney Museum of American Art, New York City. A portrait of the artist's father as the "Kansas Farmer" for which the sketch (Fig. 128) was one of the preliminary studies. Notice the idealization of the figure through the tall and heavy proportions and the grouping of farm stock and buildings around it to increase its monumental effect.*

131—ISHMAEL BUSH. *Red chalk. Illustration to* THE PRAIRIE, *by James Fenimore Cooper, Limited Editions Club, New York, 1940. "At some little distance in front of the whole, marched the individual, who, by his position and air, appeared to be the leader of the band."—*THE PRAIRIE, *page 4. It is this character of the "leader" rather than the page-long objective description of the man himself which Curry emphasizes in this illustration.*

132-3—STUDIES FOR THE PORTRAIT OF CHRIS CHRISTENSEN. *Crayon, watercolor. 1941. Two of several preliminary sketches for the portrait of Dean Christensen, which show the artist's original interest in a more forceful stride toward the left. In the finished painting the step of the central figure has been reversed so that the left leg is back rather than forward; also the companions are placed less actively in the background. The result of the change is a balance between the striding movement and the monumental stance of the tall agricultural leader.*

132-133—STUDIES FOR PORTRAIT OF CHRIS CHRISTENSEN

134. CHRIS L. CHRISTENSEN

134—CHRIS L. CHRISTENSEN. *Oil and tempera on canvas. 1941. A portrait of the Dean of Wisconsin's College of Agriculture, represented, not in the traditional flowing robes of his academic position, but in his shirt sleeves striding through the rows of hybrid corn on the experimental farm of the University. The likeness is good and the impressive proportions are those of the subject, whose six feet six inches make him tower well above his companions.*

Domestic Animals

In a radio interview broadcast from Minneapolis in the fall of 1938 Curry was asked whether he believed that the so-called "regionalism" was just another fad in which artists deliberately set out to paint local subject matter to keep in line with the trend. His answer was in the negative, but it was expressed in an extremely personal way: "Naturally there are those who wish to fall in line whenever any type of painting is publicized. However, I believe that anyone paints the things best that he understands best and those artists who are products of a certain environment should try to understand that environment. People should learn to see the beauty of their own surroundings and not feel that only the remote things are wonderful."

The beauty that Curry himself saw about him in years past can be found in the pictures he painted. The renewed concentration on the study of nature began in 1930, and by paging through the reproductions collected here one gradually understands the particular character of that beauty both as it exists in nature and in the artist who presents it in pictorial form. The landscape itself was not enough; it must be his own experience to be true. Thus at Westport it was the First Snow of a homesick dreamer. In Kansas it was the wind-swept valley of the Heart Ranch that became Spring Shower, Kansas Sunrise and Morning to an artist in process of development. To the fully matured Curry at Madison the rich harvest of the Wisconsin Landscape became the symbol of a well-ordered prosperity.

Beauty is not only formal structure but involves meanings and associations that are an integral part of the artist's vision. He loves and admires his father, and therefore idealizes him as The Stockman. In the portraits of Dean Christensen and Ishmael Bush he extends the likeness of the subject to that of an idealized leader, and the unsophisticated youth of his daughter gives her the freshness and beauty of Flora. Similarly the plants of garden and the fields develop symbolic qualities as he paints them: field corn, the oak tree, sunflowers, and the old-fashioned flowers of the farm. Even though these qualities may become commonplace by too much literary embellishment they are convincing when one is confronted by the original painting.

The studies of animals are a part of this same process of thought and research. Each object in nature is watched, analyzed, and sketched, with a constant view toward a comprehension from which the artistic form and expression can grow. Each represents a species with an individual form of its own; some of them appear a bit restricted in their possibilities of expression, or at least Curry did not use them very often in finished paintings, while others appear to be unlimited in the varying designs and uses of which they are capable.

Their characters can be followed in the reproductions: the wild terror of a jack rabbit with its beady eyes and long elastic form; the similar character of a domestic cat with its much wider and brighter eyes, softer form, and concealed savagery; the huge red-brown form of the sow with her litter of pigs lying complacently in the mud of the barnyard. Two of these types are developed to the monumental proportions they embody, namely the Stallion and the Bull (Ajax) and though one may want to recall famous parallels like the Dutch Paul Potter or the French Gericault or Rosa Bonheur, Curry's form and style are honest and original, products of the working method he advises others to follow.

Like the portraits and other themes, the form and content of such compositions as Ajax and The Stallion are self-explanatory. Reginald Marsh jokingly described Ajax, with his heavy round shoulders, short neck and round head, as a self-portrait of his friend Curry. It could just as easily be a portrait of Marsh, but Curry good-humoredly allowed that he might be right, although

Ajax would weigh a bit more than he does, even though the proportions may be somewhat similar.

The compositional possibilities of the Ajax form can be followed through a number of specific studies of cattle (Figs. 140-141), leading not only to the distinguished stance of the Ajax painting (Fig. 144), but also to the extension of that pose in a panorama design as seen in the drawing of Figure 142, and the rich circular design of Kansas Pasture (Fig. 145).

Ajax is actually a portrait, but, like the portraits of human beings which Curry has painted, it is dramatized into a monumental form of beauty and significance. The fact that such an animal can have beauty and significance is not new in the history of art. One can hardly forget, nor does Curry, Paul Potter's big bull that glowers down at the tourist as he walks into the Mauritshuis in The Hague; the terrifying bulls of Goya in the Tauromachia; or the symbolic bull that towers triumphantly over the carnal waste and destruction in Picasso's Siege of Guernica.

A similar dramatic motif appears in the art of the American frontier. In the 1830's George Catlin executed a series of drawings illustrating the dramatic and picturesque life on the prairies west of the Mississippi.* This included landscapes of the vast plains and river valleys, characteristic scenes from the primitive life of the roving Indians and hunters, and gave something of the fear and terror that one experiences in those primeval wastes. One page represents a single buffalo in much the same pose as Ajax, but looking straight out at the beholder with dark raised head, sharp horns, and fiercely shining eyes, the most terrifying menace of the prairies.

Curry knew the George Catlin portfolio, as he does the work of almost every other artist of the frontier, but had never thought of the Buffalo until reminded of it after Ajax was finished.

To Curry the bull (or buffalo) is no symbol of fear and terror

---
* George Catlin, The North American Indian Portfolio, London, 1844.

but literally, good beef: prize stock that is a product of the scientific breeding, culture, and good pasturage which the intelligent farmer must provide for the successful development of beef cattle. In a sense, therefore, it is an idealogical parallel to the successful harvest represented in the Wisconsin Landscape.

The consistency of his belief is reflected in his remarks quoted before (p. 83) at a meeting of the American Country Life Association in 1937 in which he advocated the painting of "portraits" of a prize-winning horse, a well-bred herd of cattle or an unusually fine grain or food product from the various communities of the state, to be placed in its public buildings. Such competition for high quality standards had long been a habit in annual county and state fairs. And the various points of excellence by which the stock judge makes his decision in awarding prizes—such as the long straight line of the bull's neck and back, the deep chest, full hind quarters—are usually the essential features of design and form which Curry recognizes as beautiful and tries to work into his composition.

The Stallion, by the very nature of the animal, inspired a different form. To be sure Curry did sketch him many times in the proud exhibition stance but never used the idea; the dynamic power of the animal inspired a much more expressive pose. He seems more temperamental and self-conscious and it is as such an actor that he is presented dramatically emerging from the runway into the spotlight of the arena. Curry's consistency is shown in the further development of the same character in the Belgian Stallions (Fig. 152) where the nervous group of performers is crowded into the narrow passageway in the tense moments just before they parade out in front of the crowd. In this confusion of massive forms there is a beautifully designed aesthetic order: the heavy bodies move rhythmically back and forth into the dark space and even though there are well over sixteen legs in a single line across the lower section, each form retains its allotted function in the composition. The comparison of these massive equine forms in their continuous rhythmical movement with the brittle pseudo-classical stylizations of Giorgio de Chirico is an interesting tribute to both Curry's point of view and the creative possibilities it embodies.

Notes on the Illustrations

136 to 141 inclusive—ANIMAL STUDIES. Red chalk and pen-and-ink. 1930. A selection from a book of sketches done on the Kansas farm in 1930. Some of them were later worked over into paintings, others remained simply as "studies." These simplified drawings are of interest to us because they reveal a number of specific points of concentration that are often hardly discernible in more finished compositions.

Notice in Figure 136 the careful attention given to the twists of the chicken wire whose repetitions form a decorative pattern. Like the Russian Giant sunflower (Fig. 107), the ordinary plants of the farm are studied here for possible decorative motifs: the stem and ragged leaves of the grapevine, the big planes of the lowly rhubarb's leaves.

In contrast to the rounded form of the hen notice the rooster (Fig. 138) in his noble stance as boss of the chicken yard, the stretched neck as he crows, the bobbing head and tail positions as he pecks for food. The geese in Figure 137 show entirely different possibilities with their long forms stretched in various hissing, cackling, or fluttering gestures. These three drawings were done in red chalk. The dead jackrabbit (Fig. 139), drawn from one he had shot in the field, was done in black ink. The particular fascination here is not alone the long, springy form of the animal, which the artist varies in several leaping poses at the top, but especially the weird, terrified expression of the beady eye. This attraction is noticeable in other animal studies (i.e., the hen and rooster) and continues as an important and expressive feature of later works. The same is true of the soft lustre and expressive roundness of the eye studies in Figure 140.

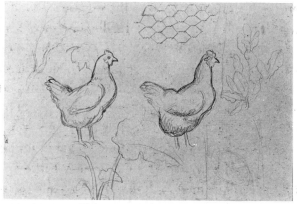

136. ANIMAL STUDIES

137. ANIMAL STUDIES

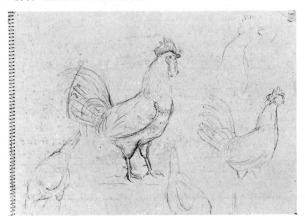

138. ANIMAL STUDIES

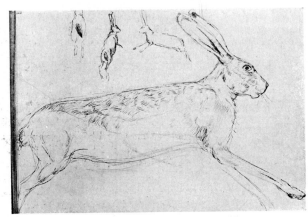

139. ANIMAL STUDIES

140. ANIMAL STUDIES

141. ANIMAL STUDIES

142. GRAZING CATTLE IN A LANDSCAPE

143. GRAZING CATTLE IN A LANDSCAPE

142-3—GRAZING CATTLE IN A LANDSCAPE. Two pen-and-ink drawings. 1933. There are several sketch books from the summer of 1933 filled with studies of prize Hereford cattle—"so fat that the rain would stand in the middle of their backs"— grazing in Kansas pastures. That characterization of rural prosperity has something of the "Peace and Plenty" idealism noted in the landscape and sunrise pictures of the same time, but the concentration here is on the animal forms—good beef cattle—as much as on the space and landscape around them.

144—AJAX. Oil and tempera on panel. 1936-40. "I shall never forget," wrote Thomas H. Benton in DEMCOURIER for April, 1941, "the picture of the big Hereford bull John showed down here in our Kansas City Museum. Our town, although it is still a sort of smoky cow-killer's town, pretty rough and ready in its basic character, is full of mincing sisters, male and female, who go in for the love of art. The tittering horrors that John's bull occasioned was a lesson. All the people who were trying to forget the manure on grandfather's boots took a crack at it. All the two-bit aesthetes, who make manners take the place of scholarship, lost their pants. But the bull was effective. It is still talked about. It was galvanic."

The idea and composition of Ajax goes back to observations and sketches of grazing Herefords he had made during the summer of 1930 (cf. Figs. 140-41). The first product was a lithograph made in 1931 which Curry mistakenly dated 1932 when it was reproduced in Thomas Craven's A TREASURY OF AMERICAN PRINTS. The painting was begun in 1934 but was continually worked over, experimented with, improved until 1940 when it was finally completed to his satisfaction.

Notice that Curry's interest is not restricted to the animal alone but includes the surrounding space as well. The central figure is raised on the crest of a hill. Its huge bulk dominates the space and is emphasized by the reduced size of the rest of the herd down the hill in the distance at the left. It is given in three-quarter view, rather than profile, with its back foreshortened into the space at the right. As the bull grazes he leans, somewhat in the scratching posture of the bull in Figure 145. The bulging sweep of such a massive neck and shoulders, together with the leaning stance and foreshortening of the form, give it a sense of strength and brute power that is further enhanced by the cloud and landscape design around it. The landscape is essentially that of the

144. AJAX (*With Birds On Back*)

145. KANSAS PASTURE

· 187 ·

146. THE STALLION

Heart Ranch. The little cow birds that habitually flutter on the backs of cattle in search of ticks, are an additional means of dramatizing the bulk. The color of the bull is a rich red-brown that is set off from the shining white of the cloud bank, luminous blue sky, and a varying blue and yellow-green of the pasture.

145—KANSAS PASTURE. *Sepia drawing. 1930. As a contrast to the panorama Curry has sketched a number of wooded landscapes into a circular or spiral design, which in this case is developed around the central figure of a bull scratching himself against a tree. The observation of such a casual and characteristic gesture made an impression on Curry, for it is this movement that determines the combined power and restraint upon which the Ajax composition is built. This drawing was actually made in 1930, though later he added the signature and date of 1936.*

146—THE STALLION. *Oil and tempera on panel. 1937. The first painting which Curry completed after his arrival in Madison as Artist in Residence. The form and expression is an interesting parallel to Ajax which he had begun three years before and was working on in his studio at the same time. Its most distinguishing features are the magnificent proportions and rich black color of the Percheron as he prances forth from the runway into the arena. The color of the stallion is a shining blue and greenish black, the effectiveness of which is due not only to the contrasting white spots in the boy's shirt, the flashing eyes, and decorations on the horse's mane, but also to the spotted white tempera underpainting, which is particularly visible under the glazes of the neck and shoulder muscles.*

147. THE STEEPLECHASER

147—THE STEEPLECHASER. Oil on canvas. 1927. An early work with a Gericault-Degas type of profile composition which Curry had painted in Paris. For that period it is extremely interesting because of its conflicting elements of preconceived "style" and a more factual sense of reality: the neck of the horse is stylized into the traditional arched design, while the jockey and derby-crowned trainer have a weight and ungainliness that is certainly not Parisian. In spite of long proportions, the leg action has more the plodding stability of a farm horse than the lean agility of a racing thoroughbred. The adjustment of the cloud design to the profile of the figure is one of Curry's favorite motifs which he habitually used in later works.

149. THE STALLION
(Preliminary Sketch)

150. THE STALLION (*Preliminary Sketch*)

151. THE STALLION (*Preliminary Sketch*)

149 to 151 inclusive—THE STALLION. *Preliminary sketches in red chalk. 1937. In making these drawings Curry spent weeks of patient study watching the boys run the giant Percherons back and forth across the oval arena of the University Stock Pavilion. The greatest effect of power seemed less evident in the straightaway runs than at the moment when the horse proudly emerges from the runway into the large open space (Fig. 151). Note however, that the prancing action represented in this sketch lacks the muscular coördination of the finished Stallion since the legs are still represented in the running position observed in the straightaway sketch of Figure 150. At the moment of the equine star's entrance into the arena there seems to be a split second's pause in which the animal's weight is balanced on the right front and left hind leg, while the opposing pair is raised in the striding action. In the pose of Figure 151 the action appears frozen and the hind leg about to break off. Again the comparison with earlier work, such as the galloping horses of Figure 11, will show the results of orderly discipline and artistic coördination which Curry had developed since the days of pure illustration. The excessive contrast in the blacks in these reproductions, particularly Figure 151, is, of course, not to be found in the original drawings and is a distortion of the luminous red chalk medium.*

152. BELGIAN STALLIONS

152—BELGIAN STALLIONS. *Oil on panel. 1938.* A composition which originated in a red chalk drawing Curry made as a cover design for the WISCONSIN COUNTRY MAGAZINE published by the agricultural students of the University of Wisconsin. It is a characteristic development from The Stallion. Included in the composition is a number of horses seen in a more frontal position as they weave back and forth in the narrow runway at the moment just before they enter the arena. The action is, therefore, much more complicated and dramatically tense than in The Stallion, where it is concentrated on an exciting release through the forward stride into the open space.

153-4—SOW AND PIGS. *Watercolors. 1930.* Two studies of pigs at mealtime that are remarkable in their soft and delicate coloration. The forms in the foreground of Figure 153 are a dark red-brown that fades to a lighter brown in the larger form of the sow behind them. In Figure 154 the whole is seen as practically a completed composition. The mass of forms in the center is painted the same luminous red-brown, the wooden fence closing off the background is a soft beige tone, and the foreground is a rich yellow. A faint sketch in the upper right corner outlines the geometrical pattern, a horizontally extended hexagon, which is the basic design enclosing the group here and was used again in Sanctuary *(Fig. 73)*.

155—HOG ASLEEP IN A MUD HOLE. *Red chalk. 1936.* Curry has always had a great admiration for hogs. Sometimes, as in this case, they are almost human. Here the hog reclines with aristocratic complacency in the seclusion of his mud hole behind the water tank.

153. SOW AND PIGS

154. SOW AND PIGS

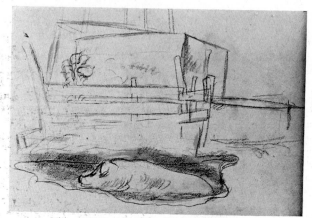

155. HOG ASLEEP IN MUD HOLE

156. CAT AND KITTENS

156—CAT AND KITTENS.
Study in charcoal. 1931.
With the same sympathy and
enjoyment that Curry drew
the pigs in the yard at his
home in Kansas, so too, he
sketched Smutty and her kittens in his Westport studio
with their characteristic soft
flowing lines and furry forms.

159 — CAT WITH A
MOUSE. Watercolor. 1931.
A softly rounded black form
represented in Figure 158,
but the artist's curiosity seems
not to be focused on the
motherly cat so much as on
the weird mystery of her
shiny yellow eyes. The wild
and blood-thirsty character of
the beast is followed through
in Figure 159 in which the
cat appears triumphantly at
the doorway, silhouetted
against a yellow and green
light, with gleaming yellow
eyes, and the mouse in her
mouth.

158. SMUTTY AND KITTENS

159. CAT WITH A MOUSE

Fighting Beasts

Having observed the isolated studies that Curry has made of separate animals, their form, capacity for movement, and general character, it is easy to see how these total characteristics logically develop into larger and more complex compositions. The pictures speak for themselves. It will be recognized that the particular character of the animal and the particular artistic problem evolve as one and the same creative process. The lean springiness of the jack rabbit is associated with the lithe and fierce movement through space of Hounds and Coyote (Fig. 168). Likewise the winged beasts of the fighting Hen and Hawk (Fig. 179) are composed as forms swooping through light and atmosphere. The lithe form and weird cruelty of the cat is associated with the fluttering color of flowers and the butterfly, in the Cat and the Butterfly (Fig. 180). In the same way the massive forms of the stallion, bull, and hog are developed into corresponding compositions that dramatize their weight and brute power (Figs. 162, 165, 173-178).

In accounting for these fighting scenes, it is clear enough that an artist of Curry's temperament would not be satisfied merely with the objective form but would seek to dramatize them in some emotional way. In addition, it will be observed that most of these works—the drawings and studies at least—were executed between 1930 and 1932, that is to say at the time of his greatest emotional stress and unhappiness in Westport. As he has often admitted to friends, the fighting scenes served as a mode of sublimation and release to a more intensive degree than even the storm scenes of the same period.

160. COYOTES STEALING PIG

Notes on the Illustrations

160—COYOTES STEALING A PIG. Lithograph. 1927. One of Curry's first lithographs, it deals with the dramatic ferocity of a life and death struggle closely related to the idea of the *Hogs Killing a Rattlesnake (Fig. 23)*. The artist had not actually seen coyotes in such an action but he had often seen pigs fighting off dogs and he had been fascinated by the fierceness with which the enraged mother defended her young. Note in contrast to the movement of forms around the central tree in the *Hogs Killing a Rattlesnake* composition, the pivot form here, the pigsty, is pushed to one side and the fighting figures circle around an open space illumined by the rising sun so that they are set off as expressive black silhouettes.

161—HOGS KILLING A RATTLESNAKE. Oil on canvas. 1930. A development of the 1925 watercolor *(Fig. 23)* whereby the action of all the forms is concentrated much more fiercely on the writhing green and yellow snake by their direct rush at it from four directions. In the watercolor this movement may seem more spontaneous through the hogs' wild rush around both sides of the tree. "In my estimation," wrote Harry Wickey, "this picture is Curry's finest to date. It fairly explodes with a wild ferocity and movement that has never been surpassed in the history of art. The subject is portrayed so powerfully that we feel we are actually witnessing the event."

162—FIGHTING HOGS. Sketch. Crayon. 1930. This sketch shows one of many experiments Curry made with the same compositional problem as in Figure 161. In this case the throwing action of the one hog is identified with both the writhing design of the snake and that of the tree trunk. The other animals seem to rush diagonally into it from all sides in an explosive pattern.

161. HOGS KILLING A RATTLESNAKE

162. FIGHTING HOGS (*Sketch*)

165. STALLION AND JACK FIGHTING

167. STALLION AND JACK FIGHTING

165—STALLION AND JACK FIGHTING. *Oil on canvas. 1930. The stallion is a shining blue-black, the jack a purplish brown. The pyramid forms are set off from the sunlit ground of salmon pink and beige wood fence. The shadow at the right is a light lavender tone, the barn wall a dull red. The ferocious action of the horse bears a close relationship with Curry's western illustrations and some of his studies of Leonardo drawings (compare the head with Figs. 40-41). One of several watercolor studies for this is in the William Rockhill Nelson Gallery of Kansas City, Missouri.*

167—STALLION AND JACK FIGHTING. *Watercolor. 1930. A study which shows variations both in conception of the subject, i.e., the kicking and biting action, as well as the composition of space and figures. Notice the shifting of the onlooking farmer's position from right to left; and note the tree, which in a preparatory drawing was used as a part of the dramatic central group similar to the Hogs Killing a Rattlesnake, and in the watercolor becomes a loose form that serves as a design to frame the central group.*

168—HOUNDS AND COYOTE. *Lithograph. 1931. A compositional idea concerned, as was Coyotes Stealing a Pig, with the fierce action of figures through space. This lithograph, and the compositional problem it involves, is one of Curry's favorites. "Notice the difference between this and the Coyotes Stealing a Pig," he says. "There the composition is open and, while the sow is fighting desperately, the coyotes are making their escape. Here the dramatic element is the impending death of the coyote. This is the end. There is no retreat. He is cornered in the vastness of the prairie."*

169-71—HOUNDS AND COYOTE. *Three sketches in pen-and-ink. 1931. From a large number of studies, these three were selected because they suggest some of the experiments which led to the final form of the lithograph, Figure 168. Out of several extremely loose and agitated drawings the form and positions of the figures become crystallized. The fierce snarls of the beasts are combined with the graceful bounds of their bodies. The vast space of prairie and sky is sketched in with a pursuing hound pushed far into the distance. In the final lithograph he is eliminated, the prairie space is no longer necessary, and the tense action is concentrated on the three figures alone.*

168. HOUNDS AND COYOTE

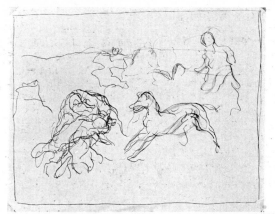

169. HOUNDS AND COYOTE (*Sketch*)

170. HOUNDS AND COYOTE (*Sketch*)

171. HOUNDS AND COYOTE (*Sketch*)

Notes on the Illustrations

173-78—FIGHTING BULLS. Sepia and red chalk. 1933. Besides the sketches of handsome big Herefords that Curry did in 1930 there are a number of small drawings of bulls fighting and goring one another. The motif, an attempt to give movement to the massive form of the Hereford, roughly parallels other fighting groups of animals: the hogs, stallions, and hounds already mentioned. He did not actually attempt to work out the problem until 1933 and, though it was never really "solved" in the form of a finished painting, this group of sketches indicates how it would be done. Notice how the action is carried through the design of the tree and landscape as well as in the opposing animals. In the later studies of the series the artist attempts to combine various action poses with a more plastic modeling of the big forms.

173. FIGHTING BULLS

174. FIGHTING BULLS

175.   FIGHTING BULLS

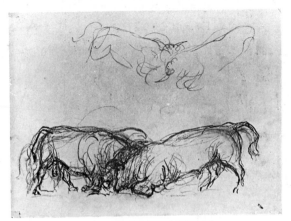

176.   FIGHTING BULLS

177.   FIGHTING BULLS

178. FIGHTING BULLS

179. HEN AND HAWK

180. CAT AND BUTTERFLY

179—HEN AND HAWK. *Oil on canvas. 1935. Collection of Mrs. C. M. Gooch, Memphis, Tenn.* Curry had often seen this. "The hawk attacks with the speed of a dive bomber—a straight shot from heaven," he said. "Ordinarily the hen would run, but here, to protect her checks, she shuts her eyes and wildly returns the attack." Mrs. Arthur B. Davis once told him that this was the most wonderful portrayal of mother love she had ever seen. The problem is a consistent variation of fighting beasts involving new possibilities of winged forms moving in light and space. Where the other compositions were all in horizontal format, this through the nature of the subject is vertical. The action comes not alone from the flutter of wings and fleeing chicks but from the contrast of heavy and lighter forms of the hen and the hawk, and the diagonal streak of brilliant silver-green light that is concentrated on them.

180—CAT AND BUTTERFLY. *Oil on canvas. 1935-38.* A strange motif based on the same "Smutty" that Curry used to watch about the studio and garden at Westport. Where in the watercolors (Fig. 158-59) the weird combination of terror and beauty was seen in the yellow-green eyes and soft rounded form of the animal alone, here it is extended into a much richer form. The cat claws fiercely at the brilliant red and yellow butterfly. A lush coloration of zinnias, phlox and ageratum embedded in a blue-green foliage surrounds the velvety black form of the cat. A black curved hose is used to begin a broken opposing diagonal through the flower bed.

· 203 ·

5

SPECTACLES

The Circus

AMERICANS LOVE EXCITEMENT and spectacular displays. The three most popular spectacles enjoyed by the American people are politics, sports, and the show. Curry's interests are not revealed in that order or in such general terms. They are clear and articulate nonetheless. The spectacle of the show to him is the circus. His sporting interest is concentrated largely on football. His political enjoyment is partly that of an interested bystander at the campaign rally and partly an artist's individualistic reaction and thinking as the spectacle rolls by.

For Curry the excitement of the spectacle is not only a normal form of amusement but also an artistic necessity. In many cases he needed a realistic stimulus to make a dramatic situation valid and convincing. That is one reason why the storm pictures, the Gospel Train, and Prayer for Grace are so effective and it appears to be what he was striving for in the hundreds of scenes from rural life that he sketched after 1929. Many of these, such as The Stockman or Mother and Father can claim universal validity. Such major spectacles on the farm calendar as the county or state fairs, the church picnics, the threshing or other seasonal group activities, or even the daily chores were not developed to the artistic proportions they actually occupy in rural life.

It cannot be said that Curry did not think of them. As a youngster he drew threshing scenes with their big machines, loaded grain wagons, and crowds of working men and horses. He even had a fight going on in the midst of one of them (Fig. 3). There were many subsequent watercolor and oil sketches of threshing scenes but no single painting was done with the concentrated effort that he had put into the separate portrait, animal, or landscape representations.

On a trip to Oklahoma in 1930 he drew a watercolor sketch of his tall cousin standing in the middle of the barnyard surrounded by his pony and cattle. They formed a remarkably striking composition. Again in 1933 he painted Early Morning Roundup which involved complicated groups of men and horses moving in space. Here, as in the Roadworkers' Camp, were beautiful designs and solutions to the artistic problems of form, light, and color. Curry approached these things from the observed detail to the compositional problem and its perfected solution. He was, however, also deeply concerned with the total dramatic and emotional spirit. He had that spirit in the Baptism and The Tornado. It was the fear that he was becoming stereotyped with his landscape and farm studies which, added to his dissatisfaction with his Westport surroundings, drove him into the glittering excitement of the "Biggest Show on Earth."

Curry had been interested in the circus long before 1932 when he joined up with the Ringling Brothers-Barnum and Bailey show on its spring tour through New England. His experience as a child, though not on any such large scale, had been a live one. It had been confined to the small amusement shows that performed for the rural picnics and county fairs of Kansas. Curry had also known the circus scenes of such old-time modernists as Seurat and Toulouse-Lautrec which were persistently exhibited in Paris at the time he was there. It is not surprising, therefore, that on his return to Westport such a subject as the State Fair (Fig. 181) should appeal to him at the same time as The Bathers, The Gospel Train, and The Tornado as a worthy subject and a characteristic American folk scene.

In contrast to these other paintings, however, the State Fair was conceived in mural terms. It is a huge canvas (92 inches by

72 inches), framed by elaborate garlands of fruit and grain, and painted in brilliant colors that have the cool luminosity of a fresco technique. In keeping with Curry's mode of procedure at that time, the total expression is the result of the careful composition of one posed and solidly modeled figure after another.

The Baptism in Kansas showed how the action of separate figures could be composed into groups, crowds, and wide spaces to result in a unified spirit and expression. In a similar way the brilliant red figure on the platform at the right of the State Fair stands out by its color and position as the key to the whole composition: it serves as a focus of attention for the beholder and leads him down into the space and the crowd. At the same time it is the center of attraction to the mass of people in the audience being addressed by the barker.

Curry used practically the same position in his High Diver (Fig. 183) as she stands demurely in the mysterious glittering light on the diving tower. The demure pose is intensified by the artist's characteristic choice of the breathless moment just before she steps up to the edge of the platform to take the dive and by the brilliant contrasts of the red-clothed figure against a dark blue sky and the bright yellow-white lights that sparkle about her.

The expression of The Medicine Man (Fig. 184) is based on the same principle, except that it is concentrated on the gestures of the main figure. The compositional idea of the gesticulating barker-salesman played an important part in the State Fair; its associations run deep into Curry's own personal life. For good or evil the profession of salesmanship is one of America's most prominent and lucrative activities. Curry himself had had a rather unsavory experience in his first job in Chicago as a shoe salesman (page 13) and he never forgot it. He tells many fantastic tales of the traveling medicine men in the rural districts of Kansas who would sell anything from chalk water to rubbing alcohol as a cure for every conceivable ailment. While the subject was realistically observed, as were the popular religious demonstrations, a considerable number of drawings (Fig. 186) reveal his experimentation to find the most effective facial expressions and characteristic gestures. It is therefore not accidental but by conscious trial-and-error experiment that he employed the same two-armed gesture used in The Gospel Train as the most effective solution to the combined pathetic and evangelistic zeal of the preaching salesman.

The number of drawings, watercolors, and even oils that Curry made in three short months with the circus is incredible. Literally hundreds of studies in a dozen different sketchbooks reflect the intensity and complete surrender of the artist to the theatrical excitement of that spectacle. Many other well-known American artists had been painting circus scenes. William Glackens, Gifford Beal, and Guy Pène du Bois had exhibited their circus pictures at the Whitney Museum in 1929. None of them however had ever gone into the subject with the desperate intensity of Curry. For Curry the circus was not simply an escape from life but to the contrary: it was a means of recovering that dynamic spirit and vitality which he feared the pedantic study of nature and artistic form was crushing from him.

Two paintings executed immediately after Curry's return to the Westport studio are perhaps the best known: The Flying Cadonas and Elephants. And they are justifiably so, for without doubt they are his most remarkable discoveries as far as expressive motif is concerned and artistically the most carefully worked out. However, there are many ideas and compositions less generally known which have remained in Curry's studio for years to be worked on, changed, and steadily improved. These, together with the many sketchbooks that one can page through, form a delightful miniature panorama of the entire show. The arrangement of the reproductions here is more or less from that point of view, for at times the artist is interested solely in the total scene and spectacle, at other times he fixes his attention on particular incidents in the performance or the side show.

As one enters from the outside there are colorful tents, gaudy bandwagons, uniforms, costumes, and waving pennants, the vast space of the tent interior, the audience waiting for the performance. After the usual parades and musical preliminaries, the show begins. There is an earsplitting fanfare: Tamara enters the arena and majestically ascends to her trapeze and aerial act (Figs. 193-198). Shining in the bright floodlights of the upper space, the world-famous Cadona brothers perform their breath-taking triple somersault and the passing leap. It was indeed breath-taking, because Curry had often watched them at practice with the safety net and on several occasions had seen the slight miscalculation that resulted in a hoarse scream and the fall (Figs. 219-220). One's attention shifts to the Reiffenach Sisters as they ride around the ring doing their acrobatic act (Fig. 224). A troup of trained horses go through their orderly maneuvers in the center ring (Fig. 236). A hurried shift of equipment and Clyde Beatty thrills the crowd with his roaring lions and daring stunts in the cage (Figs. 225-233). Then again it is the great Wallendas balancing on the high wire at the top of the tent. The clowns perform their antics with loud shouts, fireworks, and slapstick comedy. During the acts one can walk about to see the animals and side shows, and watch the actors in the runway awaiting their turn to go in or returning from the arena.

With all the gaudiness of the glittering lights, the tinsel, bright costumes, and painted faces the atmosphere has much of the romantic drama and pathos that one sentimentally enjoys in *Il Pagliacci*. In some instances like that of The Runway (Fig. 243) Curry would let himself go in contrasting the nervous excitement of performers about to enter the arena as opposed to the tragic exhaustion of the returning ones. But these are exceptions. Most of the time both the objective vision, as recorded in the first sketches, and the execution of the motif into a painting, are seen with the artist's eye for expressive form and design. These are concentrated on a number of basic problems which find their compositional and iconographical parallels in other works previously discussed.

One of these, and by far the most exciting, is the problem of swinging or catapulted muscular figures in free space. The closest that Curry had ever come to such an idea before was the lithograph of Hounds and Coyote that he had done the year before. From the selection of pencil, sepia, and watercolor sketches (Figs. 200-207) one can follow the persistent observation of swinging figures, their action, pauses, and timing as well as the brilliant color that makes his study of the scene increasingly impressive. The first group (Figs. 200-203) concerns the compact spinning forms which are finally perfected in the Whitney Museum's Flying Cadonas (Fig. 199). The second (Figs. 204-207) involves a related action of the upright twisting body as it hurls itself through the air.

The Aerialists is somewhat different in that it concentrates on the muscular majesty of a pair of figures slowly swinging through space. Notice the progression in the sketches (Figs. 215-218) from the meticulous study of the grip to the muscular structure of back and arms, to the rippling design revealed in the string of body forms as it moves with perfectly integrated precision. Some of the watercolors indicate an attempt to develop that movement in conjunction with the dizziness of glaring lights and the great heights (Figs. 217-218). In the final painting these values are reduced in importance because of Curry's persistent interest in the solid form, controlled movement, and clear space; but the watercolor studies reveal a spirited action in color and design that would rival the wildest and most dramatic of the Parisian Fauves.

A fourth group comprises dozens of sketches on what is by far the most difficult problem: a combination of tense action and

majesty that is so exhilarating to watch in such an aerial performance. The Passing Leap (Fig. 208) seems to come closest to its
adequate presentation and the drawings roughly indicate how the
crystallized form used in the final painting grew out of detailed
and sometimes confused initial observations.

One of the most spontaneous compositions of the entire circus
series is the balancing act of The Great Wallendas (Fig. 221).
From the first crayon sketch to a watercolor study of the color and
the beautifully finished oil painting, the serene tension and equilibrium of the actual performance is the essential quality of the
picture. A variation of this idea in quite a different form is the
Reiffenach Sisters (Fig. 224), with its uncertain balance of figures
held in perfect equilibrium by the clean-limbed muscular strength
and solidity so characteristic of Curry's figure compositions.

A number of drawings are concerned with attempts to compose
masses of moving forms into rhythmical designs. One case is the
semicircular grouping of tall, elegantly plumed trained horses of
Figure 236. Another is the line of powerful, gently swaying elephant trunks (Fig. 237). And a third is the circular composition
of fierce catlike beasts in Clyde Beatty's cage (Fig. 234). Of these
the Elephants is the most spontaneous and successful. Curry described the situation himself in an interview on a children's radio
program in Madison, and with due allowance for his juvenile
audience the remarks are worth quoting:

"Elephants look easy to draw but they really are not. It is
hard to get the feeling of balance and movement as well as
their bulk. If you will notice elephants are always moving and
swaying back and forth on their feet.

"I made the drawings for this picture late one afternoon.
As a matter of fact I had started to draw the Ubangi ladies
who had been brought over here from the middle of Africa.
They are the ones, you know, who wear big rings in their lips
which make them look as though they have duck bills. Well

I had no sooner started to draw than they got angry and their attendant rushed over to tell me to get out quick. So I went over to the elephants. They didn't mind.

"How should you go about drawing an elephant? Begin with the large circular shapes first: a big round egg for the body, and remember that it should be tilted up in front, for you will observe that an elephant is higher at the shoulder than the hips. Then continue with the cylindrical shapes of the legs, head, and trunk. Draw them loosely so you can get the action of the animal at once. You then can make a more careful outline of the body over these forms and even suggest shading as you go.

"When you first look at an elephant you are not conscious of the animal's eyes because they are small and usually the ears take your attention. Shortly you become aware of those shining beady eyes and it is a little disconcerting to see this brilliant animation in such a massive form. It is the same way with pig's eyes. You don't see the eye at first but then suddenly you become conscious of its gleaming presence buried in the shadow of the ear. I have tried to show this effect in many of my paintings."

With Curry's natural love of massive forms it is understandable that he could not avoid painting Baby Ruth (Fig. 242) the famous fat lady. Artistically just as fascinating is the powerful form of the hippopotamus (Fig. 240); and a number of sketches show the gaily bedecked baby elephant that was used in the clown parades.

Many of the performers became Curry's close friends. He was a great admirer of Alfredo and Lala Cadona and after performances or practice sessions they used to analyze the various positions of the act that Curry had recorded in his drawings. He often speaks of Hugo Zachini who was famous for his act of being shot out of a cannon. Zachini had once intended to be an artist and studied at the academy in Rome and, perhaps out of sympathy, offered to make a cannon man of Curry. Asked how one learned to be shot out of a cannon he blandly replied that it was easy, "just take little jumps first." Among Curry's friends were also most of the clowns and he drew many portraits of them in their elaborate make-up. Both as portrait sketches and as finished paintings they reflect the rough humor, pageantry, and human sympathy which is closely related to the spirit of such folk religious pictures as the Prayer for Grace.

Notes on the Illustrations

181—STATE FAIR. Oil on canvas. 1929. A large-sized canvas (92" x 72") which belongs with the great pictures Curry painted in Westport during 1928 and 1929: Baptism in Kansas, The Tornado, The Gospel Train, Roadworkers' Camp. The subject is no particular circus or fair but a generalization of those he used to see in Kansas and, with the exception of a few separate figure studies, was sketched directly on the canvas.

The composition is based on certain primary considerations of mural design through

181. STATE FAIR

183. HIGH DIVER

the same emphasis on a stage setting flanked by heavy baroque wing decorations of a rich dark purple. The three performers—clown, fat lady, and acrobat—are arranged across the stage, their backs toward the beholder, and the attention of the crowd below in the middle ground of the picture is being attracted by the gesticulating barker to the acrobat lady standing demurely at the right. Across the crowd to the left is another stage with a group of red-clad chorus dancers to whom another barker seeks to draw the attention of the audience.

The color, though bright and sparkling, has an even, all-over tone that retains the surface quality of the canvas in spite of the sharp recession from the stage down to the middle-ground and back to an extremely high distant horizon. The problem of design that interested Curry particularly was the relationship of a few big forms with masses of little forms—the round tent forms that are embedded in the colorful crowds of people moving, yet firmly placed in the space.

183—HIGH DIVER. Oil on canvas. 1930 (later repainted). There are a number of State Fair subjects, mostly of single figures, which Curry was working on in 1929 and 1930, two years before he went with the Ringling Brothers circus. The particular interest in subject and pose of this figure is the tense and breathless moment before the actual dive is taken. The glaring yellow light, the solidly modeled red form

184. THE MEDICINE MAN (also Aqua Vita)

against the deep blue background, the glittering reflection, and wavy design of the cloak tend to increase the dramatic effect of the pose. A second painting, begun at the same time, represents the diver the moment after she has leaped from the tower in a spectacular Fire Dive. In most of these instances when Curry reworked an earlier painting there was little revision of the drawing or composition. The changes in most cases involved a brightening and intensification of the color which in later years he felt he was better able to exploit.

184—THE MEDICINE MAN (also called "Aqua Vita"). Oil on canvas. 1931. Collection of William Benton, Chicago, Illinois. Painted in Westport from memory of the old-time medicine shows Curry used to see at home in Kansas. Like the High Diver it is related to the State Fair, not as a massed scene, but as one of the side shows in which concentration is on a single figure—the gesticulating barker-salesman. The primary emphasis in the composition is on the rotund form of the barker. It is complemented by strong horizontal forms that also emphasize the surface design: at the bottom of the picture a rich red bier with the soft white of the reclining maiden, her shining golden hair spread over a blue velvet pillow; at the top the gray scalloped awning forming a parallel horizontal design. The space and figures immediately behind the medicine man are enveloped in a warm brownish-gray atmosphere.

186. THE MEDICINE MAN (Preliminary Sketch)

186—THE MEDICINE MAN. Preliminary sketch. Black crayon. 1931. There are about a dozen of these studies. They indicate that the composition of the final painting was developed from the expression of one figure and that the artist had sketched many different poses and gestures before arriving at what he considered the most expressive form. Consequently, it is not merely a repetition of the orant gesture that he had used in The Gospel Train and Prayer for Grace, but the reconstruction of a fundamental mode of expression.

188. GENERAL SKETCHES OF THE CIRCUS

189. SKETCH OF THE CIRCUS

190. SKETCH OF THE CIRCUS

188-192 inclusive—GENERAL SKETCHES OF THE CIRCUS. Sepia, watercolor 1932. A group of detail studies which Curry used at various times for design and color composition. As such their realistic and decorative function is that of background or setting rather than any particular center of attraction. Notice in Figure 188 the general view of colorful tent tops framed by the wings crowded with figures similar to those in State Fair. The watercolor of the Big Top (Fig. 189) is notable both for the compositional spaciousness through the diagonal movement of the posts and for the brilliant color combination of bright red (the ring at the right) and light blue posts against a soft beige background. The excited and colorful crowd (Fig. 191) is

· 216 ·

191. SKETCH OF THE CIRCUS

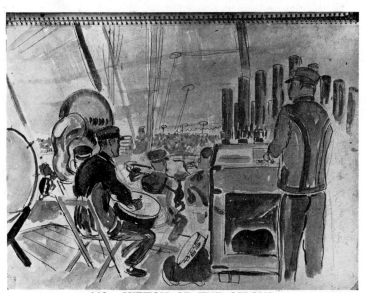

192. SKETCH OF THE CIRCUS

a composition in itself that was also used in The Runway (Fig. 243) and later in The Stallion (Fig. 146). The most important associative device for creating the festive circus atmosphere is the brass band, and it is no accident that in the many watercolor sketches of the performing musicians (Fig. 192) the instruments given greatest prominence are the drums, tuba, and steam calliope. Equally glaring—and beautiful in the original color—is the combination of a poisonous green and yellow in the uniforms, a lavender color of the horn, against the soft beige space which is punctuated by red and blue tent poles.

193. TAMARA'S ACT (Study)

194. TAMARA'S ACT (Study)

195. TAMARA'S ACT (Study)

193-198—TAMARA'S ACT. Sepia and watercolor studies. 1932. A group of sketches of an aerial act that indicates a persistent interest in the scene rather than the performance itself. The theatrical pose of the actress (Fig. 193), the bright green and blue of her costume, and even brighter orange and yellow arena floor against the same

196. TAMARA'S ACT (Study)

197. TAMARA'S ACT (Study)   198. TAMARA'S ACT (Study)

beige colored background, are striking compositional parallels to the blaring fanfare that announces Tamara's entrance into the arena.

"I was impressed by the dramatic effect," Curry says, "of this flaming beauty ascending heavenward in the brilliant spotlight, while the wretched-looking laborers in the shadows, like ancient slaves, heaved at the ropes to raise her."

199. THE FLYING CADONAS

199—THE FLYING CADONAS. *Oil and tempera on panel. 1932. Whitney Museum of American Art, New York City. Alfredo Cadona in a triple somersault as he is hurled like a spinning yellow comet through the air to the grip of his brother Lala. Notice the strong silhouette of the outstretched Lala, a bright orange-red against the glaring yellow floodlights on the post, as opposed to the deeper red spherical form of Alfredo further back in the space and light. To the orange-red forms and yellow light are opposed the bright cobalt blue tent poles and a purple rim around the floodlights, which fades into the lavender and beige tone of the background. These colors of the light and setting are the same ones noted in such a general sketch as Figure 189.*

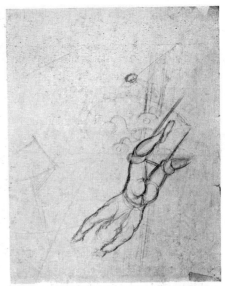

00. THE FLYING CADONAS (*Study*)   201. THE FLYING CADONAS (*Study*)

202. THE FLYING CADONAS (*Study*)   203. THE FLYING CADONAS (*Study*)

200-203—THE FLYING CADONAS. Studies. Sepia, red chalk and watercolor. 1932.
A selection from a large number of sketches that show the study of separate figures,
gestures, and positions, as well as the dramatic expressions that can be achieved through
contrasting patterns of light and dark (*Fig. 203*). Notice particularly the reversal of
the spinning Alfredo's position and the use of outstretched and clasped hands in the
pose of Lala.

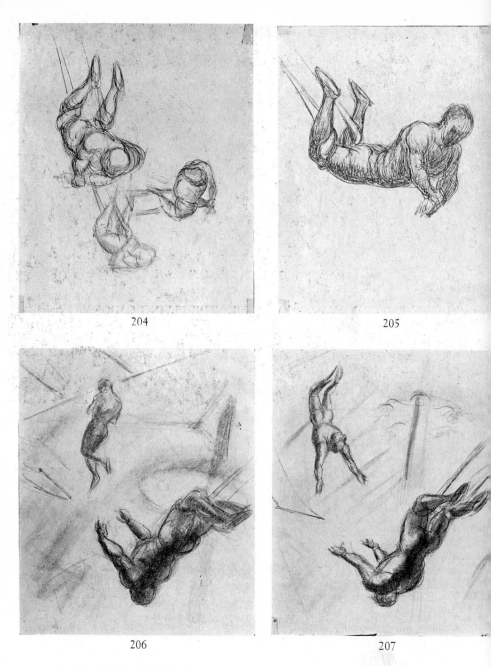

204

205

206

207

204-207—THE FLYING CADONAS. Related studies. Sepia, red chalk. 1932. The sepia sketches (Figs. 204-205) concentrate particularly on the tense moment of pause at the end of the trapeze artist's swing. In the first sketch there are several positions

208. THE PASSING LEAP

tried and in the other the correct, that is the most effective position found. This same
dramatic position of Figure 205 reappears in many succeeding sketches but is not used
in precisely the same form in any one painting. The top figure, Alfredo, in The
Passing Leap, however, is somewhat similar. The two red chalk drawings show a
varying side twist in which the movement contains something of the uncertainty of a
fall rather than the "confidence" which is so striking in the spinning somersault of
The Flying Cadonas. The comparison of these various figure positions and movements
will readily demonstrate the sincerity of Curry's statement that he watched this
act for two weeks before he finally began to get it right.

208—THE PASSING LEAP. Oil and tempera on panel. 1933. A difficult three-figure
composition related to The Flying Cadonas. In contrast, notice that the format is
horizontal and that the effectiveness of the movement is dependent on a more involved
composition of lights and other figures in a much greater space. Taken alone as in the
watercolor study (Fig. 213) they remain suspended in mid-air. The color of the figures
is a purple-red which is contrasted to the yellow light, the blue tent poles, and the
lavender-beige variations in the deep space.

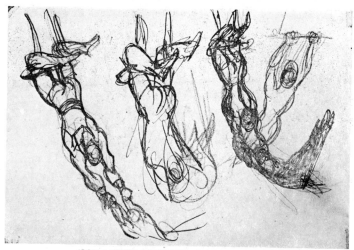

209. THE PASSING LEAP (Study)

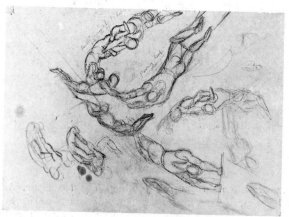

210. THE PASSING LEAP (Study)

209-13—THE PASSING LEAP. Studies. Black crayon and sepia, pencil, watercolor 1932. These, and there are hundreds of the same type, reveal something of the difficulty involved in extending the dynamic power of such a two-figure composition as The Flying Cadonas into one of a larger number. The main problem was one of correct timing and the drawings show a careful analysis of the complicated action before and after the figure is thrown. In several cases where the movement lacked clarity, the artist went over the forms vaguely suggested in the rough pencil sketches with sepia. The watercolor (Fig. 213) and the final painting (Fig. 208) indicate that the best solution was for the artist to disentangle the figures and let each one function independently. The unifying influence of space, light, and color was then used to counteract the isolated action that the more careful modeling of the forms tends to produce.

211. THE PASSING LEAP (*Study*)

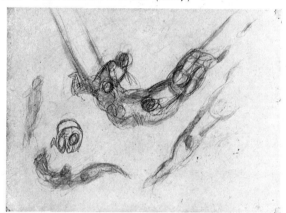

212. THE PASSING LEAP (*Study*)

213. THE PASSING LEAP (*Study*)

214. THE AERIALISTS

214—THE AERIALISTS. *Oil and tempera on panel. 1932. Collection of Dr. Arthur W. Erskine, Cedar Rapids, Iowa. A third basic compositional form that Curry had developed out of the Cadona sketches. This does not concern the dramatic catapaulting of figures through space, but the vertical sway of two connected forms (Lala Cadona and Vera Bruce) in almost majestic relaxation.*

215-218—CADONA SKETCHES USED FOR THE AERIALISTS. *Pencil, sepia, and watercolor. 1932. The rough sketches in Figure 215 again show some of the instant recordings made while watching the aerialists perform. Notice particularly the various grips, i.e., that for the passing leap, which is done first in pencil and then corrected later—often with the advice of the performers themselves—in sepia. Figure 216 is a more careful sepia study of muscular structure of the arms of the two figures,*

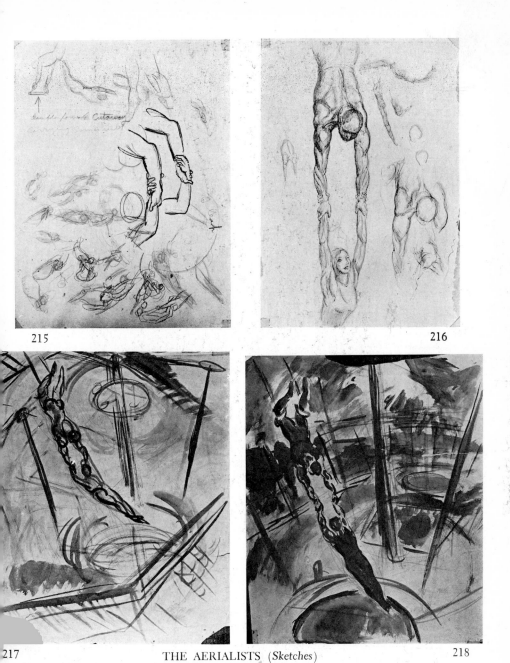

215

216

217

THE AERIALISTS (Sketches)

218

while the quick strokes and bold color of the watercolors (Figs. 217-218) suggest something of the wild excitement and tension of the lofty space and the situation. Comparison of these sketches with the final painting reveals the attempt to balance the contrasting elements of movement and control.

· 227 ·

219. AERIALIST'S FALL
(Sketch)

220. AERIALIST'S FALL
(Sketch)

219-20—AERIALIST'S FALL. Black crayon, watercolor. 1932. Not connected with the fall and death of the famous aerialist, Lillian Leitzel, but an event that frequently occurred in practice and one which was dramatically ever-present as a possibility. The motif has not been used in any easel painting but was used in a lithograph and is the central feature in the Tragedy panel of the Westport murals (Fig. 294).

221—THE GREAT WALLENDAS. Oil and tempera on panel. 1932. One of the easiest, most spontaneous and delightful compositions of the entire circus series. The balance, drawing, and arrangement of the figures did not change from the first sketch (Fig. 222) to the final painting. The same character appears in the coloration: for it is in a general soft purple to light tan tone of the space that the figures are poised, these painted a cool white that likewise tapers to a light blue at the top of the pyramidal composition.

221. THE GREAT WALLENDAS

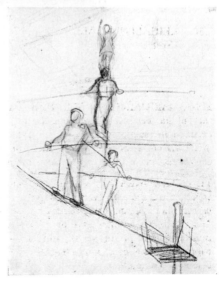

222. THE GREAT WALLENDAS
Preliminary sketch. Black crayon. 1932.

224. THE REIFFENACH SISTERS

224—THE REIFFENACH SISTERS. *Oil and tempera on panel. 1932.* A problem
in balance quite different from that of the Wallendas, not alone in the obvious subject
matter, but in the artistic means. On the rounded, unstable form of the moving horse
the balance is held through the beautifully modeled muscular forms of the riders.
The compositional balance of the Wallendas was achieved largely through the color
and linear design. Here the luminous colors of the dappled gray horse and the pink
figures with their green sashes are continued and contrasted to the smoky green and
purple of the lighted background.

225-233—STUDIES OF CLYDE BEATTY AND HIS ANIMAL ACT. Sepia and
black crayon. 1932. A series of sketches showing the famous animal trainer in various
dramatic poses, some of them significant simply as feats of daring for the benefit of
the crowds, others seen as separate parts of a routine animal performance. Notice the
close relationship between these studies and those of Curry's own cat, "Smutty." The
clawing gesture of the lion in Figures 226 and 227 appears in the Cat and Butterfly
(Fig. 180). It is natural and common to both lion and cat.

225. CLYDE BEATTY AND ANIMAL ACT (*Study*)

226. CLYDE BEATTY AND ANIMAL ACT (*Study*)

227. CLYDE BEATTY AND ANIMAL ACT (*Study*)

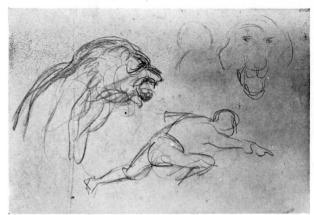

228. CLYDE BEATTY AND ANIMAL ACT (*Study*)

229. CLYDE BEATTY AND ANIMAL ACT (*Study*)

230. CLYDE BEATTY AND ANIMAL ACT (*Study*)

231. CLYDE BEATTY AND ANIMAL ACT (*Study*)

232. CLYDE BEATTY AND ANIMAL ACT (*Study*)

233. CLYDE BEATTY AND ANIMAL ACT (*Study*)

234. PERFORMING TIGER

236. PERFORMING HORSES (Study)

234—PERFORMING TIGER. Lithograph. 1932. This is the one finished composition that Curry has made from the preceding series of sketches. The central motif is the fierce sullenness of the animal under the trainer's control. Notice the circular composition with its single striding diagonal figure and towering forms in the back. The dramatic contrasts are between the sinuous striped form of the tiger, the compact lions, and the tiny figure of Clyde Beatty in their midst.

236—PERFORMING HORSES. Black crayon. 1932. The sprightly and nervous elegance of these animals is quite a contrast to the more substantial verve that is so characteristic of Curry's other horse subjects. These designs were never developed, however, except in a modified way in the horses of The Runway (Fig. 243).

237. CIRCUS ELEPHANTS

237—CIRCUS ELEPHANTS. Oil on canvas. 1932. Collection of Mrs. Grace Eustis, New York City. Circus Elephants and The Flying Cadonas are probably the best known of Curry's circus paintings. The circumstances in which he first sketched elephants and the artistic interests involved were described by Curry in the speech quoted on page 210. These remarks confirm the instant impression of spontaneity that one has when the picture is first seen. It shows a long line of massive forms receding diagonally with the wall of the tent, the huge trunks of the animals swaying rhythmically as they feed on the hay before them. There was a certain element of fear in the realistic scene that Curry wanted to retain in the composition. This is indicated in his quoted remarks wherein he describes the uncomfortable effect of the sharp, beady eyes buried as they are in the massive bulks of the elephants. The color is dominated by warm brown and by purple-gray in the overlapping and solidly modeled forms. In the foreground there is green and light ochre, the canvas tent covering in the background is the same soft beige color that has been noted before, while the bright and slightly duller blue colors of the two tent poles emphasize the clear space of the interior.

239—THE ELEPHANTS. Sketch. Watercolor. 1932. One of the preliminary studies which show both the isolated form of the elephant's head and dangling trunk and the moving pattern created by these forms in line. Notice the bull-like protrusion of the second animal and the close attention paid to contrasts in the silhouettes.

239. CIRCUS ELEPHANTS (Study)

242. BABY RUTH

242—BABY RUTH. *Oil on canvas. 1932. A composition that is somewhat related to The Medicine Man (Fig. 184) in its combination of a flat surface pattern (the scallops and curtains below and behind the figure) and a single, heavily modeled form. The dominant color is a luminous and gaudy pink in the prominent flesh tones and the lady's tinseled dress.*

240—HIPPOPOTAMUS. Black crayon. 1932.

243. THE RUNWAY

243—THE RUNWAY. *Oil on canvas. 1932. Collection of Bryn Mawr College, Bryn Mawr, Pennsylvania. A scene and a composition that seeks to give something of the general spirit of the circus mentioned in the sketches at the beginning of this series. At the same time it includes many subjects and motifs of which Curry had made a particular study. Notice the returning acrobats and riders composed in groups across the foreground, the lean and flowing design of spirited horses (compare the drawing of Fig. 236) trotting in the opposite direction, the diagonal profile pattern of the circus audience noted in the watercolor of Figure 191, and the vast, brilliantly lighted space of the central arena (sketched in Fig. 189).*

· 237 ·

244. AGONY OF THE CLOWNS

244—AGONY OF THE CLOWNS. *Oil on canvas. 1932. A simple composition based on the loose sketch of Figure 245 and a generalized audience design used as a back-drop. The title reflects the clownish humor that was as much the artist's as it was the subject's. The gaudiest red, white, and blue colors were used in the costumes of the figures and were contrasted to the softer tones characteristic of these circus interiors. The painting has been destroyed. Curry said that he did not like the color and started to repaint it. As he worked the picture "got worse and worse" until he gave it up.*

245—STUDIES OF CLOWNS. *Black crayon, sepia. 1932. A characteristic study of comic types and actions, one of a large number of similar drawings. Note particularly the attention given to realistic detail, such as the exact labeling of colors used in the clown's makeup.*

249—CLOWN AND EQUESTRIENNES. *Oil and tempera on panel. 1934-41. There are a number of these clown and equestriennes paintings which are based on the casual or excited pose of the actors awaiting their cue for the performance, and which have long remained in the studio to be worked over and repainted. This is by far the finest. Its deep, rich coloration is focused on the bright red of the clown's nose and bow tie, then is extended to the warm brown of his hat and coat, to the lush flesh tones of the girls, to the glistening green in their costumes, and finally to the cool gray-green of the surrounding horses and plumes.*

245. STUDIES OF CLOWNS

249. CLOWN AND EQUESTRIENNES

Football

We have already noted Curry's ability as a youth to run fifty- or hundred-yard dashes in good competitive time and his speed and elusiveness as a high school halfback. This experience is important as a foundation for the artist's understanding of America's most spectacular sport.

There is a natural emotional attraction to that amazing weekly spectacle of the American autumn. The college football game with its gigantic stadia filled with cheering crowds, the waving pennants and parading bands, the changing weather of the autumn season, and the integrated character of the game itself is obvious pictorial material. Curry's approach, however, was through the muscular action of the performing athlete, its coördination into the massed teamwork of eleven men, and the juxtaposition of the two teams in a rigid system of competing action laid down by the rules of the game.

There are many drawings and watercolors of football players in action. These are the result of serious study taken up on two occasions: in the east, once in 1933 when he used to see many games at Princeton and Yale and in the west at Madison in 1937 and 1938. The pen sketch of Figure 251 is characteristic of the earlier work in which certain basic problems of artistic representation are clearly seen, such as, the various actions of an end run, the poised figure of a back about to throw a forward pass, and a fullback's plunge over the goal. The movement is presented largely by means of the nervous and agitated line and its furtive repetition in an attempt to crystallize the tenseness of such split-second action. Both the problem and the technique are closely related to the sketches of the Hound and Coyote studies (Fig. 168).

The Madison sketches reveal a different means of approach. The rendering, in which the action is created through form rather than through line, is far more effective. He seems to have applied his own advice and practice, noted in the drawing of movement in Elephants (page 211), to the more dynamic form of the football player. Even in the most cursory thumbnail sketch, such as the tiny pen drawing of Figure 267, the action is seen and presented in the rounded form and not in the suggestive outline. Notice that in comparable situations, as in the line play of Figure 268, the artist chooses a dramatic moment in which the charging back is hurled into the air by the impact of the tackler. In the earlier drawing the action has already stopped, the downed man is surrounded by figures which form an agitated mass of lines rather than the clear-cut suspended form (Fig. 251).

As in the athletic studies of the circus Curry spent hours of patient observation of the men in practice and scrimmage on the playing field. He did this first in 1937 at Camp Randall stadium in Madison, where he appeared on the side lines regularly every day for three hours during the six weeks of spring practice. He continued his attendance with less regularity through that fall and the spring of the next year. During this time a great many compositional drawings and paintings were worked out. These sketches show the separate figures in their natural and prescribed positions used in training: the center holding the ball for the kick-off, a back kicking a punt, an end set to go down the field under a punt, another end in the act of receiving a forward pass. Grouped figures begin with charging linesmen and various blocking positions (Fig. 253), then develop into the regular team plays with an end run, line buck, or forward pass (Figs. 256-260).

In principle many of these artistic forms come remarkably close to those observed in the circus studies, as can be seen by comparing the spinning figure of a blocker in Figure 264 with the Flying Cadonas, or the scattered figures on an end run practically suspended in mid-air—entirely different in appearance, to be sure, yet still basically the problem attempted in the aerial performances (The Passing Leap, Figure 208).

The one really striking attempt that Curry made toward the

perfected football picture was the Goal Line Play (Fig. 268). It is based essentially on a small sepia sketch (Fig. 267) which the artist made on a pocket scratch-pad while watching the Marquette-Wisconsin game in 1937. It is a dramatic moment which most football enthusiasts have seen many times: "fourth down, the goal line to go" when, as the fullback makes a last desperate plunge to put the ball over the line, he is tackled by the opposing back and the force of the impact sends him high into the air. Around this "airplane" motif which is so spectacular in popular wrestling matches, the remaining figures are built into a heavy and powerful composition moving in groups from the right foreground to the background at the left.

When the picture was exhibited in New York it was criticized as overloaded, overworked and dull—"a monument to a lost opportunity." Curry reworked the composition through a number of stages but finally destroyed it. This was unfortunate, for if one surveys the relatively small number of football pictures in contemporary American art he will find that what Curry attempted in this picture comes much closer than any other to the strength and dramatic power that makes the game a universally recognized American sport.

In the studio one day the Wisconsin football coach, Harry Stuhldreher, was looking over some of Curry's football drawings and oil sketches. When asked what he thought about them, particularly Figure 261, he replied that the positions were perfect and he could find nothing wrong except, "When in the world did you ever see us run off a play where we managed to get that much interference out in front of the runner?"

The question brings up an interesting problem that is quite significant to the understanding of Curry's style. In teaching football strategy and developing successful plays many coaches insist that the individual play is not just an attempt to gain yardage, but is always a potential score. If the strategy of the attack does not successfully eliminate one defense player after another to give the ball-carrier an open field for the score, the play is a failure and must be tried again or varied as the case may warrant. That same point of view determines the form in many of Curry's pictures: the pose of separate figures, their grouping, and their total action must be a successful unit. The play must function in all its details toward the achievement of its desired end. That is why so many of the compositions depict such moments of "success," i.e. the ball-carrier free on an end run, the fullback plunging over the goal line, or the blocking of interference successfully executed. The same principle of "form follows function" was observed at work in the Peace and Plenty ideology of the harvest landscapes, as well as in the ideal physical perfection of Ajax and The Stallion.

Notes on the Illustrations

251—EARLY FOOTBALL SKETCH. Pen-and-ink. 1933. One of a number of early football studies which indicate something of Curry's early approach to problems of dramatic subject matter and expressive form. Such poses, gestures, and groups may have been influenced by the many photographs that cover the sports pages of every newspaper during the fall season. These sketches, however, were done directly from observation of the game itself. Similar problems of active forms in space had always interested Curry as already noted in the early illustrations and the Hounds and Coyote sketches. The artistic means by which that action is presented here is largely the same nervous and agitated line.

253-254—FOOTBALL: SEPARATE STUDIES OF BLOCKING AND LINE POSI- TIONS. Black crayon. 1938. Some of the simplest and clearest studies showing the methodical analysis of blocking players as seen from various sides (Fig. 253). Just as the coach explains a play to his team by making a diagram on the blackboard during "skull practice" so here Curry has diagrammed the position of each player on the team and indicated the line of motion for an end run. With that diagram he has included the stance of each player as the signals are being called, the shift, and finally the release of the play as the ball is snapped and the backfield men sweep around the end.

256—FOOTBALL: STUDY OF THE FORWARD PASS. Black crayon. 1938. Notice the clarity with which the passer, the various blockers defending him, and the opposing players attempting to break up the play are seen and composed into a unified action. The essence of that clarity is the plastic modeling of each figure as a form, the logical organization of each form into dynamic groups—usually pairs of figures—and then the moving groups into the larger space. The comparison of this sketch with the earlier Figure 251 demonstrates the effectiveness of Curry's conscientious and self- imposed discipline.

251. FOOTBALL SKETCHES

253. FOOTBALL: SEPARATE STUDIES BLOCKING AND LINE POSITIONS

254.   FOOTBALL: STUDIES OF BLOCKING AND LINE POSITIONS

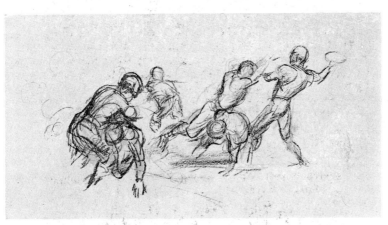

256.   FOOTBALL: STUDIES OF THE FORWARD PASS

259-260—FOOTBALL: TWO SKETCHES OF AN END RUN. *Black crayon. 1938.*
These are based essentially on the idea noted in the lower right of Figure 254.
In the many sketches of end runs there seem to be two rather conflicting modes of expression which are aptly demonstrated here: the two runners (interference and ball-carrier) are free from the struggling mass of players at the left, but that struggle is in the one instance seen as made up of pairs or small groups of opposing players; and in the other as a much more compact and unified mass (Fig. 260). In the more developed compositions of succeeding sketches and paintings one of Curry's chief interests was to extend the dynamic power of a single figure hurling itself through space to the greater

259. FOOTBALL: STUDIES OF AN END RUN

260. FOOTBALL: STUDIES OF AN END RUN

impressiveness of massed figures. That was essentially the problem involved in the development from The Flying Cadonas to The Passing Leap and it was one which Curry had been concerned with long ago in the works of Signorelli, Michelangelo, and Rubens.

261—END RUN. Oil on canvas. 1938. An oil sketch, based essentially on the two previous drawings, but with a single figure, the ball-carrier, isolated at the left, and the massed figures composed rhythmically into four groups: three in which each player of the offensive interference is taking out his opponent properly, and a fourth in which two of the defensive backs are racing to tackle the ball-carrier. The silhouetting of these red and gold forms against the light green background, their rhythmical repetition and design are values rather close to those which motivated such of the earlier sketches as Figure 251, but Curry seems not to have been satisfied with these linear designs alone, as the other sketches and oils will show (see especially Fig. 263).

261. FOOTBALL: END RUN

263. FOOTBALL: END RUN

263—END RUN. *Lithograph. 1938. Compared with the previous end run studies the composition here is much more compact and heavy. Notice, however, that the action is carefully thought out in terms of running, blocking, and tackling figures, as in the other instances.*

264.   FOOTBALL: LINE PLAYS

265.   FOOTBALL: LINE PLAYS

264-265—FOOTBALL: LINE PLAYS. Red chalk. 1938. Plays running through the
center of the line or off tackle involve vastly different problems than the more open
and spacious compositions of punts, passes, or end runs. Figure 264 was sketched during a practice scrimmage with but a few players. It shows again how Curry approached
the problem through the composition of single and grouped figures in an open space
which this time he indicated more clearly by the stripes on the ground and the Field
House in the background. The tension between figures—the halfback at the right, the
charging ball-carrier at the left, and the spinning blocker in the center—recalls again
the similar problems that Curry had studied in The Flying Cadonas and Passing Leap
compositions.

266. FOOTBALL: LINE PLUNGE

267. FOOTBALL: LINE PLUNGE (*Hurt Player*)

266—LINE PLUNGE. *Oil on canvas. 1938.* Related to the two previous sketches but more loosely composed into what appears to be four groups: a fiercely tumbling pile at the right, a string of forms receding at the left, the fullback being blocked out in the background, and the ball-carrier in the center tackled by the neck and the ankles at the same time. Like a Brueghel or Rubens Kermess composition the action swirls in arabesques diagonally from right across to the background at the left, with an

268. FOOTBALL: GOAL LINE PLAY

obvious iconographical (i.e., the figure carrying the ball) and compositional focus of attention on the central group. This is perhaps one of the best of Curry's unfinished football compositions. While many of the groups, such as the blocking figures in the left background, are developments of carefully studied poses (Fig. 253), the ferocious tumbling of groups and the total dramatic spirit is very close to that noted in some of Curry's early illustrations (e.g., Fig. 15).

267—LINE PLUNGE; HURT PLAYER. Sepia. 1938. Two quick drawings which Curry made on a small pocket sketch-pad while watching the Wisconsin-Marquette football game early in the 1938 season. Accidental observations, yet familiar to every football enthusiast, they are significant as representations of both the action and the pathos of the spectacle. With other sketches that he particularly likes, Curry has these tacked up on the wall of his studio.

268—GOAL LINE PLAY. Oil and tempera on canvas. 1938. (Now destroyed.) A large-sized canvas based on various sketches like those of Figures 265 and 266, but using as its central motif the dramatic pose of the fullback, hit head-on with such force that his body is hurled high into the air (Fig. 267). The artist's difficulty seemed to come in the over-emphasis on the separate figures and their heavily padded forms rather than muscular action. Their pattern covers almost the entire surface of the canvas and the somewhat leaden repetition of many forms tends to make the composition heavy and overloaded. The color is—or was—predominantly red and gold in the uniformed figures as contrasted with a light green and gray of the grass and the background.

Boxing

A similar logic is carried over into the art and sport of boxing. There are many studies parallel to the early football sketches (1933) which record the tension and competitive action of boxing figures far more skillfully than the earlier fighting men noted in the drawings and illustrations of Figures 15-16. In fact the combination of muscular skill and intellectual control is essentially what makes a sport of boxing rather than a fight. Curry frequently attended and sketched the university boxing contests which are among the most popular sport events in Madison. The results are not what one would expect, for instead of the athletic contest Curry was much more fascinated by the dramatic pathos of the total spectacle as it is focused on the unfortunate victim. Two of the most striking sketches are from a series made in 1940, in which the boxer is depicted flat on the canvas after having been knocked out, and then is being carried from the ring by his seconds.

So far Curry has never painted an important boxing picture. If he would, these sketches indicate that the motivation would be an emotional one of sympathy or compassion rather than one of aggressive action. There is good tradition for that point of view. It is the brutality of a wild slugging contest rather than athletic sportsmanship which characterizes George Bellows' famous painting of Firpo Knocking Dempsey out of the Ring (Whitney Museum of American Art, New York). Curry felt much the same way about it for, as far back as 1925, when he used to see the boxing matches in the 14th Street Armory, he painted a watercolor representing a bleeding boxer wilting to the canvas in a corner of the ring with the crowd jeering at him. The same pose and its expression was developed in later years to the more extensive mural symbolism of Justice Defeating Mob Violence (Fig. 297).

270. COUNTED OUT

271. BOXING STUDIES

Notes on the Illustrations

270—COUNTED OUT. Watercolor. 1925. An early watercolor which reflects Curry's reaction to the boxing match much more dramatically than any of his later studies. In contrast to the ferocious realism of fighting men, as presented by a George Bellows, Curry focuses his attention on the pathetic victim collapsing to the canvas with blood streaming from his face while the merciless crowd jeers at him.

272. BOXING STUDIES

271-272—BOXING STUDIES. *Black crayon. 1940. Two of a number of sketches drawn directly from the ringside at boxing matches held at the University Field House in Madison. In keeping with the early reaction noted in Figure 270, there seems to be no particular interest here in the athletic performance itself—there are some sketches of jabs to the face and guarding positions, to be sure—but the inspired form can be recognized in such studies as these, when the defeated boxer is knocked out cold, or is being carried to the dressing room by his seconds. It is the same reaction of sympathy and compassion that he had experienced aesthetically in Ruben's Descent from the Cross and sketched once before in the hurt football player of Figure 267.*

Politics

Curry's excursions into political subject matter have been rather conservative, which is not due to any political principles of his own, but to a number of outside circumstances. He believes that art should be understandable to the common people, but he does not believe in propaganda, particularly of the Marxist variety that so strongly influenced the social conscious painters in America after Diego Rivera's meteoric rise to popularity in the early 1930's. He deliberately avoided exploitation of controversial subjects such as those which involved Rivera at the Detroit Institute of Arts and Rockefeller Center, because he felt that the resultant publicity tended to obscure rather than enhance the artistic quality of the work.

From a spectacular point of view, however, politics in Madison offered much material which he could hardly resist. There were the constantly recurring political controversies and investigations at the university. In 1938 the famous oil trials involving the much-publicized defense of the great oil companies against Federal Government charges of conspiring to violate the Anti-Trust Laws were held in the packed Federal court room in Madison. That year, too, the governor of the state, Philip F. La Follette, staged the spectacular inauguration of his National Progressive Party at the giant University Stock Pavilion. These were all colorful displays which Curry simply had to see. He made many sketches but none of the ideas developed further than the preliminary stages. Perhaps the most impressive was the Progressive rally but the oil sketch he painted for Governor La Follette can hardly be called more than a study.

In contrast to these, other paintings of a semi-political content are remarkably convincing because they represent situations that were not theatrical displays, but were an outgrowth of his own personal feelings and experiences. One of these is the previously mentioned Return of Private Davis. The actual scene was first witnessed at home in 1918. There were related sketches made in 1926 upon visiting an American soldiers' cemetery in France. The idea was developed into a pictorial composition in 1928 (Figs. 47-48), and the painting finally completed in 1940 when it was sold to the American Legion Headquarters in Milwaukee. Its spirit is closely related to the Baptism in Kansas: a rural religious ceremony whose tragedy is intensified by the realization that this son of the fresh green Kansas prairies was sacrificed on a battlefield whose ideological remoteness was as dramatic as its geographical.

The Parade to War (Fig. 277) is a variation in reverse of the same idea: the spectacular departure of marching soldiers rather than the pathetic return of the individual victim. Finished in 1939, the preliminary sketches date from 1933 (Fig. 278). These show that the compositional idea was not merely the colorful "parade," but the striding action of the two-figured group—the young girl and her soldier-lover—the type which he had also used in the Baptism in Kansas. The identity of war with personal tragedy, suffering, and death is not only a part of Curry's experience (for he had seen and felt the effects of war even though he did not serve in the trenches) but was further stimulated by the Alfred Noyes poem, *Victory Ball* and the surge of popular disillusionment and anti-war spirit of the period that was likewise reflected in such literary works as *Journey's End, All Quiet on the Western Front*, and *Road to War*.

A third type of subject matter which somewhat belongs in this classification is the Man Hunt (Fig. 283) and The Fugitive (Figs. 284-285). The Man Hunt has all the physical qualities of a typical blood-and-thunder movie thriller as well as the artistic qualities of dramatic action. But it also embodies many personal concepts of justice and law that go back to Curry's early youth. He often describes the hoarse cries and noisy excitement of the sheriff's posse, fully equipped with baying bloodhounds and shotguns, as it rushed through the field in search of some unfortunate victim. To such dramatic action he juxtaposes, in a later panel, the trembling terror of The Fugitive, clinging with outstretched arms to the branches of a hidden tree and barely visible in a weird and unearthly light.

Both of these ideas were Curry's own, but dramatically publicized events of the years 1931 to 1934 stimulated him to a greater consciousness of their importance. He was not concerned about the nation-wide man hunts that attended the famous Lindbergh kidnapping or the Dillinger cases so much as the cause of justice involved in the many lynchings like that of the murderers of Brooke Hart in San José, California, or the various racial and political problems attending the Scottsboro case. They are important not only in themselves as the crystallization of certain basic experiences: terror, injustice, persecution, and dramatic excitement, but also because they become determining dramatic and compositional factors in his later mural work (i.e. in the Department of Justice Building, Figures 296-297).

Notes on the Illustrations

273—THE FIRST RALLY OF THE NATIONAL PROGRESSIVE PARTY. *Oil on canvas, 1938. Collection of Philip F. La Follette, Madison, Wisconsin.* An oil sketch of the famous mass meeting held in the University Stock Pavilion on April 28, 1938. The spectacle itself is perhaps important to American politics in that it represents the revival on a national scale of the Progressive Party which had been headed by the elder La Follette and since his time had functioned largely in Wisconsin state politics alone. The setting was as spectacular as the idea, with brass bands, red-sweatered ushers, flags and colored bunting decorating the hall, and centered behind the rostrum the gigantic banner with the newly devised party emblem.

274-275—PROGRESSIVE RALLY. *Sketches. Pencil and red chalk. 1938.* Two of the sketches which Curry made on a small pad indicate the general scheme which he used later in the oil sketch of Figure 273. Notice, however, the greater vitality and conviction here, which is partly due to the fresher and more vigorous drawing, but particularly to the more effective use of didactic gestures in the central figure (i.e., the raised hand of the speaker in Fig. 274, and the repetition of the pointing gesture at the top).

274. PROGRESSIVE RALLY (Sketch)

273.   FIRST RALLY OF THE NATIONAL PROGRESSIVE PARTY

275.   PROGRESSIVE RALLY (*Sketch*)

276. THE RETURN OF PRIVATE DAVIS

276—RETURN OF PRIVATE DAVIS. *Oil on canvas, 1928-1940. American Legion Headquarters, Milwaukee, Wisconsin.* In its original conception this painting belongs with the drawing and watercolor noted in Figures 47 and 48, as ideological and compositional parallels to The Bathers and Baptism in Kansas. Though exhibited at various times the canvas had remained in the artist's studio and undergone many revisions which have proven greatly to its advantage. Significant here is its contrast, both as a spectacle and as a political theme, to such a scene as the Progressive Rally. Though the two pictures have many compositional elements in common, such as the brightly colored flags, the preaching figure, and the listening crowd, this has a convincing quality which springs essentially from the artist's personal feelings and experience rather than the external display that characterizes such a political spectacle.

277—PARADE TO WAR. *Oil on canvas. 1939.* Related to the Return of Private Davis and the marching motif of The Victory Bill (see page 255). The original conception of this idea goes back to drawings of 1933. It was worked into a composition in 1938-39. The unbalanced, leftward movement is composed into three planes: the motorcycle policeman and old people in the foreground, the running youths and parading soldiers in the middle, and the massive architecture closing off the background. The color correspondingly recedes from a dark blue and purple to the luminous khaki uniforms and a light blue-gray behind. The single group of a white-clad young girl marching with death, the soldier, is the central motif and compositional point of focus.

277. PARADE TO WAR

278. PARADE TO WAR (*Preliminary Sketch*)

282. PARADE TO WAR (Preliminary Sketch)

278 and 282—PARADE TO WAR. Preliminary sketches. Pencil, red chalk. 1933-38. The first idea was that suggested in Figure 278 (1933) whereby the mass hysteria was to be expressed by the girl rushing with outstretched arms to the soldier marching in the opposite direction. At the time Curry made several drawings from models on that basis. In 1938 he reversed the idea by having the two figures clasping each other as they march in the same direction, then he added the marching columns and further integrated the movement and composition by accenting one figure to the left as a parallel to the central pair. In the final composition this is balanced through the use of light and the total dramatic effect is strengthened by the three-quarter length silhouettes in the foreground.

6

THE ARTIST AND SOCIETY

CURRY HAS NEVER SURRENDERED to the sweet seclusion of the ivory tower. This fact has been stressed in following his work and career in these pages. The esoteric experimentation with form and color was not enough. His art must be based on the realities of his personal experience. It must be comprehensible, not only to a select few, but to the many. It must mean something to society as well as to himself.

He has shared the sense of responsibility to society with many of the patrons with whom he has come in contact. Through the years their number and importance have increased. On several occasions not only individual patrons but the editors of popular news magazines have become sufficiently interested in Curry's pictorial interpretations of a given subject to use them as leads for the discussion of significant social and political problems.

The first suggestion of the sort was a request by the *Saturday Evening Post* for a painting to accompany an article on the great Ohio floods of 1937. Even though the preliminary sketch that Curry submitted was rejected, the fact that he was asked is significant both as an indication of the recognition he had already achieved and as evidence of a new point of view on the part of the magazine editors.

Curry's sketch (Fig. 75) was no reversion to the illustrator's style. It was a consistent development of his own previous conceptions which he had painted without consciousness of any particular audience.

· 261 ·

In 1941 he was commissioned by *McCall's Magazine* to paint a symbolic representation of American youth leaving home to serve in the nation's great defense industries. With the romantic nostalgia that is so characteristic of Curry, the "home" is a lush rural landscape glorified by a magnificent sunrise. Upon this idealized homeland the lone figure of a farm boy in the foreground turns his back as he strides forward toward the spectator and the unknown world of the future.

The most important of these social themes, however, came to Curry a year earlier. It is the painting of Hoover and the Flood (Fig. 286) which was commissioned by *Life* in 1940. When the commission was given its subject was prescribed by the editors in the most general terms, but in the article that accompanied the color production (published May 10, 1940) a strikingly vivid train of facts and ideas was developed with the picture as the iconographical point of departure.

These were focused on the gigantic power of the flood of 1927, the merciless destruction, misery and pathetic confusion that follow its slow and resistless movement, and the humanitarian forces of an entire nation that were organized to relieve that suffering.

The relief work was likened in the article to a military campaign against an enemy as relentless as in any war. The leader of that campaign as generalissimo of all the relief forces was the then Secretary of Commerce, Herbert Hoover.

There was some point to the emphasis on Hoover at the time the article and picture were published. After comparative obscurity since the 1936 presidential campaign Hoover suddenly loomed again as an important political personality through his renewed activity on behalf of the Republican party in the 1940 campaign, as well as an organizer for the relief of civilian sufferers among the war-ravaged countries of Europe. Leadership and humanitarian relief had been associated with Hoover's name during and after the first World War when he organized the feeding of helpless

Belgians, Russians, and central Europeans. It was his successful organization of relief forces during the great Mississippi flood of 1927 however that launched him into political power and the presidency of the nation the following year. The last sentence of the article makes one remark that illuminates both moral and social motivation of the subject by pointing out that the disaster ". . . left Herbert Hoover primed to march straight to the White House, there to function in glory a bare seven months until a man-made flood of Depression far more disastrous than any flood of God came to sweep him out."

This had to do with the iconography—subject matter—and its relationship with the political, social, and even moral background in America during the first half of the year 1940. Knowing Curry and the previous works he had painted, one can easily recognize that the artistic form and the organization of content ideas are an integrated unit. The wet misery and confusion of cattle and human beings were the central themes of Sanctuary and The Mississippi (Figs. 73-74) and appear here in a new form in the crowded flatboat and along the river shore. The ecstatic gestures of terror and divine supplication that had appeared in the Gospel Train, Mississippi, and The Fugitive are here used to give expression to the confusion of the crowds. The stabilizing forces of law and order, as in the Justice Defeating Mob Violence mural (Fig. 297) are concentrated in the three figures at the right, with the ever-present newsreel cameraman just behind them used as in The First Progressive Rally (Fig. 273) as a realistic symbol of the attending publicity and its political implications. Dramatic and human interest details, like the Red Cross workers, the mother nursing her child, and the line of admiring youngsters, accompany the event and serve to enrich the design as well as to make it realistically convincing.

To the student of modern American journalism this particular form of picture-editorial is by no means new, since it is closely related to the daily cartoon on the editorial page or the Sunday magazine supplement in most metropolitan newspapers. However, the choice of an artist who purports to paint museum pictures has not been so common except in certain pictorial magazines such as *Life* and *Fortune*, whose interests are focused on clarifying news as well as gathering the facts. New media, such as the artistic development of photography, better and cheaper color reproduction, together with a change in popular taste have contributed to a new set of conditions which place new responsibilities on the artist. Like the historian, political scientist, or news analyst, he has become a student and interpreter. He is not producing pretty pictures that will sell or appeal to popular taste. He is no longer an illustrator, but a creative realist in the deepest sense. The remarkable combination of change and continuity that has been observed both between Curry as an illustrator of 1921-25 and as an artist of 1928-41, and between the public requirements which he has sought to meet in those two periods, is indeed convincing proof of the vitality of modern America's cultural growth.

Another aspect of this closer relationship between society and the creative artist is the influence of the "museum picture" on commercial design. As a general movement it is in its infancy but its character, particularly as it concerns Curry and his art, can be described by several different examples. One curious situation appeared shortly after Curry's arrival in Madison. A suggestion was made to him that he design a seal or trade mark for the newly reorganized University of Wisconsin Press. Just at that time, it will be remembered, he had been working in the Stock Pavilion on the various drawings for The Stallion, and without a moment's hesitation he quickly sketched a magnificent Percheron, centered in a medallion against a landscape, with much the same verve and power of his Stallion composition.

For various reasons the trade mark was not used, but it is interesting to see how, in such a situation involving the birth of a new enterprise, Curry's design grew as naturally as that which was finally given permanent form in the picture of the stallion emerging into the arena. Such significant poses and expressions as this have been exploited commercially many times (e.g. Landseer's Monarch of the Glen, and Millet's The Sower) but only after they were made famous by the artist's painting.

A more venturesome spirit is reflected in two other commissions which came to Curry in 1939. One was from Russel Wright of The American Way for a textile pattern. The artist worked it out on the basis of the Osage Orange composition (Fig. 100). The other came as the result of an extensive project of the Steuben Glass Company to use designs by twenty-seven of the world's best-known modern artists. The finished pieces were presented to the public for the first time in an impressive exhibition held in New York early in 1940. This achievement was "symptomatic" as the eminent art historian Frank Jewett Mather wrote in his preface to the catalogue "of much that is going on to make America as good to look at as it is good to live in."

In 1941 Esquire commissioned Curry to paint The Light of the World, a striking pictorial interpretation of American democracy with its free farmers, workers and business men intently watching the ominous, lightning-pierced clouds and deadly conflagration across the seas. It was reproduced in full color and in its original format in the annual Christmas number of that year.

The following spring the American Tobacco Company ran an extensive series of what it called "notable paintings of the tobacco country by America's foremost artists" in the nation's leading magazines. While the central theme—tobacco—remained constant the individual interpretation given by each of these outstanding artists was a remarkable contribution to contemporary American art. Curry's was no exception. The commercial requirement that the pictorial prominence be given to the tobacco product did not prevent him from creating an intimate rural home scene that is as genuine as anything he has painted.

These various commissions are significant as indicative of new developments in American taste and patronage of the arts. They are also significant to the artist in giving him a new sense of direction, a feeling of confidence that he is a necessary and useful part of society. The best reaction is given in Curry's own words written in the spring of 1941 in the magazine *Demcourier* at Madison:

"Michelangelo is reported to have said in anger and resentment that the times were not propitious for art and artists. The same might be said for the present age. But history proves that in every age, in spite of the most adverse conditions, the world hungers for and demands art.

"Artists have been called upon to propagandize religion, political parties, social upheavals, and the status quo. And they have been required to carve and paint surfaces for purely decorative and esthetic reasons.

"My prediction is that the artist of the new day that is upon us will fulfill a double purpose. First that of propagandist for the coming social upheavals and second, strangely enough, he will be asked to give pattern to the new concepts of decoration and design. His field will increasingly embrace every phase of modern life. His imagination and talents will beautify everything: the kitchen sink, the family car, the office desk, as well as the painting that hangs on the wall or the statuary in a public building. The artist of this new day will be, perhaps, more completely a servant of the people than he has ever been in preceding generations."

283. THE MAN HUNT

Notes on the Illustrations

283—THE MAN HUNT. *Oil on canvas. 1931.* Another type of social theme that is associated more with personal concepts of justice than with politics. Curry often refers to the furious man hunts which used to rouse the neighborhood at home in Kansas. The fury and excitement raised almost to the point of fanaticism will be noticed in the physical types, here personified in the single leader, the terrified pose of the galloping horse, and the eerie color combination of purple and green used in effective contrasts.

284—THE FUGITIVE. *Lithograph. 1933.*

285—THE FUGITIVE. *Oil and tempera on canvas. 1933-1940.* A subject that is related to The Man Hunt with its dramatic interest fixed upon the trembling fugitive rather than the pursuing posse. Note the blending of tree and figure into complementary forms, the contrast of the large figure in the dark foreground as opposed to the mass of pursuers in the light of the distance, the use of the upturned negroid head and outstretched arms in a piteous gesture of prayer and terror, and the further dramatization of that terror through the vigorous design of the surrounding foliage. In the lithograph (Fig. 284) this design is emphasized by the silhouetting of the foliage in the foreground against a light background whereas in the painting, especially as recently revised (1940), that vigor is carried through the color and brush stroke over the entire canvas. The color is a deep blue, green, and brown, with a weird greenish tone of the sun that is dramatized by the bright red butterflies hovering in the foreground.

284. THE FUGITIVE
(Lithograph)

285. THE FUGITIVE

286. HOOVER AND THE FLOOD

286—HOOVER AND THE FLOOD. *Oil on canvas. 1940. Collection of* Life, Inc., *New York City.*

Commissioned by Life in the spring of 1940 as a part of that magazine's series of paintings on recent American history and reproduced in color in the issue of May 6, 1940. In the publication the significance of the theme was fully described in an accompanying text, notably the public service rendered by Herbert Hoover as relief organizer during the disastrous Mississippi flood of 1927, the public recognition of which eventually led to his election as President of the United States.

The contrasting ideas of order and chaos inherent in the subject are the motivating elements of the composition. The pictorial vocabulary by which the subject is made comprehensible can be recognized from many of Curry's previous works. Notice that the general scheme—a circular mass of figures out of which a single group emerges— is that used in the lithograh, Baptism in Big Stranger Creek (Fig. 58). The pathetic poses and gestures of rain-soaked cattle in a flood had been used in Sanctuary (Fig. 73). The terror, confusion, and prayerful gratitude of flood refugees, as expressed in the ecstatic gestures of the two central figures, were motifs that appeared in The Mississippi (Fig. 74). The rigid, military confidence and order expressed in the three standing figures at the right is again a motif used with a similar context in the Department of Justice murals (Fig. 297). The association of the newsreel camera and publicity is another element that is an important item to this theme which has been similarly used in the Progressive Rally sketch (Fig. 273).

Curry intended that these motifs and their associations should be easily recognized. It is their integration into a spacious composition that swirls in a gigantic circular sweep from the foreground to the left and around to the distance—with the Hoover group as the stabilizing hub—that gives the subject its effectiveness.

287. GLASS PLATE WITH
CORN SHOCK (*Design
Steuben Glass Inc.*) .

288. COTTON DRAPERY
FABRIC (*Design for Russel
Wright's American Way*)

287—GLASS PLATE WITH CORN SHOCK DESIGN. *Steuben Glass Inc., 1939.*
The corn shock design was made about the same time as the Self-Portrait lithograph
of Figure 115 in which the same motifs are used as a part of the decorative back-
ground.

288—COTTON DRAPERY FABRIC. *1940. For Russel Wright's The American*
Way, Inc. A textile design executed by Curry as an all-over pattern based on the
Osage orange composition (Fig. 100); an exuberant spray of green branches against a
yellowish-peach background.

7

MURAL DECORATIONS

First Attempts

THE ARTIST PAINTING MURALS has quite a different task than when painting easel pictures. The differences are both technical and psychological. Technically it is not the actual medium—i.e. whether the artist uses fresco, oil, or tempera to paint with—that is important as much as his skillful control over that medium. In mural decoration the areas to be painted are usually much larger than in easel pictures; the design is more limited by the space and the architectural conditions surrounding it. Moreover, the artist is not free to paint whatever he wishes, but must respect the requirements of the patron, commissioners, or public for whom the work is done. He does not paint the picture and then offer it for sale, as he does in the case of an easel painting. He is commissioned to perform a task in accordance with certain stipulations, like any architect, contractor, or craftsman. His freedom is based on the intelligent recognition of these limitations.

The remark was made earlier that the wall maps painted in 1928 were the starting point for Curry's style as a muralist. This is what was meant: in the case of the two walls of the Boring Travel Agency (Figs. 289a-289b), the request was for maps that could be clearly read, could take the variously colored ribbons which indicated each tour route, and would attract interest through the characteristic place illustrations as well as the general design. Knowing these requirements, and something of Curry's background and personality through his previous work, one can recognize the artist's personal handwriting cropping out, particularly in his manner of handling those motifs close to his own experiences, such as the cowboy and buffalo figures or the picturesque landscapes.

Compared to the formidable character of the Boring murals the overmantel panel he painted for Mr. Seward Prosser (Fig. 290) is much more informal and domestic: the design includes both a detail map of Wood's Hole and the near-by Cape Cod region, as well as the characteristic features—Bartholomew Gosnold, Pilgrims, and the sea—that are associated with local tradition.

These wall maps were painted in 1928. The similarity with such of his contemporary painting as the Baptism in Kansas, the Bathers, the Return of Private Davis sketch and the Battle of Amazons, was not one of external characteristics of "style," but an internal one involving the artist's psychological attitude toward a given problem. The phenomenal development of Curry's mural style in the succeeding twelve years can be followed in the reproductions. It is, of course, not only a matter of artistic growth and technical mastery, but also a complex development involving government patronage, popular recognition and acclaim, and the personal efforts of farsighted individuals in making the mural commissions possible for him.

In the mural painted in 1931 for the Washington Centennial Exposition (Labor of the Common People for the Success of the Revolution, Fig. 291), Curry took the first word of the prescribed title as the central motif and gave it a dignity that has been a part of the artist's repertoire through the ages, from the Labors of the Month themes of medieval art to Millet, Hodler and the mural artists of modern times. The difficulty with his design is that it is too heavy and overloaded. Many of the ideas, however, are unique and among Curry's favorites, such as the mother with her child seated at the spinning wheel, the cat, kettle, vine, and house combination used as one frame at the left, and the standing Plainsman at the right. These stage-wing designs, as well as the general compositional scheme, are closely related to the State Fair (Fig. 181) which, through its dimensions, color, and figure-design, is far more "mural" in conception than an easel painting.

Westport High School

Those compositional ideas are most completely integrated in the Westport murals, which he painted in 1934 under local sponsorship. The frescoes occupy the two slightly recessed walls flanking the stage of the small high school auditorium. The choice of a theatrical subject matter and the obvious contrasts of Tragedy and Comedy grew logically out of this setting. In addition, the choice of the various character-ideas in each scene was governed by popular interest. Curry intended that they should be easily recognized and should carry associations from popular experience: there is hardly an American who does not know the antics of Charlie Chaplin or the story of Uncle Tom's Cabin, and though few may have seen an aerialist's fall, the tense consciousness of that possibility is certainly a common experience.

The color and design function on the basis of that recognizability of subject matter. Through the overlapping of forms—the theater boxes and stage lights as opposed to the central figures, and the use of contrasting lights and colors—an effect of depth is achieved similar to the State Fair, in which the forms move with the greatest of ease. The stylization of the musical comedy performers (Fig. 295) suggests a relationship with similar motifs by Seurat and Toulouse-Lautrec, which Curry knew just as he had known their circus pictures. Comparison with those early French modernists, however, will emphasize two features which are significant and characteristic of Curry's style: one is the plastic modeling of the figures and their moving composition in the space through arabesques and a luminous atmospheric color. The other is a matter of character-portrayal—a form of realism by which the subject-type is able to speak as well as the artistic medium. Seurat's faces are usually lost in a shadow, or enveloped in the atmosphere of light and color that he loves. Here the sprightly humor of Mickey Mouse, the good-natured wit of Will Rogers, or the pathetic sweetness of the popular crooners are an integral part of that vital expression which, to Curry, is the popular theater.

In Curry's mind the most distinctive technical feature of these Westport murals is the rich and luminous coloration. He had never before attempted a mural in true fresco and, like many other artists at that time, he wanted to try it out. In doing so, his interests were not focused on the atmospheric spot coloration of Seurat, but the combination of solid form and luminous color of Piero della Francesca. The solidity and strength of many of Curry's later works (e.g. John Brown) are due to some extent to the intelligent understanding of the monumental strength for which Piero was striving.

Notes on the Illustrations

288a—PLAINSMAN, PIONEER FAMILY, SURVEYORS. Design for a mural. Watercolor on brown paper. 1925. One of Curry's earliest attempts at a mural design. It was painted for no particular place or person, but simply as an experiment during the same time that he did The Lightning and Hogs Killing a Rattlesnake. The pioneer and frontier type of subject matter reveals "what at that time I thought a genuinely American mural art should be." Though there is a tremendous difference in technical ability between this and the perfected murals of later years the basic iconographical principles have remained the same.

289a—WALL MAP OF EUROPE. Oil on canvas (10′ x 16′). 1928. Office of the James Boring Travel Agency, New York City.

289b—WALL MAP OF NORTH AMERICA. Oil on canvas (10′ x 16′). 1928. Office of the James Boring Travel Agency, New York City.
These two designs represent Curry's first mural decorations. The basic fact to be remembered here is the combined decorative and commercial problem. The latter called for a large and clearly legible map, capable of taking the different colored ribbons that indicated the agency's tours. Having practically forgotten these murals long ago as "early attempts," Curry looks at them today with considerable interest, both as designs and as commercial projects successfully performed. In addition he recognizes many inventions which he was quite proud of at the time. Notice the bizarre decorations emanating from the sun and moon in Figure 289a, and the sunrise design of

288a. PLAINSMEN, PIONEERS, SURVEYORS (Mural Design)

Figure 289b against which the high-towered city panaroma is outlined. A characteristic personal touch is the prominent silhouette of the cock from the tower of the Hecksher Building (upper right of Figure 289b). Looking over the small easel-like paintings that frame the maps as decorative illustrations one will find many conventional types and scenes, but also many personal motifs readily recognized as Curry's own and which he has used in other works. No sophisticated "pinxit," but a straightforward "John Steuart Curry made this map" identifies the artist at the bottom of each painting.

290—OVERMANTEL DECORATION IN THE SUMMER HOME OF SEWARD PROSSER. Wood's Hole, Massachusetts. Oil on canvas. 1929. (27" x 92"). A wall map over the mantelpiece in a private home naturally involved a different set of requirements than those for the business office of the Boring Travel Agency. The result is a much more informal conception and freer design. This can be seen in the luminous pattern of light and clouds over the curved horizon from moon to sun at the top, and the continuation into the cloud design of the side pictures. Curry's persistent interest in space and dramatic action can be recognized especially in the "Moby Dick" and clipper ship motifs at the right.

291—LABOR OF THE COMMON PEOPLE TOWARD THE SUCCESS OF THE REVOLUTION. Oil on canvas (10' x 14'). 1931. (Now destroyed.) This mural was commissioned for the Centennial Exposition held in Washington, D. C. in 1932. The rather expansive title was not Curry's idea but was given to him by the commissioners.

One will recognize many of the labor motifs that were prescribed by the subject, i.e., the mother at the spinning wheel, the grain sower, the reaper, blacksmiths, shipbuilders. Some of these have their historical parallels, such as Millet's and Van Gogh's Sower, and Winslow Homer's Reaper (The Veteran, Collection Adelaide Milton de Groot). These figures, well posed and plastically modeled, are not isolated motifs, but

289a.   WALL MAP OF EUROPE (Mural Design)

are woven into a moving pattern over the entire wall. The silhouette patterns of foliage and frontiersman are favorite devices for framing a scene in order to drop the action back into space. Curry used it again in the Westport frescoes.

292—ANCIENT INDUSTRY. Oil on canvas. 1936. Norwalk High School.

293—MODERN HAT INDUSTRY. Oil on canvas. 1936. Norwalk High School. Two murals painted in 1935-6 under the sponsorship of the Public Works of Art Project and dealing with local subject matter. The design is more related to the Washington Labor for the Revolution murals than to the Westport frescoes. In conversations Curry seldom mentions them, believing that they are less successful than any of the others.

294—TRAGEDY. Fresco (8' x 13'). 1934. Auditorium of Westport High School, Westport, Connecticut.
295—COMEDY. Fresco (8' x 13'). 1934. Auditorium of Westport High School, Westport, Connecticut.
    These murals were Curry's first attempts in the technique of true fresco, and while they are remarkably successful from many points of view, they have remained his only ones in that medium up to the present time. They are situated on either side of the stage platform in an auditorium which measures about 50 x 90 feet. In keeping with their location the composition is developed from recognizable subjects, beginning

289b. WALL MAP OF NORTH AMERICA (Mural Design)

(Fig. 295) with Charlie Chaplin on the cinema screen, Mutt and Jeff, Popeye the Sailor, and other comic-strip characters in the box at the left. Rose O'Neill and her famous Kewpie doll are at the right. Mickey Mouse, Will Rogers, Amos 'n Andy, clowns and musical comedy showgirls are in the center space. Portraits of John and Kathleen Curry, occupying the lower boxes, flank the composition like stage wings.

The content of Tragedy *(Fig. 294)* can be followed in much the same way. Suspended in the central spotlight is the tragic motif of the Aerialist's Fall *(Fig. 219)*. In a sweeping yellow diagonal, parallel to that of the showgirls in the opposite fresco, is represented the death of little Eva, while Pagliacci slumps at the foot of her bed and Uncle Tom prays at her side. Behind is the galloping Erlkönig and Lady Macbeth and, at the footlights, Hamlet soliloquizes over Yorick's skull. In the boxes below are portraits of the Shakespearian actor, Moffett Johnston and his wife Winifred, while above at the left can be recognized the dramatist Eugene O'Neill and the novelists Sherwood Anderson and Theodore Dreiser.

The essential feature of the content is just this recognizability; the associative power of each subject is stimulated by the remarkable composition in light and color. There is a host of colors of every description, but it is organized on the basis of a dark and luminous red in the boxes and curtains of the foreground as opposed to a green of the backdrop. Between these the brilliant reds, greens, whites, pink and yellow make an exciting pattern that recedes up into the space behind the footlights. In execution the Comedy was undertaken first, the Tragedy later, and if one examines the color of the original painting carefully the technical mastery of the fresco medium will be found considerably improved in the second fresco.

290. OVERMANTEL DECORATION; SUMMER HOME SEWARD PROSSER

291. LABOR OF THE COMMON PEOPLE

292. ANCIENT INDUSTRY, NORWALK HIGH SCHOOL (Mural)

293. MODERN HAT INDUSTRY, NORWALK HIGH SCHOOL (*Mural*)

294. TRAGEDY (*Mural Westport High School*)

295. COMEDY (*Mural Westport High School*)

Department of Justice

The two murals for the Department of Justice building in Washington were already begun in Westport before the artist moved to Madison. He set them up on huge stretchers in his new studio and continued work there until the following spring (1937), then completed the task in Washington after the canvases were fixed to the wall.

In the iconography of American art there is no subject more significant and representative of American ideals than Westward Migration. It is not the abstract "Migration" theme that Orozco painted on the walls of Baker Library at Dartmouth, but a "Westward" Migration which has its foundation in the historic expansion of the nation from the eastern seaboard across an entire continent, and which has developed into an ideal source of artistic inspiration since Colonial times. There are variations of the theme among the works of Thomas Cole and Emanuel Leutze, but the actual source of Curry's interpretation can be found in his own knowledge and experience of the pioneer West as expressed in his previous works, from the early illustrations to The Ne'er Do Well and the idealized portrait of his father as The Stockman.

It is no accident that the key figure of the composition is the grim-faced pioneer father in the center. Curry is frank in expressing his love for the old-time western tales of pioneer leaders: scouts like handsome Buffalo Bill Cody and Wild Bill Hickok. His father often described his own struggles with the unfenced prairies when he first migrated to Kansas. The central figure is not a portrait of his father, Buffalo Bill, or anyone else but a character-type such as he had seen in many westerners and had portrayed in the sketch of Figure 307. The remarkable fortitude and depth of character in the face of the pioneer mother—which actually began as a portrait of the artist's wife—is to be understood from this same point of view. The various problems involved in the compositional scheme and their final synthesis can be followed in the preliminary sketches illustrated in Figures 299-303.

For the opposite wall Curry originally submitted a sketch representing The Liberation of the Slaves (Fig. 308). It was refused by the authorities on the ground that it might stir up racial controversy. Though Curry did not resent the action, he was disappointed not to be able to realize a remarkably fine theme and composition. Later, however, he was to use it for the decoration of the Law Library at the University of Wisconsin.

The idea of the Liberation of the Slaves was an outgrowth of such religious demonstrations that Curry had represented in the Baptism in Kansas, The Gospel Train, and the Mississippi. Its primitive unrestrained enthusiasm is in marked contrast to the grim determination of the Westward Migration, yet the composition, with its expressive group toward the center, its movement from the heavy storm clouds at the left to the radiant and idealistic sunshine at the right, forms an effective parallel and counterpart to the opposite wall.

Nevertheless the new plan was probably worth the effort. Once again the artist went back into his own work and experience for a theme which he could expand into monumental proportions. Justice Defeating Mob Violence is a development of the lynching theme which Curry had painted in The Fugitive (Fig. 285) with its terror-stricken Negro hiding in a tree as the armed posse and bloodhounds approach from the distance, and again in the Man Hunt (Fig. 283) with its angry mob of pursuers led on the trail by bloodhounds. Curry, as a boy, had been impressed by a story his father told: how bandits robbed the local bank and the entire community turned out with guns and dogs to hunt the criminals.

The simpler narrative of the earlier scenes is here transformed into a dramatic situation: on the one side a motely crowd of raging men, armed with guns, bloodhounds, and the ready noose, seething with fury and excitement as they rush up the steps from a flaming background; while at the right, backed by the columns of tradition and the forces of law and order, stands the solitary, commanding figure of the robed judge, at once protecting the cowering fugitive and restraining the unbridled passion of the mob.

Looking at the picture from the point of view of content alone one cannot help but be impressed by the deep-felt sympathy and compassion of the underdog which the artist has tried to present. It is not merely the tear-jerking romanticist's play on the emotions, neither is it the realist's bold statement of facts. It is a real situation taken from life, which every thinking person knows, intensified and raised to a universally recognizable concept of "justice." Curry's compassion and intensity has almost a religious fervor. He has expressed it many times in such pictures as the Baptism, The Gospel Train, and Liberation of the Slaves. It is certainly not accidental that the closest parallel is to be found in the dramatic religious miracles painted by Peter Paul Rubens, as for example The Miracles of St. Francis Xavier in the Vienna State Museum.

That this human sympathy is an inseparable part of the artist's life and artistic character is shown in his other works and the preliminary sketches for this one. Notice that in one of the studies for the Justice composition (Fig. 309) the figure of the judge is represented in the impulsive gesture of a father bending to comfort the fugitive and at the same time with outstretched hand protecting him from the pursuers. Something of that character of compassion expressed through a two-figure group will be found in Rembrandt's early etching of the Return of the Prodigal Son which Curry knew and liked, though he was not thinking of it when he did this sketch.

Curry's composition, as can be seen from these preliminary studies, is built up from single figures and their intrinsic expressions. The idea is essentially that of a helpless beaten victim presented years before (1925) in the watercolor Counted Out (Fig. 270). He developed it with fresh studies from posed models, one of which (the red chalk drawing of Fig. 311) in its simple pathos and depth of feeling is comparable only to the beautiful sketch of the weeping woman for the Prayer for Grace (Fig. 56) and to similar cringing figures of Orozco's fresco of The Trench in the National Preparatory School of Mexico City which was mentioned before (page 66) as one of Curry's favorites. In the final composition the father-protector implication is reshaped into a concept of protection yet of stately dignity and wisdom: the protecting hand is still there, but the figure is straightened up into a magnificent expression of strength and composure.

A few of the salient features of the composition can be quickly pointed out. As a complement to the opposite Westward Migration where the figures are composed around a central group, the composition here is divided to either side by the nature of the subject. To the order and upright dignity of one side is contrasted the heterogeneous grouping of the lawless mob. In the division of the whole panel, and through the confusion on the left especially, one can follow the artistic order: the arched back and forward thrust of the bloodhound is repeated in the outline of the exhausted fugitive; the automobile headlights not only glare on the crowd but furnish an illumination about the boy and triad of leaders, modeling them as moving forms in the space. Perspective is used, not only for the illusion of a third dimension, but to strengthen the total expression. Curry habitually uses a low horizon as a means of giving a more monumental effect to forms in the foreground. Hence the mob scrambles up the stairs from the left and from the background to the platform in the center, while sharp foreshortening of the steps at the right emphasizes from the opposite direction that same empty space in which the climax of the scene, namely the dramatic tension between judge and the mob, is held taut.

Curry's principle of parallelism is used here, as in the moving figures of the Migration panel, to remarkable effect. The repeti-

tion of striding legs and slanting bodies is especially marked among
the figures at the left and continues to the fugitive and the half
stride of the judge. An opposite slanting pattern is given in the
parallel rifles of the soldiers at the right and repeated in the figures
of the crowd. The awkwardness of the death figure holding the
noose, with his extended elbows and the thrusting figure beside
him, is not alone to suggest the brute force of animal nature, but
also to carry out and combine these parallel patterns. Likewise
several X-patterns, such as the diagonal silhouette of the mob and
the slanting arm of the judge are intended to bind the composition together. The wavy pattern of the judge's sleeve is repeated
in the noose of the would-be executioner, hence the artist had to
make him left-handed. The same function is performed by the
outline of the bloodhound repeated in that of the collapsing
fugitive.

Curry's coloration is rooted in the time-honored principles of
solidity of form, luminosity of color, and unity of composition
used in his easel pictures. The entire color composition is based
on a light ochre underpainting over the whole canvas. Every succeeding color is built up on this single tone, beginning with the
ochre and silver-gray color of the columns and steps at the right
and continuing in the gray-green of the figures receding in the
distance. The forms are beautifully modeled, with the solid weight
of sculpture. Luminous and irridescent flesh tones are particularly
remarkable on the back of the fugitive, where pearly gradations
of yellow-gold move into cool greenish-blue tones and a shining
purple in the shadows. The red on his back and feet is not just
the red of blood, but is composed into this reddish-purple of the
shadows. A quite different effect is to be found where the glaring
yellow of the headlights strikes the olive-brown of the rope-carrier's
chest, producing a fascinating combination of yellow, bright
salmon, and greenish variations. A bright orange-salmon color
behind the screeching figures at the left is continued in a diagonal

line of light salmon flames back of the distant central figures.

Curry, like many other serious artists of that time, was to some extent imbued with a spirit popularly called "social conscious-ness." But he was not following any party line. In one of the background figures someone pointed out an upraised fist which looked like a Communist salute. He immediately put a club in the fist to eliminate the association. This was his own interpreta-tion of a social problem.

Justice Defeating Mob Violence is not merely a protest against lynching or any contemporary phase of injustice that might be prevalent at a given moment. It is rather an idealization of justice —the character and composition of the judge group is evidence enough to prove the point—which everyone, regardless of political creed or social standing cannot help but recognize. It is not a symbol, then, but a universal situation, valid in the past as it will be in the future. It is an encouragement to a present generation to keep striving toward that ideal which has motivated legal pro-cedure through ages of the past. The artistic medium is therefore not an aesthetic or mental exercise, but a means by which the fire of that ideal is rekindled. The roots of this point of view have already been suggested in Curry's earliest approaches to the prob-lem of illustration. There are critics who have disparagingly ignored or condemned this work as mere "illustration"; if it is so, then the Night Watch of Rembrandt and the Surrender of Breda by Velasquez will have to be reclassified under that designation.

These ideas were set down in Curry's own direct manner in an address he gave before the Madison Art Association on January 19, 1937, only a few weeks after he had taken up residence in Wisconsin. While it repeats many things he had expressed before and was to express afterwards, it is quoted in full at this point because it most adequately reflects his attitude toward the prob-lem of public art projects at the time he was actually at work on the Washington murals.

"You have been told that the subject of my address would be American painting. This address as I have prepared it seems primarily to deal with my own painting and my own personal reactions to my immediate environment. You may think this strange, my work being but a small part of American art, but I extenuate this by the fact that I am not really informed properly to speak on such an extensive subject, so to be honest about the matter this address is personal and anything I may say consider it as such.

"The ushering in of the Roosevelt Administration and the New Deal emphatically ushered in a new deal in American painting. I believe that the present administration's program sponsoring painting, sculpture, music, and the drama is of tremendous importance to the American art of the present and of the future.

"In the instance of painting there has been nothing comparable to it in magnitude. The Mexican and Russian revolutionary governments have sponsored programs of painting, but on a much reduced scale. Fascist Italy has watered the plant of painting with a gentle rain of gold on the top-most leaves.

"This large scale projection of painting onto the walls of our public buildings has startled the public. It has been startled into liking or disliking it and for the first time realized that painting was something that could exist outside a museum.

"In our younger days we heard art and painting referred to in Baccalaureate sermons, Commencement speeches, and the like, where flights of oratory were let loose. Art as a reality was as foreign as Chinese.

"Now it is different. Try to realize this—that within these few years there has been an absolute revolution in the symbol and subject matter of American painting, and particularly in that of mural art for our public buildings.

"You have in the Capitol building here in Madison perfect examples of the so-called 'Court House decoration.' The state can be complimented for obtaining the best of the time and period. But contrast this with the decoration now being done for the Federal buildings of the present day. With one sweep the classical lady with flowing robes is gone; gone too is the noble youth posed in a noble attitude doing nothing. In fact the whole tableau and stagy set-up is swept aside and we have in its place a presentation of people doing things. The noble female is reduced, if you will, to a presentation more mundane. That luscious arm and empty posed hand emerging from flowing drapery now holds a business-like broom. In the Capitol's legislative chamber you have a large mural presenting early settlers, a Missionary Father, a Civil War group with flag, and posed in the center a group of lovely females in different attitudes amid huge pine trees expressing something—I don't know what.

"Well, the beautiful maidens are still in Wisconsin, but the pine trees are no more. If this mural had been presented in truth, the early settlers, Civil War veterans, and beautiful ladies would have been shown whacking down the pine trees and the Missionary Father shown praying for the future of the state.

"I am well aware that the foundation that pays my way here comes from those pine trees, but in this matter we are all not blameless. The American Farmer is presented in mural art as a beautiful, noble, and fairly intelligent-looking fellow. My own family have been farmers for generations, and as you can see by the representative before you, were beautiful and noble, but from the amount of good top soil they and their farmer neighbors have sent down the Mississippi or up in the air, I doubt their wisdom.

"You may be sure the heirs and administrators of the Brittingham estate, the farmers of Wisconsin, the governing powers of the state, and the University would approve of a propaganda by art of any nature that would aid in preserving the natural resources. To illustrate this different conception and viewpoint I cite the work I am doing now for the Department of Justice Building in Washington, and the reason I cite my own work is that I know more about it.

"In the first panel I have been given the subject, 'The Migration from the Atlantic to the Pacific, Bringing Justice and the Settlement of the Land.' I have shown the pioneer father, the mother, the child, the boys, the dogs, oxen, wagons, the soldier, the scout, the bad men, the prairie fire, and the cultivated land. I have not made these people ugly, but true to the general type of our first settlers. Neither have I idealized them into the symbolical ladies with wings holding aloft books, scales and wands in the ever present and gentle breeze that blows through the draperies and ribbons of the old decoration.

"In the second panel, 'Justice Defeating Mob Violence,' I have used for the properties of my theme the mob, vicious death with the rope, the projecting limb of the tree, the glaring auto light, the hysterical women, the bloodhound, the clubs, the guns, the horses, the upraised clenched fists of the bloodthirsty. Opposite these is the black-robed figure of the Justice, at his feet the fugitive, behind him the arm of the law, the Department of Justice man, the militia; and behind them the pillars of the Court—with these properties I have endeavored to give a dramatic story with the reality of the day, and at the same time so organized that they will fit in an art form that will give them authority and so that they will as decorations give an added luster to the building, and to their setting. From the full-sized cartoons which I have tried in place I know they will do this.

"I wish to point out to you the vastly more difficult problem which we as painters today face than that which faced the Coxes, Blashfields, and the Simmonses of a few years ago.

"They had no problem of idea. It was a set thing; it was the triumph of the virtues; learning, the law, justice were symbolized by the same well-developed young lady in robes and a nice young man thrown in now and then to nullify the impression that this scene was from the Isle of Lesbos. Because they avoided the realities of life their art form remained static; their only problem was a rearrangement of their certain few props; and because they were a close monopoly, they had no competition and their work never changed.

"Our work today lacks their refined elegance, our line is cruder, the mass more insistent, the prop is unpainted. We have moved with that great part of America which has surged good-naturedly around and past the ballyhooers of the status quo and to the attractions at the other end of the fair ground. The artists of today have the opportunity to use the alive and vital issues as subject matter, and they are doing it. This classification has been applied to many of us who have been painting only recently, but in truth there have been American artists since the primitive days painting the life and spirit of their times. We owe a great debt to such forerunners as Nast, Eakins, Ryder, Pyle, Homer, and of our present day, Bellows and Sloan.

"Grant Wood, under the banner of regional art, has tried to make people realize that painting is something that can be enjoyed here and now by you and you. That you might have artists alive and producing in your own neighborhood, that you might even be proud of their works, that you might even be the artists, that art need not be something that is sent out from Chicago, New York, or Paris for your edification.

"In the minds of many Americans, including critics, painters and esthetes, any American artist is fore-ordained and predestined to damnation. They may have a few patronizing words for the painter who exhibits some mannerism of the popular foreign mode, but this is all; so I say it is a better part to die with the wolves than to be dragged out and slain with the beautiful lambs.

"The social, political, and economic disturbances of the times have brought forth those artists who, taking their themes from these issues, have produced telling and effective works for the cause of social and political justice. I need not here enumerate the other and various phases of our painting Renaissance. Just give us time. Give us ten years, and if we can escape the paralyzing hand of war, we will accomplish something even in that short time.

"It has been reported that my reason for joining the circus, discarding for the time-being my Midwest subject matter, was to sharpen my technique of drawing and obtain a livelier skill in painting. I may have given these as reasons, but the real reason was that I had become restless in my environment and felt the need for a new viewpoint of life. The action and the color of the circus appealed, and I made the opportunity to carry out my idea of first hand observation.

"It is for this same reason that I came to Wisconsin. For the past few years I have felt the need to enliven my imagination by new contacts with American life.

"The idea of a "resident artist" fitted in with the educational ideal that the University of Wisconsin had conceived.

"I am glad to be associated with the College of Agriculture. While in my youth I fled from the arms of agriculture to the more seductive charms of art; now I return. It is the University's hope that the farm youth of the state will gain through my efforts a conception of painting, and those with a special talent will be encouraged to actual study of drawing and painting. To this end they have the whole-hearted coöperation in the University of the Departments of Art Education and Art History, and back of that the lively interest and appreciation of the people of the state.

"However, the people of Wisconsin can be assured of this— I do not come here to wreak good on them. To the interested citizens, I will appreciate your interest in my work, and to the artists, I will give my most sincere advice, if it is wanted, and very gladly.

"I approached the life of the circus looking for dramatic action, color, and lively personalities. I found them. I came to Madison looking for dramatic action, color, and lively personalities. I have found them. Thomas Benton after returning to Missouri said to me that he believed that in the next ten years the economic and political power of the nation would shift to the Middle West. I believe this will happen, and I expect to see Wisconsin in the center of one of the most colorful periods of American history.

"As I have said, I was asked to come here because of my painting, and not because of anything I have said or written. My only influence will be through my work, and I am sure my experience here will enliven my conceptions.

"I have great sympathy for the artist and his problems, and particularly for the young artist. In reality it is a single problem; it is the problem of self; the expression of self. When we are young we turn blindly from this light to that light, seeking the means to express ourselves, borrowing for the time the mannerisms of this master and that master, assuming the cloak of this school or that school. My sincere advice to the young artist is that first he should acquire knowledge; and most important, a knowledge of drawing and structure, learn how the figure is constructed first and be able to paint, if you will, a solid academic figure, and this need not be a stupid literal performance either. I have had students tiring of this advice burst forth, and as they invariably put it 'wish to express themselves'—and invariably they assumed the mannerisms of some one of the masters of the so-called School of Paris; and to those who feel that this is a heavenly transfiguration, let me point out this fact—that these masters in their beginning had an excellent and more or less thorough training in the academic actualities. This basis has given their adaptations and distortions the authority which their less schooled imitators lack. It is pleasant, though, to escape the old iron fetters for those golden chains.

"My sole interest and conception of subject matter deals with American life, its spirit and its actualities. In this day paintings of religious nature are uncalled for either by the churches or by the people. At this time paintings of a purely decorative nature have little appeal. I myself have had no struggle for or with a subject matter. Likewise I have not been worried by the fear that my art form would or would not fit the prevalent esthetic style, knowing that there is no subterfuge of mannerisms in which to hide with my deficiencies and in which I would not soon be found out.

"From my experience I advise that you sharpen your tools of craft, look behind the flashy and popular contemporary or stylish vogue to their sources, and paint pictures and then more pictures. It takes from five to ten years to develop a competent baseball player or prize fighter. A skilled acrobat goes into training at the age of three and reaches his best at about twenty-four—so in this art of painting you can allow yourself at least ten years of work before you can in your own mind feel the freedom and satisfaction of a controlled craft.

"Every artist has within him that 'still small voice.' When he has slighted or fumbled his work, it speaks to him. Even though the voices of beguiling friends make a comforting din, it speaks to him. Likewise when he has done well and endures

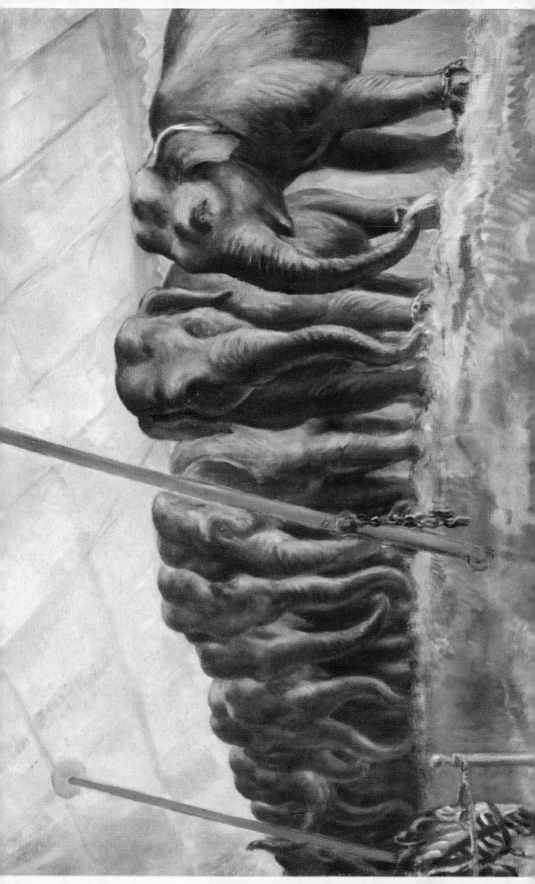

CIRCUS ELEPHANTS

the slights of neglect and the darts of unjust and stupid criti-cism, the voice speaks to him and he is given courage.

"Some of us look forward to a great and alive American art. We look forward to a great and alive art in the Middle West, but be reminded of this—the great art is within yourself—within your own heart is the secret of the power that will attract your fellow men. Bring this power forth and with it you bring life to the despised and long neglected subject. With this power you give a brilliant radiance to the old and hack-neyed idea. So I say to you, your greatness will not be found in Europe or in New York, or in the Middle West, or in Wisconsin, but within yourself; and realize now that for the sincere artist there is no bandwagon that goes the whole way, no borrowed coat of perfect fit, and no Jesus on whose breast to lay your curly head."

What is said in this speech coincides with what an analysis of the work itself demonstrates: a remarkable clarity of purpose and ideals as well as a confidence of expressive form. That clarification —artistic maturity—has been described before in the Baptism in Kansas. The Department of Justice murals represent its extension into the greater, more responsible problems of mural decoration. Here Curry's mural style is crystallized.

Notes on the Illustrations

296—WESTWARD MIGRATION. *Oil and tempera on canvas. (20' 6" x 8' 6")
1936-37. Department of Justice Building, Washington, D. C.*

297—JUSTICE DEFEATING MOB VIOLENCE. *Oil and tempera on canvas,
(20' 6" x 8' 6") 1936-37. Department of Justice Building, Washington, D. C.*
  In these two works Curry felt that he had perfected a mural style which would match in its way the recognized style of his easel paintings. Here were fully expressed the principles with which he could challenge the courthouse style of the Blashfields, the Simmonses, and Kenyon Coxes who had controlled the public commissions for over two generations (see page 293). With these Curry begins an impressive series of murals which have maintained a remarkably high standard of quality.

The two pediment-like murals are placed high on opposite ends of a monumental elevator hall on the fifth floor of the new Department of Justice Building. They are brilliantly illuminated by artificial light which is further enhanced by the simple design and the silver leaf of the surrounding ceiling and walls. In their location the spectator has to look up rather sharply to see them, a factor which Curry has used in the composition of both murals. In the one case it is the central group of the pioneer family striding over the crest of a hill which recedes down into the space toward the left. In the other case it is the tense space before the courthouse steps which recedes down into the flaming space toward the right. The language and development of these two expressive elements—the striding group and the dramatized space—can be followed in the preliminary studies, Figures 299-303, 309.

In Westward Migration the round-faced figure at the right with the corncob pipe is a self-portrait of the artist. The central figure holding the lyncher's rope in the Justice mural was originally depicted as a hard, bony-faced character, which Curry then changed to a death's head as it appears in this photograph. Later on he decided against it and covered the gruesome face with a mask similar to that on the mounted figure just behind him.

299-303—WESTWARD MIGRATION. Preliminary studies. Crayon, watercolor, oil. 1936. Notice two primary considerations indicated in the first sketch (Fig. 299): one, the sweeping movement of the design from right to left (below), the other a concentration on a central figure group with complementary forms to the right and left, of which the latter is somewhat lighter in weight to accentuate the forward movement. Figure 301 shows one stage in the crystallization of those three groups. In Figure 302 the concentration is on the single group of the pioneer family with horses and wagons receding to left and right over an unbalanced triangular area. The mother here does not look back, as in the previous design, but ahead with a resultant emphasis on the forward action. Figure 303 represents a balance between all the preceding elements which Curry retained in the final design.

304-307—WESTWARD MIGRATION. Detail studies. Crayon, pen-and-ink, and watercolor. 1936. Once the general design is clarified each figure is carefully constructed with studies from the model. Figures 304 and 306 show drawings from the nude for correct and convincing anatomical structure. Then they are sketched in costume with details involving historical or realistic subject matter given careful attention for their factual authenticity. Finally, there are numerous studies in character portrayal (Fig. 307). Notice that in the studies of the pioneer woman the sunbonnet of the first sketches is pushed back and an exceedingly refined, strong character-type is used in the final painting.

308—LIBERATION OF THE SLAVES. Oil sketch on paper. 1936. Collection of Lloyd K. Garrison, Madison, Wisconsin. This was one of the original designs which Curry had intended for the wall opposite the Westward Migration. It was rejected, however, by the authorities on grounds of possible racial prejudice and controversy. Its expression is based on various gestures and motifs noted before in The Gospel Train and The Mississippi, but Curry's chief interests here—and his disappointment in not being able to use it—were in both the idea (i.e., Freedom) and the moving, pyramidal composition receding into space similar to that of the opposite wall.

296.   WESTWARD MIGRATION   (*Mural Dep't Justice*)

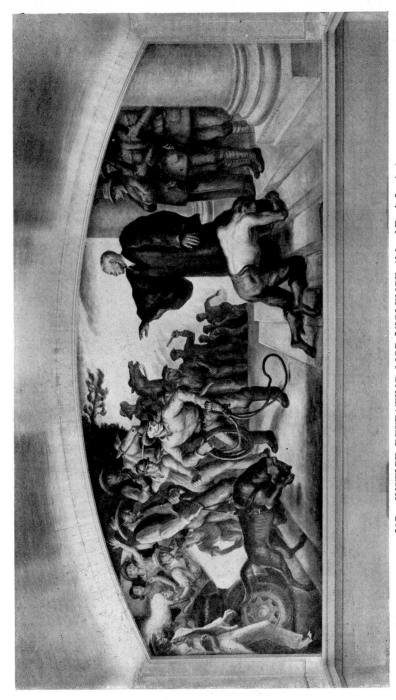

297.　JUSTICE DEFEATING MOB VIOLENCE　(*Mural Dep't Justice*)

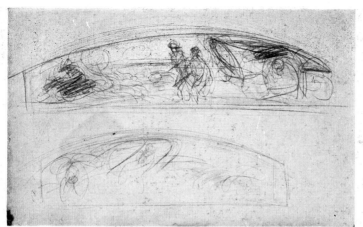

299. WESTWARD MIGRATION (*Preliminary Sketch*)

300. WESTWARD MIGRATION (*Preliminary Sketch*)

301. WESTWARD MIGRATION (*Preliminary Sketch*)

302. WESTWARD MIGRATION (*Preliminary Sketch*)

303. WESTWARD MIGRATION (*Preliminary Sketch*)

304-305. WESTWARD MIGRATION (*Detailed Sketches*)

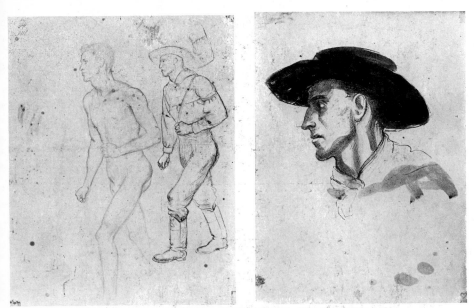

306-307. WESTWARD MIGRATION (*Detailed Sketches*)

308. LIBERATION OF THE SLAVES

309. JUSTICE DEFEATING MOB VIOLENCE (Sketch)

310. JUSTICE DEFEATING MOB VIOLENCE (Sketch)

309 to 314, incl. JUSTICE DEFEATING MOB VIOLENCE. Preliminary studies. Red chalk, crayon, oil. 1936. One of the first studies for the new composition (Fig. 309) shows a clear definition of the dramatic tension between the excited mob and the restraining judge facing one another from opposite sides of the space. The group at the right is here conceived in the more compassionate attitude of the fatherly judge protecting with one hand the victim and warding off the pursuers with the other. As the studies from models progressed the figure of the judge became straightened up and was given more power and dignity. The pose and psychological conception of the victim is based on that of the wilting figure in Counted Out (Fig. 270), but is developed from that cringing pose to the stumbling movement of Figure 312 which then is combined with the relentless parallel design of the bloodhound on the opposite side (Fig. 314). Every detail of the important figures was carefully studied from reality. Curry even took a special trip to the police barracks at Ridgefield, Connecticut, to study the movement of bloodhounds and after many sketches of the type seen in Figure 313, the expressive lunge of Figure 314 was achieved.

312. JUSTICE DEFEATING MOB VIOLENCE (*Sketch*)

313. JUSTICE DEFEATING MOB VIOLENCE (*Sketch*)

314. JUSTICE DEFEATING MOB VIOLENCE (*Sketch*)

Department of the Interior

The second commission for the Federal Government in Washington was for two murals in the Department of Interior. They represent historical facts which have a characteristic symbolism and whose significance is enhanced by their dramatic juxtaposition. One is a form of Westward Migration in the representation of that famous day—twelve o'clock noon on April 22, 1889—when the Oklahoma Territory was opened to homestead settlement and some twenty thousand prospective settlers rushed into the new land to stake their claims. The other represents the homestead itself, with all the typical features that make up the blessed peace, happiness, and potential prosperity of ensuing rural life.

Comparing the two murals one can again recognize many familiar artistic and factual motifs that are essential to Curry's mode of expression: the swift action of galloping figures, the peaceful quietude of the home with fence builders, plowed field, vegetable garden, chickens, and the prairie spaces bathed in the life-giving warmth of the sun. These compositional motifs, too, were factual and symbolic. Many of them appear again and are specifically described as such by Curry in his notes for the murals in the State Capitol at Topeka (Figs. 319-321).

The most distinctive feature, however, grows out of the architectural limitations of the corridor in which they are placed. The proportions are extremely long and narrow. Since there is only a limited area for the spectator before the picture Curry designed the ground as an apparent extension of the corridor floor. One has the illusion that he is actually standing in the scene. The result is a panorama type of composition, which, as a form of mural design, reveals unlimited possibilities for further development.

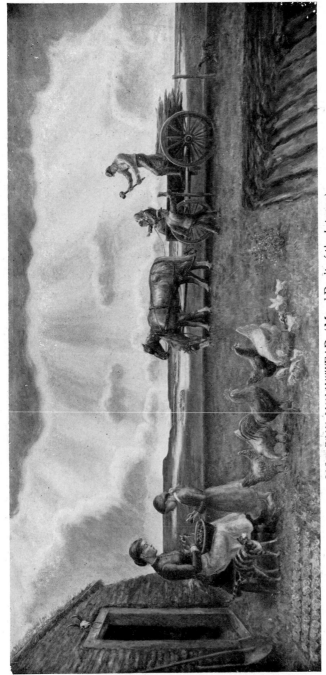

315. THE HOMESTEAD (*Mural Dep't of the Interior*)

316. OKLAHOMA LAND RUSH (*Mural Dep't of the Interior*)

Notes on the Illustrations

315—THE HOMESTEAD. *Oil and tempera on canvas (9' 2" x 19' 8"). 1938. Department of Interior, Washington, D. C.*

316—THE OKLAHOMA LAND RUSH. *Oil and tempera on canvas (9' 2" x 19' 8"). 1938. Department of Interior, Washington, D. C.*

The location of these two murals in a narrow enclosed corridor is rather unfortunate but Curry has done his best in adjusting the composition to these restrictions. The murals cover the wall practically from ceiling to floor, the figures are slightly under life-size, the horizon line is located just below the spectator's eye level, so that one has the feeling of actually standing in the picture as he looks at it. That impression of reality is more compelling through the dramatic contrast of violent action and pastoral peace which the two scenes present.

The spirit of The Homestead is one of peace and grandeur: the mother and daughter peeling potatoes before the open door of their sod hut, the house cat and the chickens, vegetable garden and plowed field spreading out across the foreground. Further back the father in his Union cap is driving the fence post which his son holds for him. The team and wagon is set off against the vast prairie with its distant farms, meandering stream and low-lying buttes. Over the whole plain is a spring freshness that grows from the rich soil to the magnificent heavens above it.

In contrast to this the opening of the frontier affords the artist innumerable possibilities for dramatic action, humor, and the swift movement of forms through space.

In both pictures the symbolism is based on historical fact as well as artistic function. Mother and child, family cat, chickens, garden plants, and spring landscape were all motifs which he had previously dealt with as a part of rural life. The Fence Builders was his first exhibited painting and represents the historic transition from the unbounded prairie of the west to the cultivated farm. For every detail of the land rush picture Curry did his usual experimentation and careful research: the bicycles and wagons, as well as the costumes of the period, the locomotive and even the chronicled girl in green who rode on it (used only in sketches). The opening of the Oklahoma Territory is another case of a historical fact here made symbolic of the eternal frontier spirit.

Kansas State Capitol

The commission to decorate the walls of the Kansas State Capitol at Topeka is in many ways one of Curry's greatest triumphs—a triumph that had nothing to do with politics, personal promotion, or official government patronage, but came directly from his reputation as an artist. The funds were raised by popular subscription through a committee of prominent citizens, including Governor Walter A. Huxman, William Allen White, Henry J. Allen, Jack Harris, and Paul Jones. Through the progress of the work, the artist's relations with the mural commission were marked by a spirit of mutual pride and respect which is indeed provocative.

With the exception of the Westport frescoes all Curry's murals have been painted in oil on canvas. In most cases his method was to make a series of preliminary sketches in small and large scale on the spot where the murals were to be placed, then work out the compositions on the final canvas stretched on a temporary frame in his studio. When the regular routine of painting—the sizing, white ground, yellow prime, design, modeling of figures in tempera and successive glazes in color—has been worked through, the canvas is fixed to the wall with casein glue (Department of Justice murals), white lead (Department of Interior murals), or an arobol formula (Topeka). The final painting is then gone over carefully to make proper color and lighting adjustments in accordance with the conditions of the surrounding architecture.

The following description of the technical methods used in the Topeka murals was written by John T. Mathiesen, a young artist who worked with Curry as assistant on the project for the Kansas State Capitol:

"The time-honored method of enlarging a preliminary sketch to final size, as, say, for a mural painting, has been the use of corresponding squares. Thus, if the sketch be one-twelfth of the size of the final product, it is ruled into one-inch squares, and the wall to be decorated into one-foot squares. The sketch is then copied freehand, square by square. The result varies in accuracy according to the ability, patience, judgment, and desire of the executor. If the area involved is large, the process is necessarily either very slow or very inexact or, worse, both.

"Today a faster and more precise system is used by certain muralists. The principle is simple and must certainly long have been evident to anyone giving the matter a thought. A detailed sketch is first made to scale, preferably in black and white. This is photographed, and a standard lantern-slide made from the negative. An ordinary lecture-room type projector is then used to throw an enlarged image of the sketch upon the wall to be painted. The image may rapidly be traced off in charcoal. The artist is thus freed from the necessity of considering first one picture, then another, and the result may well be a freely-drawn, unstilted rendition, in spite of the fact that a coldly mechanical process was used in the making.

"If the mural is very large, space limitations may make it impossible to set up the projector far enough away from the wall to permit one slide to cover all of it; in this event, the preliminary sketch may be photographed in sections, and each section enlarged to full slide size. Each section is then projected and traced individually. Since such factors as parallax, lens distortion, and exact adjustment of the projector enter in, it cannot be expected that each section will match perfectly with that adjoining; if, however, a reasonable amount of care is taken, the final product will tie up remarkably well and such minor corrections as may be called for may be readily made freehand. This method was used on the murals done by John Steuart Curry in the statehouse at Topeka, Kansas, where, in the case of the larger panels, measuring eleven and a half by upwards of thirty feet, it was necessary to project in eight sections per wall. A great saving in time and labor was effected, and the results were most satisfactory."*

In presenting his first oil sketches to the commission for its approval in 1937 Curry wrote out a few notes explaining their symbolism and purpose (quoted with the illustrations, Figures 319-321). The opportunity to use many of these motifs—such as the corn, wheat, the fence builders, the peaceful farm—in this

---

* Demcourier, Madison, Wisconsin, April, 1941.

particular setting in the capitol building of an agricultural state, represents the culmination of a lifetime's activity.

Of the two gigantic conceptions of what might be called War and Peace the most unique achievement is the one mural in the east corridor of the Tragic Prelude, with its dramatic figure of John Brown. The spirit and purpose of that figure in its compositional surroundings can be traced from The Gospel Train (Fig. 50) and the first design for the Department of Justice mural (Liberation of the Slaves, Figure 308). Its tremendous power comes not only from the strong characterization of the head, the towering distortion of the figure over the surrounding groups, the brilliant coloration and plastic modeling, but also because it is the climactic figure of a sweeping mural panorama, backed by the towering figures of Padre Padilla, Coronado, and the Plainsman; behind them the vast prairies of thundering herds, fires, and the tornado.

What Curry saw in the character of John Brown is perhaps best expressed in the opening paragraphs of a pamphlet which the artist had in his library. It describes John Brown's life as told by an aged negro who had remembered him from boyhood and whose family had been liberated through the efforts of Brown.

"John Brown, The Traitor
John Brown, The Fanatic
John Brown, The Martyr

"Thus has this man, one of the most dramatic characters of all times, been denounced and acclaimed. But regardless of the varying estimates of him, the great outstanding fact of his life and death is that it was he who crystallized sentiment which brought about the onslaught against the greatest curse which this nation has ever known, and its final eradication— human bondage.

"Born of parents whose ancestors came to this country on the Mayflower, in whom the Puritanic influence was the predominating passion, the very atmosphere of his early environ-

SANCTUARY

ment and training fitted him preëminently to crusade against the pernicious system of slavery. The traitor in him led him to disregard the laws of the land, if need be, to overthrow this system which, unless eliminated, would eventually destroy the nation's civilization. The fanatic in him could see but one course to pursue, regardless of all the obstacles which might be thrown in the way of accomplishing his purpose. The martyr in him made him subjugate every desire for human comforts and pursue the course for which he believed he was appointed by God. While the United States of America remains, the name of John Brown will be perpetuated as the man who, when the nation was stagnating and threatening to disintegrate, pointed the way to renewed strength and virility."*

Political controversy prevented the completion of the murals, specifically the eight panels of the central rotunda which depict scenes from the life of the Kansas homesteader. The actual point at issue was whether or not the expensive Italian marble slabs should be removed from the wall to make way for Curry's mural. This the legislative committee refused to do.

Behind the refusal, however, were objections which, as they developed in the press, involved two main issues. One was a very human and somewhat trivial questioning of Curry's adherence to factual details. Critics contended that pigs' tails do not curl when they eat; skunks' tails curl up over their backs when they walk and are not straight as he had painted them; or the red color of Curry's Hereford bull was too red and not "natural-like." For the most part Curry welcomed this type of criticism. He can make mistakes and is willing to sit out in the barnyard, watch the animals and make new sketches in order that these details be accurate and convincing. Even from the sketches reproduced here one can see

---

* Alfred W. Santay, A Brief Sketch of the Life of John Brown, the Martyr-Emancipator. Watertown, New York, 1934.

for himself how many times the details, of pigs, skunks and cattle have been studied before. Their tails may be both curled or straight. Their colors may vary in brightness. That being so, the artist is at liberty to choose those values which can be most advantageously worked into his pictorial design.

The other issue involved in the controversy was the more serious one of historical interpretation. Objections were raised especially to the blood on John Brown's hands, the prairie fires and tornados in the Kansas landscape, and "those atrocities on that wall of horror" in general. Patiently Curry has tried to explain that he wanted "to get into his pictures the iron that is in the Kansas people; not a soft, soppy presentation." John Brown did have blood on his hands—perhaps not literally, but blood was shed by his acts. His presentation of John Brown in general is not as a traitor to his country but as a "man who, when the nation was stagnating and threatening to disintegrate, pointed the way to renewed strength and virility." The heart-rending years of indecision before America's entry into World War II could well afford such a statement as this. To the seamy side of history and the destruction symbolized by tornado and prairie fire, Curry juxtaposed a likewise symbolical peace and prosperity, so that he cannot be accused of presenting only the sordid side of Kansas history.

The public shares a responsibility in these matters. The artist made an honest attempt to fulfil the requirements of his job. The least a critic can do is to look at the work and judge it on its own merits.

317. THE TRAGIC PRELUDE (*Topeka Mural*)

317-a. THE TRAGIC PRELUDE (*Topeka Mural*)

Notes on the Illustrations

317-317a—THE TRAGIC PRELUDE. *Oil and tempera on canvas.* 1940. *Sections of the east and north walls of the East Corridor, State Capitol, Topeka, Kansas.*

318a-318—KANSAS PASTORAL. *Oil and tempera on canvas.* 1940. *Sections of the north and west walls of the West Corridor, State Capitol, Topeka, Kansas.*

319—PRELIMINARY SKETCH FOR THE TRAGIC PRELUDE. *Oil on canvas.* 1938.

320—PRELIMINARY SKETCH FOR KANSAS PASTORAL. *Oil on canvas.* 1938. *(South and west walls of the West Corridor.)*

The following is Curry's own description of his murals in the State Capitol of Kansas, written to accompany these sketches as they were presented to the legislative commission for its official sanction:

"Since undertaking the project of murals for the State Capitol I have received many suggestions relating to subject matter and the mode of approach. In such a situation the court of last appeal must be the artist himself.

"The theme I have chosen is historical in more than one sense. In great measure it is the historical struggle of man with nature. This struggle has been a determining factor in my art expression. It is my family's tradition and the tradition of a great majority of Kansas people. And though I fully realize the importance of Kansans in the fields of politics and the various phases of education and human welfare, these phases are removed from my vital experience and that experience is necessary for me to make a forceful art expression.

"Back of the historical allegory is the great backdrop of the phenomenon of nature, and to those who live and depend upon the soil for life and sustenance this phenomenon is God."

TRAGIC PRELUDE

"East and north wall of East Corridor *(22' x 11' 6")* fronting on the Governor's Office.

"In the words of William Allen White, the period depicted in these two panels was a 'tragic prelude to the tragic years to come.'

"At the left of the East Corridor door Coronado and Padre Padilla, the Franciscan missionary, look out across the Kingdom of Quivera, above which float the omnipresent buzzards.

"To the right of the archway stands the figure of the plainsman and buffalo hunter —behind him the slain buffalo—and behind them the thundering herds of buffalo pursued by Indians, and behind all a lurid sun which lights the scene on both walls.

"Centered on the north wall *(31' x 11' 6")* is the gigantic figure of John Brown. In his outstretched left hand the word of God and in the right a 'Beecher's bible.' Beside him, facing each other, are the contending free-soil and pro-slavery forces. At their feet, two figures symbolic of the million and a half dead of the North and South.

"In this group is expressed the fratricidal fury that first flamed on the plains of Kansas, the tragic prelude to the last bloody feud of the English-speaking people. Back of this group are the pioneers and their wagons on the endless trek to the West, and back of all the tornado and the raging prairie fire, fitting symbols of the destruction of the coming Civil War."

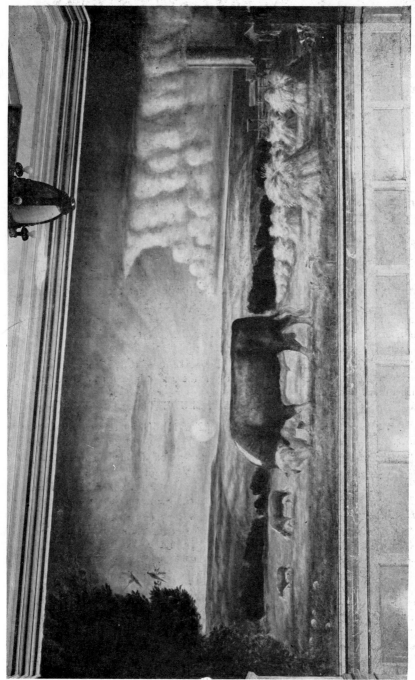

318-a. KANSAS PASTORAL (*Topeka Mural*)

318. KANSAS PASTORAL (Topeka Mural)

319. TRAGIC PRELUDE *(Preliminary Sketch)*

320. KANSAS PASTORAL *(Preliminary Sketch)*

Notes on the Illustrations

321—SKETCHES FOR FOUR OF THE PROPOSED PANEL DECORATIONS IN THE ROTUNDA, STATE CAPITOL, TOPEKA, KANSAS. *Oil on canvas.* 1938.

Curry's own description of these continues:

THE ROTUNDA *(11' 6" x 7' 5").*

"These panels being grouped in separate pairs offer a problem in design—the designs are paired in idea and composition and preserve a common horizon line. These designs as submitted are not yet completed and must be understood from that point of view.

"In the large detail sketch of these spaces some suggestion of how a sculptured figure would enhance the effect is given, and the effect with the marble removed from above the wainscoting is also shown.

"The panels at right of East Corridor Entrance:

(1) THE HOMESTEAD: Before the wooden shack sits the prairie wife paring potatoes. The child investigates the process; beside her the kitten; beyond the wide expanse of open country.

(2) BUILDING THE BARBED WIRE FENCES: The building of the barbed wire fences ushered in a new era. Behind their barbs grew up a different civilization and doomed forever the roving life of the cattleman and wandering hunter.

"The panels at left of East Corridor Entrance:

(1) THE PLAGUES: Like ancient Egypt, Kansas is at times beset by plagues: in this panel is depicted drought and grasshoppers. In the foreground on the parched earth stand the stalks of stripped and withered corn; before the blazing sun floats the cloud of hoppers.

(2) SOIL EROSION AND DUST: Sheet erosion and the shoe-string gully are two of the great calamities of our nation, and in the Midwestern plains can be added wind erosion. In the foreground of this panel is the clutching hand of erosion directed toward the abandoned farm home. Beyond is the threatening cloud of dust. This panel is designed as a significant warning and voices the concern of government and educational forces interested in preserving the nation's resources.

"Two panels at right of West Corridor Entrance:

CORN AND WHEAT: In these two panels are two basic products of our fruitful land: wheat and corn.

"Two panels at left of West Corridor Entrance:

(1) COMMEMORATING THE SACRIFICE OF LIFE OF THOSE WHO FORGED WESTWARD ON THE OLD SANTA FE TRAIL: This depicts the burial of a child. Before the rising sun the pioneer minister with raised hand pronounces the last benediction. Surrounding him the fellow travelers, back of them the wagons hitched and ready to proceed westward.

(2) THE GREAT CATTLE DRIVES: This panel depicts the great herds that for thirty years were driven from Texas to the roaring rail points of central and western Kansas.

KANSAS PASTORAL

"West Corridor off Rotunda: In this comparatively quiet corridor is portrayed Kansas in the time of fruitful harvest. In color and tone, and their unlimited possibilities of

321. SKETCHES FOR ROTUNDA DECORATIONS IN TOPEKA

322. TRAGIC PRELUDE (Preliminary Study)

expression, will be portrayed the overpowering sensuousness of the land at sunset and in its time of abundant harvest.

"On the north wall (22′ x 11′ 6″) are two spaces portraying the industry of the oil fields. Here are shown the oil rig and refinery which again demonstrate the tremendous resources of the state.

"On the west wall stand the ten-foot figures of the young farmer, his wife and children, and back of them the ideal unmortgaged farm home; back of that the night and evening sky.

"On the long wall to the south (29′ x 11′ 6″) a great reach of the Kansas landscape. In the foreground the Hereford bull, wheat field, feeding steers and hogs, a grain elevator, doves in Osage orange trees. Behind all these are fields of corn and grain running back to the distant hill and the setting sun framed by the great turreted cloud to the north.

"I have been accused of seeing only the dark and seamy side of my native state. In these panels I shall show the beauty of real things under the hand of a beneficent Nature—and we can suppose in these panels that the farm depicted is unmortgaged, that grain and cattle prices are rising on the Kansas City and Chicago markets—so that we as farmers, patrons, and artists can shout happily together, 'Ad Astra Per Aspera.' "

322—PRELIMINARY STUDY FOR THE TRAGIC PRELUDE. Oil on canvas. 1938.

324. TRAGIC PRELUDE (Full-Scale Drawing)

324—FULL-SCALE DRAWING FOR THE TRAGIC PRELUDE. Charcoal. 1940.

325—JOHN BROWN. Red chalk. 1939. Collection of Dr. Kent Tenney, Madison, Wisconsin.

In concept and artistic realization the Topeka John Brown is Curry's greatest single achievement in the field of mural painting. These six illustrations suggest its development along a creative pattern somewhat similar to that noted in the studies for the Department of Justice murals.

The basic composition is that of the first project (Liberation of the Slaves) Curry had made for the Department of Justice, with a group of figures on a raised ground before the space. Here a greater emphasis is put on the central form, his size is double that of the surrounding figures, the arm gesture is changed from one of prayerful appeal to a more deliberate and compelling, earth-directed force. That patriarchal power is further dramatized by the spacious prairie and the relentless slow-moving migration across it, the gigantic tornado and prairie fire clouds which loom overhead.

The earlier sketches (Fig. 322) are primarily concerned with the expressive composition, which, when the artist actually gets to the problem of the full-scale wall two years later, is developed by studies in greater movement and the conscientious rebuilding of each single figure into the total complex (Fig. 324).

At the same time Curry did a great deal of actual research into the history of John Brown and the varying aspects of that famous character as a fanatic, a traitor, and a

325. JOHN BROWN (Detail of Tragic Prelude)

self-appointed martyr to a great cause. Here, then, his attention is focused not on The Tragic Prelude theme, but on the specific, human character of the leader, which is first crystallized in the magnificent drawing of Figure 325. Comparison of this with the oil study (Fig. 322) and the final painting shows how the two forms—the character-portrait and the compositional form — are fused into a perfected monumental expression.

329—THE PLAINSMAN. Red chalk study for the Kansas State Capitol mural. 1940. An excellent drawing and figure composition, closely related to some of the illustrations Curry was doing for Cooper's The Plainsman during the same period.

330—STUDY FOR THE KANSAS FARMER. West Corridor of the Kansas State Capitol. Charcoal. 1940. A carefully studied drawing from the model showing again the persistent thoroughness with which the artist built his figures from the skeleton to the anatomical nude to the final denim-clad form. Note the difference in vitality and expressive power between this figure and its counterpart in the schematic sketch of Figure 320.

331—PORTRAIT STUDY FOR THE FARMER'S WIFE. In the West Corridor of the Kansas State Capitol. Red chalk. 1940. No idealization but an actual portrait of a young working woman whose physical type Curry felt expressed the character he sought in the completed mural composition.

330. KANSAS FARMER
(Study for Topeka Mural)

329. THE PLAINSMAN
(Study for Topeka Mural)

331. KANSAS FARMER'S WIFE (Portrait Study)

University of Wisconsin

Since 1940 Curry has undertaken a series of mural decorations in various buildings in Madison, particularly on the University of Wisconsin campus. The first project was sponsored by the Brittingham Fund. Part of it is completed on the second floor of the new Biochemistry Building in the College of Agriculture, and represents benefits of biochemical research to agricultural life and to society. The most distinctive feature in its compositional form is the lively movement of a large number of figures from the picture space practically into the area where the spectator stands. It has many of the panorama features noted in the Department of Interior compositions, but in the dramatic concentration of movement and light on the central space and the spectator it has achieved a far more compelling emotional effect.

The second part of this project is a mural design planned for the graduate seminar room of the same building. The scheme calls for the portrayal of chemical cycles against a background of Wisconsin landscape.

Early in 1942 he finished a group of four mural decorations for the First National Bank in Madison, being, as the institution's announcement expressed it, "a sort of gift to itself and to the community" on the occasion of its eighty-seventh birthday. They represent typical Wisconsin scenes from the surrounding lake country: a farm landscape with shocked corn, a distant view of the city and its capitol in early autumn, and two smaller scenes of corn and pheasants.

A magnificent pediment-shaped space was provided on the end wall of the main reading room in the new Law School Library on the university campus. The subject Curry chose was the one given him for one of the walls in the Department of Justice building in Washington—"The Freeing of the Slaves and the

Coming of the New Immigrants." The original sketch shows a motley procession of slaves and immigrants moving from the country and the ships toward a central group climaxed by a gaunt negro figure. This he simplified into a more factual content and plastic composition by developing the contrasting elements of chaos and order, sunlight and storm, into an Emancipation Proclamation. For political reasons the Fine Arts Commission did not feel this was appropriate for Washington and, as already mentioned, the design was rejected.

Curry had always been proud of the idea. It was an appropriate theme for the decoration of a room constantly in use by law faculty and students, and he was happy for the opportunity to execute the project at this time. For in its original conception of the new America emerging from the trials of civil war it gives expression to the same ideals of freedom and democracy being so drastically threatened in the present World War. That is essentially the same spirit expressed in the Light of the World and the Topeka murals.

It is an ideal of "Justice and Freedom for All" that is at once factual and inspirational. Here is Curry's expression of a subject matter which "deals with American life, its spirit and its actualities."

"Just give us time," he had said to his Madison audience back in 1937, "give us ten years . . . and we will accomplish something!" Indeed, one can look back at the lofty winged ladies of the court-house decorations and recognize that something has been accomplished.

So, this record of work comes to an end. It is incomplete because John Steuart Curry is a living artist who must continue to add daily to his Pageant of America.

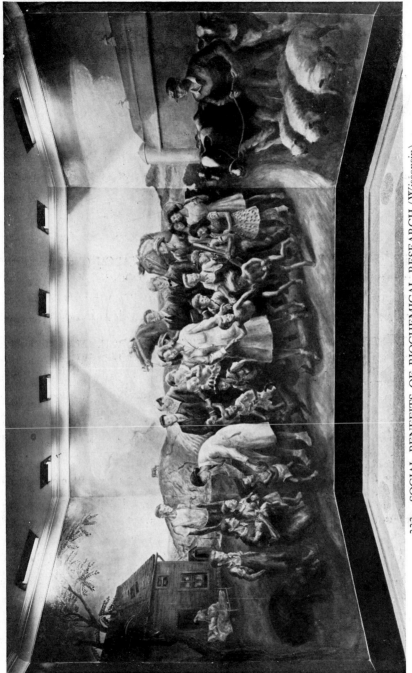

332. SOCIAL BENEFITS OF BIOCHEMICAL RESEARCH (*Wisconsin*)

333. SOCIAL BENEFITS OF BIOCHEMICAL RESEARCH (Preliminary Sketch)

Notes on the Illustrations

332—SOCIAL BENEFITS OF BIOCHEMICAL RESEARCH. Oil and tempera on canvas. (9' x 14' 4") 1941. Biochemistry Building, University of Wisconsin. The first mural commission Curry received at the University of Wisconsin. It is located in a rather restricted octagonal stair landing on the second floor of the new building devoted to research in agricultural biochemistry. The content is composed in a didactic scheme of contrasts: dilapidated farm house with its sick bed, undernourished family, and unhealthy stock, in contrast to a sleek modern barn and well-fed cattle on the opposite side of the wall. In the center a parade of life-sized figures surges forward as symbolic of a healthy, vigorous society, led by the uniformed research workers and, characteristically, a delightful, motley crew of husky American youngsters.

Due to the limited space the composition is based on a compact organization of figures in the manner, as Curry expresses it, of the "early Italians" (i.e., Mantegna and Benozzo Gozzoli). Composed in accordance with specially designed floodlights in the ceiling, the color is soft and luminous, with the forms bathed in an atmospheric light creating the space.

333—PRELIMINARY SKETCH FOR THE WISCONSIN BIOCHEMISTRY MURAL. Crayon. 1941. This drawing reveals the initial interest in a compact mass of figures out of which a central group led by the nurse and children, rushes forward. Notice the use of tree and animal figures at the sides as framing designs, the focusing of light on the central group, and the vigorous Stallion motif in the horses' heads showing up behind the figures. Notice, too, in the finished composition of Figure 332 how the separate figures have achieved greater freedom of movement and expression in the space.

334. FARM STOCK   335. CORN AND TOBACCO

334—BENEFITS OF BIOCHEMICAL RESEARCH: FARM STOCK. Oil and tempera on canvas. *(9' x 4' 7")* 1941. Biochemistry Building, University of Wisconsin.

335—BENEFITS OF BIOCHEMICAL RESEARCH: CORN AND TOBACCO. Oil and tempera on canvas. *(9' x 4' 7")* 1941. Biochemistry Building. University of Wisconsin.

   These two decorations face the larger mural of Figure 332 in comparable positions to the left and right. The open space between them leads to the stair well. In both designs the same contrasting motifs are carried through: the diseased chickens, pig, and calf below, as opposed to the lustily crowing rooster, the galloping calf, and healthy cattle in the yard; the scientifically cultivated plants bathed in light, with the undernourished growth in the shadow. The tall, long-leaved corn stalks whipped in the breeze *(Fig. 334)* is probably the finest design that Curry has ever made of that favorite motif.

336. WISCONSIN SCENE
(*Madison Mural*)

337. WISCONSIN SCENE
(*Madison Mural*)

338. WISCONSIN SCENE (Madison Mural)

339. WISCONSIN SCENE (Madison Mural)

340. FREEING THE SLAVES (Watercolor)

336-339—WISCONSIN SCENES. Murals in the lobby of the First National Bank, Madison, Wis. Oil and tempera on canvas. Sizes 30" x 42" (Figs. 336 and 337) and 70" x 92" (Figs 338 and 339). 1941. Commissioned by Thomas Hefty, president of the First National Bank, these murals represent characteristic views from the environs of the city. "There was no monumental idea here," says Curry. "My idea was simply to present familiar scenes that would be pleasant to look at."

340—FREEING THE SLAVES. Watercolor. 1936. Curry's first idea for the Department of Justice mural which he then changed to the more factual and historical Civil War theme (Fig. 308). Particularly interesting here is the association of the liberated negro slaves in America with the stream of immigrants from Europe in a unified concept of America as the Land of the Free. Much the same concept in another form appeared later in the Light of the World (page 265).

341—FREEING OF THE SLAVES. Oil and tempera on canvas. Library of the Law School, University of Wisconsin, Madison. 1942. Size 37' x 14' (center), 11' high at sides. Based on the rejected sketch for the Department of Justice (Fig. 308), this mural is exceedingly impressive, particularly when seen in its original setting. In contrast to the similar John Brown design the expression here is concentrated on the ecstatic prayer of gratitude revealed in the gaunt central figure.

341. FREEING THE SLAVES (University of Wisconsin Mural)

PART III

A CONTEMPORARY EVALUATION

A CRITIC'S OPINION

THE FOREGOING CHAPTERS, together with the descriptive notes on the illustrations, are largely restricted to the content and form of Curry's pictures and the various ideas that are associated with them. Critics' opinions are variable in their judgment and significance. Nevertheless I should like to venture a few remarks in conclusion which may be of some value to the reader in surveying the material presented and in making his own judgment. They are not inspired by Curry but by his work; they do not purport to decide the aesthetic value of the artist's achievement, but to suggest what I think are the main characteristics of his art as an expression of our times. This chapter, therefore, is to be understood as a purely personal discussion. The reader may reject or consider it as he sees fit.

Before Curry arrived in Madison to take up his duties as Artist in Residence at the University of Wisconsin, I knew him only through some of his work, principally the Baptism, the Tornado, the Flying Cadonas, and a few drawings. I admired the clarity of his draughtsmanship, the extraordinary sense of coloration, the dramatic power of his subject matter, and I venture to say that critics were fairly well in agreement on the excellence of Curry's work from these three points of view. Since that time, however, I have had ample opportunity to know him personally, to watch him work and to discuss the endless problems of pictures, techniques, artistic purposes and functions within the frame of the society we call our own.

John Steuart Curry is quiet and unassuming, an excellent conversationalist when he is in the mood and possessed of an infectious good nature that sometimes bubbles forth at the most unexpected moments. He is not an artist who paints merely to sell pictures. As I grew to know him intimately I became more and more impressed by the clarity and breadth of the artistic ideal that motivates his work. In the past he was not always certain of just how he would achieve that ideal; but he worked unceasingly, and the record shows the many oscillations along the steady path of progress in the direction of his goal.

The ideal? Baldly stated, it is the creation of a distinctly American art that is both modern and native. You would say that there is nothing extraordinary about such an obvious and praiseworthy notion because it is precisely the goal sought by hundreds of other practising artists in America, and has a tradition which goes back many generations in the cultural pattern of this country.

Curry has never felt or said that he was unique in his point of view. In fact, he has often mentioned such other artists as George Bellows, Howard Pyle, and John Sloan, whom he considered well along on the road toward the same goal. And when, in the early 1930's, the public began to associate him with Charles Burchfield, Thomas Benton, Grant Wood, Reginald Marsh, and a number of others, under the banner of Regionalism, he had no particular objection since most of them were his friends and he fully appreciated the sincerity of their point of view, as they did of his.

Unique, however, was the fact that here was a farm boy whose courageous career had led him from rural Kansas to the metropolitan art centers of Chicago, New York, and Paris, yet whose intrinsic character and training did not permit him to discard the one cultural pattern which was his own, for the more spectacular glitter of another which was not. Whether as a professional illustrator, or art student in Paris, or studio artist in Westport, he still wanted to paint the things he knew and loved best: the actual objects, scenes, tragedies, and ambitions of life and people on the land from which he grew. His development was not from one class of society or region to another, but was an inner growth of character which finds more and more articulate expression in his art.

This is something different from what was generally understood as Regionalism. Its primary concern is neither with subject matter nor geographical location alone, but with an attitude which strengthens the associative power of a subject and is controlled by the artistic form through which it is presented. Moreover, that form is no set formula or "style" which can be applied to any number of situations; it is something that must be recognized in the intrinsic structure of the object itself. Prerequisite for this attitude is a rigid adherence to fact and a quality of imagination in the artist which can visualize the expressive possibilities it embodies.

For the catalogue of Curry's one-man show at the Wisconsin Union in Madison (1937) I wrote an essay in which I tried to characterize this attitude as Factual Romanticism. I meant neither the literary dramatics of nineteenth century art nor the artificial stylization of the contemporary Parisian Neo-Romanticism but an emotional state wherein unlimited flights of imagination could be set off by realistic fact and controlled by an artistic form. I still think it is an adequate characterization—not of Curry's painting, to be sure—but of the psychological methods involved in its creation.

When Curry read my essay he looked at me with a wry smile and remarked: "So I'm a Factual Romanticist, eh?" He shook his head. "The critics are all the same; they're always looking for a label to pin onto people."

Perhaps he is right. Through the years the slogans have been forgotten and Curry's reputation has steadily grown. It is a reputation that is based partly on his name, partly on his position as "artist in residence" at a great university, but more on his pictures and the endless train of ideas they set in motion; ideas that vary from the approaching storms of the Tornado and John Brown to the expressions of strength and self-confidence found in The Kansas Stockman and Westward Migration.

When, some three years ago, I began setting down in manuscript form the material I had gathered on Curry, I was curious to know whether the impact of Curry's first successful works on contemporary artists had the same inspired character as that noted in the press reviews (page 62). I asked Harry Wickey what he and other friends of Curry thought about the pictures in the first one-man show at the Whitney Studio Club in 1930. This was not a matter of searching for complimentary remarks from Curry's artist friends. Usually they are the most accurate when it comes to the critical analysis of a picture, and the most brutally frank in their denunciation of faults or pretensions when it is warranted.

Wickey did not hesitate to say that the work was not all of the same quality, but as a whole, he felt that "here was an exhibition where the paintings gave an expression to dynamic aspects of life in terms that were both vital and original. Contrasted to the product of many of his contemporaries whose lack of courage and vision limited their subjects to crooked apples in crooked vases on crooked tables, Curry's paintings contained subjects of every type, and these were expressed in the most robust terms. It took courage and the vision of the true artist for an unknown man to strike out boldly in the direction Curry took.

"The three pictures which we considered the finest in that exhibition were the Tornado, Roadmakers Camp, and Baptism in Kansas. That Tornado seemed almost symbolical; it struck some of us as being a tornado for the art world that would scatter or obliterate much of the rubbish that cluttered the walls of the art galleries. It did just this thing, if not wholly, at least partially, for this picture more than any other contemporary painting gave a knock-out blow to the School of Paris and all its American imitators. Here was a picture that portrayed man and the elements working under full steam, without a hitch in the artist's vision or technique to come between the onlooker and the actuality of the scene presented. Curry's comprehension of forms and the subject is such that the work carries the conviction of life expressing itself, instead of a concoction of ways and means of producing a picture. One is convinced that the story Curry paints actually happened. It seems to me that this fulfills Walt Whitman's hope and prophecy of a truly great native art growing out of American life."

To me these remarks are extremely revealing. Though made years afterward, they express in an even more personal and forceful way the same impact which these pictures made on the art critics as recorded in their press comments. Not only that, but if you would talk to Harry Wickey today and, I would wager, many others like him, you would find that the experience of the Tornado, the Hogs Killing a Rattlesnake, or the Baptism in Kansas is something that is alive, growing, and imperishable, even more vital now than it was when the pictures were first seen. There is a difference between this type of reaction and the "contemporaneousness" recorded in the art criticisms of the time. That living permanence of an experience is precisely what Curry sought to give.

The controversial problems of aesthetic creed have absorbed the energies of both artists and critics far beyond their proper proportions. To my mind—and I think history has fairly well demonstrated the fact—what Wickey calls the rubbish in the art galleries, will eventually disintegrate through its own lifelessness, regardless whether produced by imitators of the School of Paris or of the American Scene.

One fact that has impressed me since I have known Curry personally is his extraordinary reticence in criticising the work of contemporary artists. I have often tried to draw him out with comments on circus, farm, or folk scenes, done by other painters, most of whom he knows. He might criticise specific pictures from a technical point of view, but he studiously avoids the type of personal antagonism that often reaches the headlines of the press and even more often the intimate discussions of the studio. When he does criticise it is from an ideological point of view and, as in the case of his first Madison lecture when he ridiculed the Blash-field murals in the local state capitol, the criticism was based on his own statement—already embodied in pictorial form in his Washington murals—of what he felt genuine mural decoration should be.

Under the stress of contemporary events it is not too much to hope for a certain degree of professional ethics and idealism among artists such as that which already exists in the professions of law, medicine, and education. In those fields established standards of personal integrity and social responsibility have long been recognized as necessary and prerequisite to the successful performance of the individual in his chosen profession. As a pro-fession the art of painting has existed as long as any of the others, if not longer. It has been organized before, and in fact some of the periods of its greatest flowering were precisely those in which the aesthetic and economic organization was the most complete. To survive some sort of order must be achieved again. From my own impressions of the past few years it seems to me that a spirit of mutual respect and aesthetic coördination has already made remarkable headway among certain artists—not the tightly bound political or studio groups, to be sure, but isolated individuals scattered over the entire country. In most cases they are motivated by a genuine patriotism, looking forward to an American art which, as Curry said, could be worthy of foreign respect. The spirit in which this coördination is taking place is neither one of mutual back-slapping nor criticism, but a recogni-tion of common goals and shortcomings. The attitude seems to me to be most honestly expressed in a recent remark made about

Curry by Reginald Marsh: "The stream of creation that flows through Curry's work is the backbone of sound American culture. It reflects our situation: robust, feet on the ground, simple in contrast to Picasso and the fall of Madrid and Paris and disintegration. Curry is not suave like Picasso. He fumbles; he is incomplete. Through his imperfections his work is more interesting than many a slick perfectionist's: I feel that Curry and I have many and similar faults to overcome. . . ." *

With such an attitude artistic stagnation—the prelude to disintegration—is simply not possible in America.

In summarizing the art of John Steuart Curry it might be profitable to recall some of the observations already made in the text. The amazing variety of subject matter and artistic means renders a critical definition of his work difficult if not impossible. Often he is spoken of as a realist, while at the same time his interest in abstract form, the strict discipline of the academy, and in certain historical traditions lead one to characterize him as a stylist of some sort.

If you analyze his work from these points of view you will probably find that his realism embodies a fixation on detailed facts which somehow have a capacity for expansion into universal experience. Notice the untiring concern with physical types—most of them actual portraits—like the habitués of the Paris cafés, the rural characters of such folk demonstrations as the Baptism and the Gospel Train, the glittering ladies of the circus. They are not seen satirically neither with the eye of a reformer, but completely and objectively as they are; their artistic validity and expression grows with the comprehension of the scene into which they are composed. Similarly, the portraits of plain folk—his mother and father, or the young working woman in Madison—acquire a beauty which is uniquely expressed in The Stockman, the Westward Migration and the pastoral scene of the Topeka murals.

* *Demcourier*, Madison, Wisconsin, April, 1941.

As in the case of his physical types Curry picks human situations that are real and factual—he can always tell you exactly where he saw it happen—yet they are also symbolic of universal experience. The idea-portrait of the folks at home could be developed to the pioneer family of the Homestead or the pastoral peace of the farm home in the Topeka mural. The Man Hunt expanded into the Justice Defeating Mob Violence. The fanatical pathos of the Gospel Train could grow to the magnificent proportions of the Liberation of the Slaves and the John Brown murals.

So it is with the hundreds of objects that make up life's setting and provide its combined economic and spiritual embellishment. The farm with its multitude of living things is developed from studies of minute details into monuments to nature at its richest: the gigantic Kansas Pastoral, the Stallion, Ajax, Spring Flowers, Corn, and the countless other forms he has so often used.

Curry's "style" cannot be divorced from the reality of these objects except insofar as the artistic form grows out of the intrinsic structure of the thing he seeks to portray. By so working Curry has isolated and clarified for himself certain basic modes of expression which likewise were capable of expansion into universal meaning. Among his earliest drawings you will find a dramatic interest in charging Rough Riders, galloping wild horses, and fighting men as well as delicate flower studies. Search this background and you will find, besides the favorable circumstances of heredity and environment, the twin phenomena of the child-like primitive and the popular in a style which was carried into his illustration work without change of basic character.

Curry did not set out to draw these things deliberately in any set way. He simply did them and as he looks back at the work today he recognizes pictorial qualities that he still likes and seeks to develop. Academic training, Europe, and the greater self-discipline of the studio arts gave him confidence. Where he could do nothing but grope his way along before, now he became conscious of the artistic means by which he could achieve the expression he wanted.

By paging through the illustrations one can follow the attack, mastery, and exploitation of specific problems: from studies of a single nude figure and its anatomical analysis to the tense High Diver and the Farm Worker (Topeka). Pairs of figures that he used to draw as blood-and-thunder fighters become refined through the study of Signorelli drawings, then developed into the Bathers and the Baptism in Kansas. The fascination in great masses of charging figures seems to have held him from his earliest youth (the Rough Riders) and reappears as one of his finest murals in the exciting panorama of the Oklahoma Land Rush. With little knowledge of Neo-Impressionism or Van Gogh the youthful Curry painted radiant watercolors with pure color laid on in bold and vigorous strokes to form a sweeping pattern (the Straw Stack). The emotional power of pattern and brilliant color he later combined with the irridescence of a glazed technique to create the magnificent Wisconsin Landscape. The expressiveness of space and proportion were problems of specific concentration which can be followed through many of his best works.

The discovery of essentials in both form and content was his own achievement. That is one reason why he does not feel obligated to tradition or the Old Masters and can look at them as equals rather than with the archaeologically bended knee. The process, however, calls forth a third element which has always been paramount in Curry's mind and that is the element of function. The problems of the "what" and the "how" in the criticism of his art can be readily found in the pictures, but the "what for" is a more complicated matter.

There are a number of his remarks in the previous quotations which suggest what he considers to be the function of art. Knowing his temperament, the most useful purpose to him, obviously, was to express himself, to get something off his chest. The story of his earlier struggles will convince one that he does not consider art an easy way to make a living. But there were certain loftier ideals and purposes which he felt art and his painting should serve. On his arrival at Wisconsin he said he hoped he could bring to farm people an understanding and love for their environment through an art that they could understand. He saw no reason why art should not be used as propaganda to promote the cause of social and political justice and he cited many inspired realists in the American tradition who served that function.

From what has been seen of his work this is not idle talk. Through the years Curry's technical means, as well as his style and subject matter, have been directed toward the public at large rather than individuals who might buy his pictures. Disregarding the more profitable trade of small pictures that would fit into the private home, his important pictures are usually of large size and are intended for the public museum.

The design and color is such that the work has something of a mural character and will not aesthetically break a hole through the wall. He will make great sacrifices for the privilege of doing murals in public buildings because he feels that is where his work belongs. When the opportunity presents itself he is anxious to do illustrations for books and magazines, even commercial designs, because he feels by that means he is able to do the greatest good for the greatest number of people.

All of these things, it seems to me, add up to the conclusion that here is one artist who in his own way has succeeded in identifying himself with the character and vitality of our time. He is not the only one, and would be the last one in the world to claim for himself the sole honor of expressing the America of today; but with the same privileges open to any other artist he has accomplished the expression of that bit which he has known and experienced.

The experiences which speak through some of his works of

the last twelve years have a way of touching all of us. The Tornado was more than a weather disturbance, for it characterized the terror of the worst economic disaster this country had ever witnessed. The Sunrises and exuberant landscapes came on the crest of the rising hopes and ideals of a new government that followed the storm. And the John Brown embodies the fanatical terror and impending chaos of an even greater debacle.

These motifs are not coincidental, neither are they obvious "illustrations" of contemporary events, but genuine expressions of the spirit behind those events. It has often been said that in 1929 people felt something was going to happen; after the depression came prosperity and a new deal; and the world-shattering fury of the war period beginning in 1939 strikes again at the foundations of American culture. The analogy, conceived as early as 1936, between the tense state of contemporary affairs before Pearl Harbor and that of pre-Civil War days is so logical—especially in Kansas—that it could hardly be avoided. Several years later it was used to characterize the national emergency in President Roosevelt's third Inaugural address.

Somehow artists have a way of perceiving these things long before the statesmen and politicians. A remarkably similar case— which Curry never knew until long after the John Brown designs were completed—is the equally magnificent and contemporary mural of José Clemente Orozco in the Government Palace of Guadalajara. There the single, piteously outstretched figure is almost engulfed in the torrential flood of world catastrophe. Curry's John Brown towers above the confusion as a symbol of iron strength and vitality. Though their solutions of the problem differ, their perception of this tragic state of world affairs is the same.

We in the United States owe a great deal to the Mexican artists in this process of cultural clarification. In the course of our future artistic development we would do well to recognize the affinity of our problems as well as the differences. The mutual understanding and cultural solidarity of a total America like that of our own United States is the ideal at stake.

Lastly it is essential to recognize that such expressions are discovered and developed through artistic means. The oft-mentioned orant gesture was not discovered in a Medieval history book but in the dramatic reality of the Gospel Train and the Medicine Man. In later works the form was varied and grew to the Liberation of the Slaves and the John Brown. The same principles can be found at work in the other murals and many of the paintings. In thus reiterating Curry's artistry I choose again to emphasize the Kansas State Capitol murals because, from every point of view, they are without question the greatest mural achievements in America today. They represent recognizable symbols of War and Peace. They express not only the ghastly fury of destruction but also the courage, confidence and potential strength of a rural America—indeed all America—to survive the storm.

INDEX

(* indicates the names of works of John Steuart Curry)

1999--